THE MODERN LIBRARY
of the World's Best Books

Ah, Wilderness!

AND TWO OTHER PLAYS

*The publisher will be pleased to send, upon request,
an illustrated folder listing each volume in*
THE MODERN LIBRARY

EUGENE O'NEILL

Ah, Wilderness!

AND TWO OTHER PLAYS

❋

All God's Chillun Got Wings

AND

Beyond the Horizon

The Modern Library
NEW YORK

Library of Congress Catalog Card Number: 64-11995

THE MODERN LIBRARY

is published by

RANDOM HOUSE, INC.

BENNETT CERF • DONALD S. KLOPFER

MANUFACTURED IN THE UNITED STATES OF AMERICA

CONTENTS

Ah, Wilderness!

❁

A PLAY IN FOUR ACTS

To

GEORGE JEAN NATHAN

Who also, once upon a time,
in peg-top trousers went the pace that kills
along the road to ruin

CHARACTERS

NAT MILLER, *owner of the* Evening Globe

ESSIE, *his wife*

ARTHUR

RICHARD

MILDRED   } *their children*

TOMMY

SID DAVIS, *Essie's brother*

LILY MILLER, *Nat's sister*

DAVID MC COMBER

MURIEL MC COMBER, *his daughter*

WINT SELBY, *a classmate of Arthur's at Yale*

BELLE

NORAH

BARTENDER

SALESMAN

SCENES

ACT ONE

Sitting-room of the Miller home in a large small-town in Connecticut—early morning, July 4th, 1906.

ACT TWO

Dining-room of the Miller home—evening of the same day.

ACT THREE

SCENE I: Back room of a bar in a small hotel—10 o'clock the same night.

SCENE II: Same as Act One—the sitting-room of the Miller home—a little after 11 o'clock the same night.

ACT FOUR

SCENE I: The Miller sitting-room again—about 1 o'clock the following afternoon.

SCENE II: A strip of beach along the harbor—about 9 o'clock that night.

SCENE III: Same as Scene I—the sitting-room—about 10 o'clock the same night.

ACT ONE

SCENE—*Sitting-room of the Miller home in a large small-town in Connecticut—about 7:30 in the morning of July 4th, 1906.*

The room is fairly large, homely looking and cheerful in the morning sunlight, furnished with scrupulous medium-priced tastelessness of the period. Beneath the two windows at left, front, a sofa with silk and satin cushions stands against the wall. At rear of sofa, a bookcase with glass doors, filled with cheap sets, extends along the remaining length of wall. In the rear wall, left, is a double doorway with sliding doors and portières, leading into a dark, windowless, back parlor. At right of this doorway, another bookcase, this time a small open one, crammed with boys' and girls' books and the best-selling novels of many past years—books the family really have read. To the right of this bookcase is the mate of the double doorway at its left, with sliding doors and portières, this one leading to a well-lighted front parlor. In the right wall, rear, a screen door opens on a porch. Farther forward in this wall are two windows, with a writing desk and a chair between them. At center is a big, round table with a green-shaded reading lamp, the cord of the lamp running up to one of five sockets in the chandelier above. Five chairs are grouped about the table—three rockers at left, right, and right rear of it, two armchairs at rear and left rear. A medium-priced, inoffensive rug covers most of the floor. The walls are papered white with a cheerful, ugly blue design.

Voices are heard in a conversational tone from the dining-room beyond the back parlor, where the family are just finishing breakfast. Then MRS. MILLER'S *voice, raised commandingly,* "Tommy! Come back here and finish your milk!" *At the same moment* TOMMY *appears in the doorway from the back parlor—a chubby, sun-burnt boy of eleven with dark eyes, blond hair wetted and plastered down in a part, and a shiny, good-natured face, a rim of milk visible about his lips. Bursting with bottled-up energy and a longing to get started on the Fourth, he nevertheless has hesitated obediently at his mother's call.*

TOMMY (*calls back pleadingly*): Aw, I'm full, Ma. And I said excuse me and you said all right. (*His* FATHER'S *voice is heard speaking to his mother. Then she calls:* "All right, Tommy," *and* TOMMY *asks eagerly*) Can I go out now?

MOTHER'S VOICE (*correctingly*): May I!

TOMMY (*fidgeting, but obediently*): May I, Ma?

MOTHER'S VOICE: Yes. (TOMMY *jumps for the screen door to the porch at right like a sprinter released by the starting shot.*)

FATHER'S VOICE (*shouts after him*): But you set off your crackers away from the house, remember! (*But* TOMMY *is already through the screen door, which he leaves open behind him.*)

(*A moment later the family appear from the back parlor, coming from the dining-room. First are* MILDRED *and* ARTHUR. MILDRED *is fifteen, tall and slender, with big, irregular features, resembling her father to the complete effacing of any pretense at prettiness. But her big, gray eyes are beautiful; she has vivacity and a fetching smile, and everyone thinks of her as an attractive girl. She is dressed in shirtwaist and skirt in the fashion of the period.*)

(ARTHUR, *the eldest of the Miller children who are still living home, is nineteen. He is tall, heavy, barrel-chested and muscular, the type of football linesman of that period, with a square, stolid face, small blue eyes and thick sandy hair. His manner is solemnly collegiate. He is dressed in the lastest college fashion of that day, which has receded a bit from the extreme of preceding years, but still runs to padded shoulders and pants half-pegged at the top, and so small at their wide-cuffed bottoms that they cannot be taken off with shoes on.*)

MILDRED (*as they appear—inquisitively*): Where are you going today, Art?

ARTHUR (*with superior dignity*): That's my business. (*He ostentatiously takes from his pocket a tobacco pouch with a big Y and class numerals stamped on it, and a heavy bulldog briar pipe with silver Y and numerals, and starts filling the pipe.*)

MILDRED (*teasingly*): Bet I know, just the same! Want me to tell you her initials? E.R.! (*She laughs.* ARTHUR, *pleased by this insinuation at his lady-killing activities, yet finds it beneath his dignity to reply. He goes to the table, lights his pipe and picks up the local morning paper, and slouches back into the armchair at left rear of table, beginning to whistle "Oh, Waltz Me Around Again, Willie" as he scans the headlines.* MILDRED *sits on the sofa at left, front.*)

(*Meanwhile, their mother and their* AUNT LILY, *their father's sister, have appeared, following them from the back parlor.* MRS. MILLER *is around fifty, a short, stout woman with fading light-brown hair sprinkled with gray, who must have been decidedly pretty as a girl in a round-faced, cute, small-featured, wide-eyed fashion.*

*She has big brown eyes, soft and maternal—a bustling,
mother-of-a-family manner. She is dressed in shirtwaist
and skirt.*)

(LILY MILLER, *her sister-in-law, is forty-two, tall, dark
and thin. She conforms outwardly to the conventional
type of old-maid school teacher, even to wearing
glasses. But behind the glasses her gray eyes are gentle
and tired, and her whole atmosphere is one of shy
kindliness. Her voice presents the greatest contrast to
her appearance—soft and full of sweetness. She, also,
is dressed in a shirtwaist and skirt.*)

MRS. MILLER (*as they appear*): Getting milk down him is
like— (*Suddenly she is aware of the screen door standing half open*) Goodness, look at that door he's left open!
The house will be alive with flies! (*Rushing out to shut
it*) I've told him again and again—and that's all the good
it does! It's just a waste of breath! (*She slams the door
shut.*)

LILY (*smiling*): Well, you can't expect a boy to remember
to shut doors—on the Fourth of July. (*She goes diffidently to the straight-backed chair before the desk at
right, front, leaving the comfortable chairs to the others.*)

MRS. MILLER: That's you all over, Lily—always making excuses for him. You'll have him spoiled to death in spite
of me. (*She sinks in rocker at right of table*) Phew, I'm
hot, aren't you? This is going to be a scorcher. (*She
picks up a magazine from the table and begins to rock,
fanning herself.*)

(*Meanwhile, her husband and her brother have appeared from the back parlor, both smoking cigars.* NAT
MILLER *is in his late fifties, a tall, dark, spare man, a
little stoop-shouldered, more than a little bald, dressed*

*with an awkward attempt at sober respectability im-
posed upon an innate heedlessness of clothes. His long
face has large, irregular, undistinguished features, but
he has fine, shrewd, humorous gray eyes.*)

(SID DAVIS, *his brother-in-law, is forty-five, short and
fat, bald-headed, with the puckish face of a Peck's Bad
Boy who has never grown up. He is dressed in what
had once been a very natty loud light suit but is now a
shapeless and faded nondescript in cut and color.*)

SID (*as they appear*): Oh, I like the job first rate, Nat.
Waterbury's a nifty old town with the lid off, when
you get to know the ropes. I rang in a joke in one of my
stories that tickled the folks there pink. Waterwagon—
Waterbury—Waterloo!

MILLER (*grinning*): Darn good!

SID (*pleased*): I thought it was pretty fair myself. (*Goes
on a bit ruefully, as if oppressed by a secret sorrow*) Yes,
you can see life in Waterbury, all right—that is, if you're
looking for life in Waterbury!

MRS. MILLER: What's that about Waterbury, Sid?

SID: I was saying it's all right in its way—but there's no
place like home. (*As if to punctuate this remark, there
begins a series of bangs from just beyond the porch outside, as TOMMY inaugurates his celebration by setting off
a package of firecrackers. The assembled family jump
in their chairs.*)

MRS. MILLER: That boy! (*She rushes to the screen door
and out on the porch, calling*) Tommy! You mind
what your Pa told you! You take your crackers out in
the back yard, you hear me!

ARTHUR (*frowning scornfully*): Fresh kid! He did it on
purpose to scare us.

MILLER (*grinning through his annoyance*): Darned youngster! He'll have the house afire before the day's out.

SID (*grins and sings*)

> "Dunno what ter call 'im
> But he's mighty like a Rose—velt."

(*They all laugh.*)

LILY: Sid, you Crazy! (SID *beams at her.* MRS. MILLER *comes back from the porch, still fuming.*)

MRS. MILLER: Well, I've made him go out back at last. Now we'll have a little peace. (*As if to contradict this, the bang of firecrackers and torpedoes begins from the rear of the house, left, and continues at intervals throughout the scene, not nearly so loud as the first explosion, but sufficiently emphatic to form a disturbing punctuation to the conversation.*)

MILLER: Well, what's on the tappee for all of you today? Sid, you're coming to the Sachem Club picnic with me, of course.

SID (*a bit embarrassedly*): You bet. I mean I'd like to, Nat—that is, if—

MRS. MILLER (*regarding her brother with smiling suspicion*): Hmm! I know what that Sachem Club picnic's always meant!

LILY (*breaks in in a forced joking tone that conceals a deep earnestness*): No, not this time, Essie. Sid's a reformed character since he's been on the paper in Waterbury. At least, that's what he swore to me last night.

SID (*avoiding her eyes, humiliated—joking it off*): Pure as the driven snow, that's me. They're running me for president of the W.C.T.U. (*They all laugh.*)

MRS. MILLER: Sid, you're a caution. You turn everything into a joke. But you be careful, you hear? We're going to have dinner in the evening tonight, you know—the best shore dinner you ever tasted and I don't want you coming home—well, not able to appreciate it.

LILY: Oh, I know he'll be careful today. Won't you, Sid?

SID (*more embarrassed than ever—joking it off melodramatically*): Lily, I swear to you if any man offers me a drink, I'll kill him—that is, if he changes his mind! (*They all laugh except* LILY, *who bites her lip and stiffens.*)

MRS. MILLER: No use talking to him, Lily. You ought to know better by this time. We can only hope for the best.

MILLER: Now, you women stop picking on Sid. It's the Fourth of July and even a downtrodden newspaperman has a right to enjoy himself when he's on his holiday.

MRS. MILLER: I wasn't thinking only of Sid.

MILLER (*with a wink at the others*): What, are you insinuating I ever—?

MRS. MILLER: Well, to do you justice, no, not what you'd really call— But I've known you to come back from this darned Sachem Club picnic— Well, I didn't need any little bird to whisper that you'd been some place besides to the well! (*She smiles good-naturedly.* MILLER *chuckles.*)

SID (*after a furtive glance at the stiff and silent* LILY— *changes the subject abruptly by turning to* ARTHUR): How are you spending the festive Fourth, Boola-Boola? (ARTHUR *stiffens dignifiedly.*)

MILDRED (*teasingly*): I can tell you, if he won't.

MRS. MILLER (*smiling*): Off to the Rands', I suppose.

ARTHUR (*with dignity*): I and Bert Turner are taking Elsie and Ethel Rand canoeing. We're going to have a picnic lunch on Strawberry Island. And this evening I'm staying at the Rands' for dinner.

MILLER: You're accounted for, then. How about you, Mid?

MILDRED: I'm going to the beach to Anne Culver's.

ARTHUR (*sarcastically*): Of course, there won't be any boys present! Johnny Dodd, for example?

MILDRED (*giggles—then with a coquettish toss of her head*): Pooh! What do I care for him? He's not the only pebble on the beach.

MILLER: Stop your everlasting teasing, you two. How about you and Lily, Essie?

MRS. MILLER: I don't know. I haven't made any plans, Have you, Lily?

LILY (*quietly*): No. Anything you want to do.

MRS. MILLER: Well, I thought we'd just sit around and rest and talk.

MILLER: You can gossip any day. This is the Fourth. Now, I've got a better suggestion than that. What do you say to an automobile ride? I'll get out the Buick and we'll drive around town and out to the lighthouse and back. Then Sid and I will let you off here, or anywhere you say, and we'll go on to the picnic.

MRS. MILLER: I'd love it. Wouldn't you, Lily?

LILY: It would be nice.

MILLER: Then, that's all settled.

SID (*embarrassedly*): Lily, want to come with me to the fireworks display at the beach tonight?

MRS. MILLER: That's right, Sid. You take her out. Poor Lily never has any fun, always sitting home with me.

LILY (*flustered and grateful*): I—I'd like to, Sid, thank you. (*Then an apprehensive look comes over her face*) Only not if you come home—you know.

SID (*again embarrassed and humiliated—again joking it off, solemnly*): Evil-minded, I'm afraid, Nat. I hate to say it of your sister. (*They all laugh. Even* LILY *cannot suppress a smile.*)

ARTHUR (*with heavy jocularity*): Listen, Uncle Sid. Don't let me catch you and Aunt Lily spooning on a bench tonight—or it'll be my duty to call a cop! (SID *and* LILY *both look painfully embarrassed at this, and the joke falls flat, except for* MILDRED *who can't restrain a giggle at the thought of these two ancients spooning.*)

MRS. MILLER (*rebukingly*): Arthur!

MILLER (*dryly*): That'll do you. Your education in kicking a football around Yale seems to have blunted your sense of humor.

MRS. MILLER (*suddenly—startledly*): But where's Richard? We're forgetting all about him. Why, where is that boy? I thought he came in with us from breakfast.

MILDRED: I'll bet he's off somewhere writing a poem to Muriel McComber, the silly! Or pretending to write one. I think he just copies—

ARTHUR (*looking back toward the dining-room*): He's still in the dining-room, reading a book. (*Turning back—scornfully*) Gosh, he's always reading now. It's not my idea of having a good time in vacation.

MILLER (*caustically*): He read his school books, too, strange as that may seem to you. That's why he came out top of his class. I'm hoping before you leave New Haven they'll find time to teach you reading is a good habit.

MRS. MILLER (*sharply*): That reminds me, Nat. I've been meaning to speak to you about those awful books Richard is reading. You've got to give him a good talking to— (*She gets up from her chair*) I'll go up and get them right now. I found them where he'd hid them on the shelf in his wardrobe. You just wait till you see what— (*She bustles off, rear right, through the front parlor.*)

MILLER (*plainly not relishing whatever is coming—to* SID, *grumblingly*): Seems to me she might wait until the Fourth is over before bringing up— (*Then with a grin*) I know there's nothing to it, anyway. When I think of the books I used to sneak off and read when I was a kid.

SID: Me, too. I suppose Dick is deep in Nick Carter or Old Cap Collier.

MILLER: No, he passed that period long ago. Poetry's his red meat nowadays, I think—love poetry—and socialism, too, I suspect, from some dire declarations he's made. (*Then briskly*) Well, might as well get him on the carpet. (*He calls*) Richard. (*No answer—louder*) Richard. (*No answer—then in a bellow*) Richard!

ARTHUR (*shouting*): Hey, Dick, wake up! Pa's calling you.

RICHARD'S VOICE (*from the dining-room*): All right. I'm coming.

MILLER: Darn him! When he gets his nose in a book, the house could fall down and he'd never—

(RICHARD *appears in the doorway from the back parlor, the book he has been reading in one hand, a finger marking his place. He looks a bit startled still, reluctantly called back to earth from another world.*)

(He is going on seventeen, just out of high school. In appearance he is a perfect blend of father and mother, so much so that each is convinced he is the image of the other. He has his mother's light-brown hair, his father's gray eyes; his features are neither large nor small; he is of medium height, neither fat nor thin. One would not call him a handsome boy; neither is he homely. But he is definitely different from both of his parents, too. There is something of extreme sensitiveness added—a restless, apprehensive, defiant, shy, dreamy, self-conscious intelligence about him. In manner he is alternately plain simple boy and a posey actor solemnly playing a role. He is dressed in prep school reflection of the college style of ARTHUR.*)*

RICHARD: Did you want me, Pa?

MILLER: I'd hoped I'd made that plain. Come and sit down a while. *(He points to the rocking chair at the right of table near his.)*

RICHARD *(coming forward—seizing on the opportunity to play up his preoccupation—with apologetic superiority)*: I didn't hear you, Pa. I was off in another world. *(*MILDRED *slyly shoves her foot out so that he trips over it, almost falling. She laughs gleefully. So does* ARTHUR.*)*

ARTHUR: Good for you, Mid! That'll wake him up!

RICHARD *(grins sheepishly—all boy now)*: Darn you, Mid! I'll show you! *(He pushes her back on the sofa and tickles her with his free hand, still holding the book in the other. She shrieks.)*

ARTHUR: Give it to her, Dick!

MILLER: That's enough, now. No more roughhouse. You sit down here, Richard. *(*RICHARD *obediently takes the chair at right of table, opposite his father)* What were you planning to do with yourself today? Going out to the beach with Mildred?

RICHARD (*scornfully superior*): That silly skirt party! I should say not!

MILDRED: He's not coming because Muriel isn't. I'll bet he's got a date with her somewheres.

RICHARD (*flushing bashfully*): You shut up! (*Then to his father*) I thought I'd just stay home, Pa—this morning, anyway.

MILLER: Help Tommy set off firecrackers, eh?

RICHARD (*drawing himself up—with dignity*): I should say not. (*Then frowning portentously*) I don't believe in this silly celebrating the Fourth of July—all this lying talk about liberty—when there is no liberty!

MILLER (*a twinkle in his eye*): Hmm.

RICHARD (*getting warmed up*): The land of the free and the home of the brave! Home of the slave is what they ought to call it—the wage slave ground under the heel of the capitalist class, starving, crying for bread for his children, and all he gets is a stone! The Fourth of July is a stupid farce!

MILLER (*putting a hand to his mouth to conceal a grin*): Hmm. Them are mighty strong words. You'd better not repeat such sentiments outside the bosom of the family or they'll have you in jail.

SID: And throw away the key.

RICHARD (*darkly*): Let them put me in jail. But how about the freedom of speech in the Constitution, then? That must be a farce, too. (*Then he adds grimly*) No, you can celebrate your Fourth of July. I'll celebrate the day the people bring out the guillotine again and I see Pierpont Morgan being driven by in a tumbril! (*His father and* SID *are greatly amused;* LILY *is shocked but, taking her cue from them, smiles.* MILDRED *stares at him in puzzled wonderment, never having heard this particular line before. Only* ARTHUR *betrays the outraged reaction of a patriot.*)

ARTHUR: Aw say, you fresh kid, tie that bull outside! You ought to get a punch in the nose for talking that way on the Fourth!

MILLER (*solemnly*): Son, if I didn't know it was you talking, I'd think we had Emma Goldman with us.

ARTHUR: Never mind, Pa. Wait till we get him down to Yale. We'll take that out of him!

RICHARD (*with high scorn*): Oh, Yale! You think there's nothing in the world besides Yale. After all, what is Yale?

ARTHUR: You'll find out what!

SID (*provocatively*): Don't let them scare you, Dick. Give 'em hell!

LILY (*shocked*): Sid! You shouldn't swear before—

RICHARD: What do you think I am, Aunt Lily—a baby? I've heard worse than anything Uncle Sid says.

MILDRED: And said worse himself, I bet!

MILLER (*with a comic air of resignation*): Well, Richard, I've always found I've had to listen to at least one stump speech every Fourth. I only hope getting your extra strong one right after breakfast will let me off for the rest of the day. (*They all laugh now, taking this as a cue.*)

RICHARD (*somberly*): That's right, laugh! After you, the deluge, you think! But look out! Supposing it comes before? Why shouldn't the workers of the world unite and rise? They have nothing to lose but their chains! (*He recites threateningly*) "The days grow hot, O Babylon! 'Tis cool beneath thy willow trees!"

MILLER: Hmm. That's good. But where's the connection, exactly? Something from that book you're reading?

RICHARD (*superior*): No. That's poetry. This is prose.

MILLER: I've heard there was a difference between 'em. What is the book?

RICHARD (*importantly*): Carlyle's "French Revolution."

MILLER: Hmm. So that's where you drove the tumbril from and piled poor old Pierpont in it. (*Then seriously*) Glad you're reading it, Richard. It's a darn fine book.

RICHARD (*with unflattering astonishment*): What, have you read it?

MILLER: Well, you see, even a newspaper owner can't get out of reading a book every now and again.

RICHARD (*abashed*): I—I didn't mean—I know you— (*Then enthusiastically*) Say, isn't it a great book, though —that part about Mirabeau—and about Marat and Robespierre—

MRS. MILLER (*appears from the front parlor in a great state of flushed annoyance*): Never you mind Robespierre, young man! You tell me this minute where you've hidden those books! They were on the shelf in your wardrobe and now you've gone and hid them somewheres else. You go right up and bring them to your father! (RICHARD, *for a second, looks suddenly guilty and crushed. Then he bristles defensively.*)

MILLER (*after a quick understanding glance at him*): Never mind his getting them now. We'll waste the whole morning over those darned books. And anyway, he has a right to keep his library to himself—that is, if they're not too— What books are they, Richard?

RICHARD (*self-conscious*): Well—there's—

MRS. MILLER: I'll tell you, if he won't—and you give him a good talking to. (*Then, after a glance at* RICHARD, *mollifiedly*) Not that I blame Richard. There must be some boy he knows who's trying to show off as advanced and wicked, and he told him about—

RICHARD: No! I read about them myself, in the papers and in other books.

MRS. MILLER: Well, no matter how, there they were on his shelf. Two by that awful Oscar Wilde they put in jail for heaven knows what wickedness.

ARTHUR (*suddenly—solemnly authoritative*): He committed bigamy. (*Then as* SID *smothers a burst of ribald laughter*) What are you laughing at? I guess I ought to know. A fellow at college told me. His father was in England when this Wilde was pinched—and he said he remembered once his mother asked his father about it and he told her he'd committed bigamy.

MILLER (*hiding a smile behind his hand*): Well then, that must be right, Arthur.

MRS. MILLER: I wouldn't put it past him, nor anything else. One book was called the Picture of something or other.

RICHARD: "The Picture of Dorian Gray." It's one of the greatest novels ever written!

MRS. MILLER: Looked to me like cheap trash. And the second book was poetry. The Ballad of I forget what.

RICHARD: "The Ballad of Reading Gaol," one of the greatest poems ever written. (*He pronounces it Reading Goal* [*as in goalpost*].)

MRS. MILLER: All about someone who murdered his wife and got hung, as he richly deserved, as far as I could make out. And then there were two books by that Bernard Shaw—

RICHARD: The greatest playwright alive today!

MRS. MILLER: To hear him tell it, maybe! You know, Nat,

the one who wrote a play about—well, never mind—
that was so vile they wouldn't even let it play in New
York!

MILLER: Hmm. I remember.

MRS. MILLER: One was a book of his plays and the other
had a long title I couldn't make head or tail of, only it
wasn't a play.

RICHARD (*proudly*): "The Quintessence of Ibsenism."

MILDRED: Phew! Good gracious, what a name! What
does it mean, Dick? I'll bet he doesn't know.

RICHARD (*outraged*): I do, too, know! It's about Ibsen,
the greatest playwright since Shakespeare!

MRS. MILLER: Yes, there was a book of plays by that Ibsen
there, too! And poems by Swin something—

RICHARD: "Poems and Ballads" by Swinburne, Ma. The
greatest poet since Shelley! He tells the truth about real
love!

MRS. MILLER: Love! Well, all I can say is, from reading
here and there, that if he wasn't flung in jail along with
Wilde, he should have been. Some of the things I simply couldn't read, they were so indecent— All about—
well, I can't tell you before Lily and Mildred.

SID (*with a wink at* RICHARD—*jokingly*): Remember, I'm
next on that one, Dick. I feel the need of a little poetical
education.

LILY (*scandalized, but laughing*): Sid! Aren't you
ashamed?

MRS. MILLER: This is no laughing matter. And then there
was Kipling—but I suppose he's not so bad. And last
there was a poem—a long one—the Rubay— What is
it, Richard?

RICHARD: "The Rubaiyat of Omar Khayyam." That's the
best of all!

MILLER: Oh, I've read that, Essie—got a copy down at the office.

SID (*enthusiastically*): So have I. It's a pippin!

LILY (*with shy excitement*): I—I've read it, too—at the library. I like—some parts of it.

MRS. MILLER (*scandalized*): Why, Lily!

MILLER: Everybody's reading that now, Essie—and it don't seem to do them any harm. There's fine things in it, seems to me—true things.

MRS. MILLER (*a bit bewildered and uncertain now*): Why, Nat, I don't see how you— It looked terrible blasphemous—parts I read.

SID: Remember this one: (*He quotes rhetorically*) "Oh Thou, who didst with pitfall and gin beset the path I was to wander in—" Now, I've always noticed how beset my path was with gin—in the past, you understand! (*He casts a joking side glance at* LILY. *The others laugh. But* LILY *is in a melancholy dream and hasn't heard him.*)

MRS. MILLER (*tartly, but evidently supressing her usual smile where he is concerned*): You would pick out the ones with liquor in them!

LILY (*suddenly—with a sad pathos, quotes awkwardly and shyly*): I like—because it's true:

> "The Moving Finger writes, and having **writ,**
> Moves on: nor all your Piety nor Wit
> Shall lure it back to cancel half a Line,
> Nor all your Tears wash out a Word of it."

MRS. MILLER (*astonished, as are all the others*): Why, Lily, I never knew you to recite poetry before!

LILY (*immediately guilty and apologetic*): I—it just stuck in my memory somehow.

RICHARD (*looking at her as if he had never seen her before*): Good for you, Aunt Lily! (*Then enthusiastically*) But that isn't the best. The best is:

> "*A Book of Verses underneath the Bough,*
> *A Jug of Wine, A Loaf of Bread—and Thou*
> *Beside me singing in the Wilderness—*"

ARTHUR (*who, bored to death by all this poetry quoting, has wandered over to the window at rear of desk, right*): Hey! Look who's coming up the walk— Old Man McComber!

MILLER (*irritably*): Dave? Now what in thunder does that damned old— Sid, I can see where we never are going to get to that picnic.

MRS. MILLER (*vexatiously*): He'll know we're in this early, too. No use lying. (*Then appalled by another thought*) That Norah—she's that thick, she never can answer the front door right unless I tell her each time. Nat, you've got to talk to Dave. I'll have her show him in here. Lily, you run up the back stairs and get your things on. I'll be up in a second. Nat, you get rid of him the first second you can! Whatever can the old fool want— (*She and* LILY *hurry out through the back parlor.*)

ARTHUR: I'm going to beat it—just time to catch the eight-twenty trolley.

MILDRED: I've got to catch that, too. Wait till I get my hat, Art! (*She rushes into the back parlor.*)

ARTHUR (*shouts after her*): I can't wait. You can catch up with me if you hurry. (*He turns at the back-parlor door—with a grin*) McComber may be coming to see if your intentions toward his daughter are dishonorable, Dick! You'd better beat it while your shoes are good!

(*He disappears through the back-parlor door, laughing.*)

RICHARD (*a bit shaken, but putting on a brave front*): Think I'm scared of him?

MILLER (*gazing at him—frowning*): Can't imagine what — But it's to complain about something, I know that. I only wish I didn't have to be pleasant with the old buzzard—but he's about the most valuable advertiser I've got.

SID (*sympathetically*): I know. But tell him to go to hell, anyway. He needs that ad more than you.

(*The sound of the bell comes from the rear of the house, off left from back parlor.*)

MILLER: There he is. You clear out, Dick—but come right back as soon as he's gone, you hear? I'm not through with you, yet.

RICHARD: Yes, Pa.

MILLER: You better clear out, too, Sid. You know Dave doesn't approve jokes.

SID: And loves me like poison! Come on, Dick, we'll go out and help Tommy celebrate. (*He takes* RICHARD's *arm and they also disappear through the back-parlor door.* MILLER *glances through the front parlor toward the front door, then calls in a tone of strained heartiness.*)

MILLER: Hello, Dave. Come right in here. What good wind blows you around on this glorious Fourth?

(*A flat, brittle voice answers him: "Good morning,"* *and a moment later* DAVID MC COMBER *appears in the doorway from the front parlor. He is a thin, dried-up little man with a head too large for his body perched on a scrawny neck, and a long solemn horse face with deep-set little black eyes, a blunt formless nose and a tiny slit of a mouth. He is about the same age as* MILLER *but is entirely bald, and looks ten years older. He is dressed with a prim neatness in shiny old black clothes.*)

MILLER: Here, sit down and make yourself comfortable. (*Holding out the cigar box*) Have a cigar?

MC COMBER (*sitting down in the chair at the right of table—acidly*): You're forgetting. I never smoke.

MILLER (*forcing a laugh at himself*): That's so. So I was. Well, I'll smoke alone then. (*He bites off the end of the cigar viciously, as if he wished it were* MC-COMBER's *head, and sits down opposite him.*)

MC COMBER: You asked me what brings me here, so I'll come to the point at once. I regret to say it's something disagreeable—disgraceful would be nearer the truth—and it concerns your son, Richard!

MILLER (*beginning to bristle—but calmly*): Oh, come now, Dave, I'm sure Richard hasn't—

MC COMBER (*sharply*): And I'm positive he has. You're not accusing me of being a liar, I hope.

MILLER: No one said anything about liar. I only meant you're surely mistaken if you think—

MC COMBER: I'm not mistaken. I have proof of everything in his own handwriting!

MILLER (*sharply*): Let's get down to brass tacks. Just what is it you're charging him with?

MC COMBER: With being dissolute and blasphemous—with deliberately attempting to corrupt the morals of my young daughter, Muriel.

MILLER: Then I'm afraid I will have to call you a liar, Dave!

MC COMBER (*without taking offense—in the same flat, brittle voice*): I thought you'd get around to that, so I brought some of the proofs with me. I've a lot more of 'em at home. (*He takes a wallet from his inside coat pocket, selects five or six slips of paper, and holds them out to* MILLER) These are good samples of the rest. My wife discovered them in one of Muriel's bureau drawers hidden under the underwear. They're all in his hand-writing, you can't deny it. Anyway, Muriel's confessed to me he wrote them. You read them and then say I'm a liar. (MILLER *has taken the slips and is reading them frowningly.* MC COMBER *talks on*) Evidently you've been too busy to take the right care about Richard's bringing up or what's he's allowed to read—though I can't see why his mother failed in her duty. But that's your misfortune, and none of my business. But Muriel is my business and I can't and I won't have her in-nocence exposed to the contamination of a young man whose mind, judging from his choice of reading mat-ter, is as foul—

MILLER (*making a tremendous effort to control his tem-per*): Why, you damned old fool! Can't you see Rich-ard's only a fool kid who's just at the stage when he's out to rebel against all authority, and so he grabs at everything radical to read and wants to pass it on to his elders and his girl and boy friends to show off what a young hellion he is! Why, at heart you'd find Rich-ard is just as innocent and as big a kid as Muriel is! (*He pushes the slips of paper across the table con-temptuously*) This stuff doesn't mean anything to me —that is, nothing of what you think it means. If you believe this would corrupt Muriel, then you must believe she's easily corrupted! But I'll bet you'd find she knows a lot more about life than you give her credit for—and can guess a stork didn't bring her down your chimney!

MC COMBER: Now you're insulting my daughter. I won't forget that.

MILLER: I'm not insulting her. I think Muriel is a darn nice girl. That's why I'm giving her credit for ordinary good sense. I'd say the same about my own Mildred, who's the same age.

MC COMBER: I know nothing about your Mildred except that she's known all over as a flirt. (*Then more sharply*) Well, I knew you'd prove obstinate, but I certainly never dreamed you'd have the impudence, after reading those papers, to claim your son was innocent of all wrongdoing!

MILLER: And what did you dream I'd do?

MC COMBER: Do what it's your plain duty to do as a citizen to protect other people's children! Take and give him a hiding he'd remember to the last day of his life! You'd ought to do it for his sake, if you had any sense—unless you want him to end up in jail!

MILLER (*his fists clenched, leans across the table*): Dave, I've stood all I can stand from you! You get out! And get out quick, if you don't want a kick in the rear to help you!

MC COMBER (*again in his flat, brittle voice, slowly getting to his feet*): You needn't lose your temper. I'm only demanding you do your duty by your own as I've already done by mine. I'm punishing Muriel. She's not to be allowed out of the house for a month and she's to be in bed every night by eight sharp. And yet she's blameless, compared to that—

MILLER: I said I'd had enough out of you, Dave! (*He makes a threatening movement.*)

MC COMBER: You needn't lay hands on me. I'm going. But there's one thing more. (*He takes a letter from his wallet*) Here's a letter from Muriel for your son. (*Puts it on the table*) It makes clear, I think, how she's come to think about him, now that her eyes have been opened. I hope he heeds what's inside—for his own good and yours—because if I ever catch him hanging about my place again I'll have him arrested! And don't think I'm not going to make you regret the insults you've heaped on me. I'm taking the advertisement for my store out of your paper—and it won't go in again, I tell you, not unless you apologize in writing and promise to punish—

MILLER: I'll see you in hell first! As for your damned old ad, take it out and go to hell!

MC COMBER: That's plain bluff. You know how badly you need it. So do I. (*He starts stiffly for the door.*)

MILLER: Here! Listen a minute! I'm just going to call *your* bluff and tell you that, whether you want to re-consider your decision or not, I'm going to refuse to print your damned ad after tomorrow! Put that in your pipe and smoke it! Furthermore, I'll start a campaign to encourage outside capital to open a dry-goods store in opposition to you that won't be the public swindle I can prove yours is!

MC COMBER (*a bit shaken by this threat—but in the same flat tone*): I'll sue you for libel.

MILLER: When I get through, there won't be a person in town will buy a dishrag in your place!

MC COMBER (*more shaken, his eyes shifting about fur-tively*): That's all bluff. You wouldn't dare— (*Then finally he says uncertainly*) Well, good day. (*And turns and goes out.* NAT *stands looking after him. Slowly the anger drains from his face and leaves him looking a bit sick and disgusted.* SID *appears from the back par-*

lor. He is nursing a burn on his right hand, but his face is one broad grin of satisfaction.)

SID: I burned my hand with one of Tommy's damned firecrackers and came in to get some vaseline. I was listening to the last of your scrap. Good for you, Nat! You sure gave him hell!

MILLER (*dully*): Much good it'll do. He knows it was all talk.

SID: That's just what he don't know, Nat, The old skin-flint has a guilty conscience.

MILLER: Well, anyone who knows me knows I wouldn't use my paper for a dirty, spiteful trick like that—no matter what he did to me.

SID: Yes, everyone knows you're an old sucker, Nat, too decent for your own good. But McComber never saw you like this before. I tell you you scared the pants off him. (*He chuckles.*)

MILLER (*still dejectedly*): I don't know what made me let go like that. The hell of skunks like McComber is that after being with them ten minutes you become as big skunks as they are.

SID (*notices the slips of paper on the table*): What's this? Something he brought? (*He picks them up and starts to read.*)

MILLER (*grimly*): Samples of the new freedom—from those books Essie found—that Richard's been passing on to Muriel to educate her. They're what started the rumpus. (*Then frowning*) I've got to do something about that young anarchist or he'll be getting me, and himself, in a peck of trouble. (*Then pathetically helpless*) But what can I do? Putting the curb bit on would make him worse. Then he'd have a harsh tyrant to defy. He'd love that, darn him!

SID (*has been reading the slips, a broad grin on his face —suddenly he whistles*): Phew! This is a warm lulu for fair! (*He recites with a joking intensity*)

> "My life is bitter with thy love; thine eyes
> Blind me, thy tresses burn me, thy sharp sighs
> Divide my flesh and spirit with soft sound—"

MILLER (*with a grim smile*): Hmm. I missed that one. That must be Mr. Swinburne's copy. I've never read him, but I've heard something like that was the matter with him.

SID: Yes, it's labelled Swinburne—"Anactoria." Whatever that is. But wait, watch and listen! The worst is yet to come! (*He recites with added comic intensity*)

> "That I could drink thy veins as wine, and eat
> Thy breasts like honey, that from face to feet
> Thy body were abolished and consumed,
> And in my flesh thy very flesh entombed!"

MILLER (*an irrepressible boyish grin coming to his face*): Hell and hallelujah! Just picture old Dave digesting that for the first time! Gosh, I'd give a lot to have seen his face! (*Then a trace of shocked reproof showing in his voice*) But it's no joking matter. That stuff *is* warm—too damned warm, if you ask me! I don't like this a damned bit, Sid. That's no kind of thing to be sending a decent girl. (*More worriedly*) I thought he was really stuck on her—as one gets stuck on a decent girl at his age—all moonshine and holding hands and a kiss now and again. But this looks—I wonder if he is hanging around her to see what he can get? (*Angrily*) By God, if that's true, he deserves that licking Mc-

Comber says it's my duty to give him! I've got to draw the line somewhere!

SID: Yes, it won't do to have him getting any decent girl in trouble.

MILLER: The only thing I can do is put it up to him straight. (*With pride*) Richard'll stand up to his guns, no matter what. I've never known him to lie to me.

SID (*at a noise from the back parlor, looks that way——in a whisper*): Then now's your chance. I'll beat it and leave you alone—see if the women folks are ready upstairs. We ought to get started soon—if we're ever going to make that picnic. (*He is halfway to the entrance to the front parlor as* RICHARD *enters from the back parlor, very evidently nervous about* MC COMBER'S *call.*)

RICHARD (*adopting a forced, innocent tone*): How's your hand, Uncle Sid?

SID: All right, Dick, thanks—only hurts a little. (*He disappears.* MILLER *watches his son frowningly.* RICHARD *gives him a quick side glance and grows more guiltily self-conscious.*)

RICHARD (*forcing a snicker*): Gee, Pa, Uncle Sid's a bigger kid than Tommy is. He was throwing firecrackers in the air and catching them on the back of his hand and throwing 'em off again just before they went off —and one came and he wasn't quick enough, and it went off almost on top of—

MILLER: Never mind that. I've got something else to talk to you about besides firecrackers.

RICHARD (*apprehensively*): What, Pa?

MILLER (*suddenly puts both hands on his shoulders— quietly*): Look here, Son. I'm going to ask you a question, and I want an honest answer. I warn you beforehand if the answer is "yes" I'm going to punish you and punish you hard because you'll have done something no boy of mine ought to do. But you've never lied to me before, I know, and I don't believe, even to save yourself punishment, you'd lie to me now, would you?

RICHARD (*impressed—with dignity*): I won't lie, Pa.

MILLER: Have you been trying to have something to do with Muriel—something you shouldn't—you know what I mean.

RICHARD (*stares at him for a moment, as if he couldn't comprehend—then, as he does, a look of shocked indignation comes over his face*): No! What do you think I am, Pa? I never would! She's not that kind! Why, I—I love her! I'm going to marry her—after I get out of college! She's said she would! We're engaged!

MILLER (*with great relief*): All right. That's all I wanted to know. We won't talk any more about it. (*He gives him an approving pat on the back.*)

RICHARD: I don't see how you could think— Did that old idiot McComber say that about me?

MILLER (*joking now*): Shouldn't call your future father-in-law names, should you? 'Tain't respectful. (*Then after a glance at* RICHARD's *indignant face— points to the slips of paper on the table*) Well, you can't exactly blame old Dave, can you, when you read through that literature you wished on his innocent daughter?

RICHARD (*sees the slips for the first time and is overcome by embarrassment, which he immediately tries to cover up with a superior carelessness*): Oh, so that's why. He found those, did he? I told her to be careful—

Well, it'll do him good to read the truth about life for once and get rid of his old-fogy ideas.

MILLER: I'm afraid I've got to agree with him, though, that they're hardly fit reading for a young girl. (*Then with subtle flattery*) They're all well enough, in their way, for you who're a man, but— Think it over, and see if you don't agree with me.

RICHARD (*embarrassedly*): Aw, I only did it because I liked them—and I wanted her to face life as it is. She's so darned afraid of life—afraid of her Old Man— afraid of people saying this or that about her—afraid of being in love—afraid of everything. She's even afraid to let me kiss her. I thought, maybe, reading those things —they're beautiful, aren't they, Pa?—I thought they would give her the spunk to lead her own life, and not be—always thinking of being afraid.

MILLER: I see. Well, I'm afraid she's still afraid. (*He takes the letter from the table*) Here's a letter from her he said to give you. (RICHARD *takes the letter from him uncertainly, his expression changing to one of apprehension.* MILLER *adds with a kindly smile*) You better be prepared for a bit of a blow. But never mind. There's lots of other fish in the sea. (RICHARD *is not listening to him, but staring at the letter with a sort of fascinated dread.* MILLER *looks into his son's face a second, then turns away, troubled and embarrassed*) Darn it! I better go upstairs and get rigged out or I never will get to that picnic. (*He moves awkwardly and self-consciously off through the front parlor.* RICHARD *continues to stare at the letter for a moment—then girds up his courage and tears it open and begins to read swiftly. As he reads his face grows more and more wounded and tragic, until at the end his mouth draws*

*down at the corners, as if he were about to break into
tears. With an effort he forces them back and his face
grows flushed with humiliation and wronged anger.*)

RICHARD (*blurts out to himself*): The little coward! I
hate her! She can't treat me like that! I'll show her!
(*At the sound of voices from the front parlor, he
quickly shoves the letter into the inside pocket of his
coat and does his best to appear calm and indifferent,
even attempting to whistle "Waiting at the Church."
But the whistle peters out miserably as his mother,
LILY and SID enter from the front parlor. They are
dressed in all the elaborate paraphernalia of motoring
at that period—linen dusters, veils, goggles, SID in a
snappy cap.*)

MRS. MILLER: Well, we're about ready to start at last,
thank goodness! Let's hope no more callers are on the
way. What did that McComber want, Richard, do you
know? Sid couldn't tell us.

RICHARD: You can search me. Ask Pa.

MRS. MILLER (*immediately sensing something "down" in
his manner—going to him worriedly*): Why, whatever's the matter with you, Richard? You sound as if
you'd lost your last friend! What is it?

RICHARD (*desperately*): I— I don't feel so well—my stom-
ach's sick.

MRS. MILLER (*immediately all sympathy—smoothing his
hair back from his forehead*): You poor boy! What
a shame—on the Fourth, too, of all days! (*Turning to
the others*) Maybe I better stay home with him, if he's
sick.

LILY: Yes, I'll stay, too.

RICHARD (*more desperately*): No! You go, Ma! I'm not
really sick. I'll be all right. You go. I want to be alone!

(*Then, as a louder bang comes from in back as* TOMMY *sets off a cannon cracker, he jumps to his feet*) Darn Tommy and his darned firecrackers! You can't get any peace in this house with that darned kid around! Darn the Fourth of July, anyway! I wish we still belonged to England! (*He strides off in an indignant fury of misery through the front parlor.*)

MRS. MILLER (*stares after him worriedly—then sighs philosophically*): Well, I guess he can't be so very sick—after that. (*She shakes her head*) He's a queer boy. Sometimes I can't make head or tail of him.

MILLER (*calls from the front door beyond the back parlor*): Come along folks. Let's get started.

SID: We're coming, Nat. (*He and the two women move off through the front parlor.*)

Curtain

ACT TWO

SCENE—*Dining-room of the* MILLER *home—a little after 6 o'clock in the evening of the same day.*

The room is much too small for the medium-priced, formidable dining-room set, especially now when all the leaves of the table are in. At left, toward rear, is a double doorway with sliding doors and portières leading into the back parlor. In the rear wall, left, is the door to the pantry. At the right of door is the china closet with its display of the family cut glass and fancy china. In the right wall are two windows looking out on a side lawn. In front of the windows is a heavy, ugly sideboard with three pieces of old silver on its top. In the left wall, extreme front, is a screen door opening on a side porch. A dark rug covers most of the floor. The table, with a chair at each end, left and right, three chairs on the far side, facing front, and two on the near side, their backs to front, takes up most of the available space. The walls are papered in a somber brown and dark-red design.

MRS. MILLER *is supervising and helping the Second Girl,* NORAH, *in the setting of the table.* NORAH *is a clumsy, heavy-handed, heavy-footed, long-jawed, beamingly good-natured young Irish girl—a "greenhorn."*

MRS. MILLER: I really think you better put on the lights, Norah. It's getting so cloudy out, and this pesky room is so dark, anyway.

NORAH: Yes, Mum. (*She stretches awkwardly over the table to reach the chandelier that is suspended from the* middle of the ceiling and manages to turn one light on —*scornfully*) Arrah, the contraption!

MRS. MILLER (*worriedly*): Careful!

NORAH: Careful as can be, Mum. (*But in moving around to reach the next bulb she jars heavily against the table.*)

MRS. MILLER: There! I knew it! I do wish you'd watch—!

NORAH (*a flustered appeal in her voice*): Arrah, what have I done wrong now?

MRS. MILLER (*draws a deep breath—then sighs helplessly*): Oh, nothing. Never mind the rest of the lights. You might as well go out in the kitchen and wait until I ring.

NORAH (*relieved and cheerful again*): Yes, Mum. (*She starts for the pantry.*)

MRS. MILLER: But there's one thing— (NORAH *turns apprehensively*) No, two things—things I've told you over and over, but you always forget. Don't pass the plates on the wrong side at dinner tonight, and do be careful not to let that pantry door slam behind you. Now you will try to remember, won't you?

NORAH: Yes, Mum. (*She goes into the pantry and shuts the door behind her with exaggerated care as* MRS. MILLER *watches her apprehensively.* MRS. MILLER *sighs and reaches up with difficulty and turns on another of the four lights in the chandelier. As she is doing so,* LILY *enters from the back parlor.*)

LILY: Here, let me do that, Essie. I'm taller. You'll only strain yourself. (*She quickly lights the other two bulbs.*)

MRS. MILLER (*gratefully*): Thank you, Lily. It's a stretch for me, I'm getting so fat.

LILY: But where's Norah? Why didn't she—?

MRS. MILLER (*exasperatedly*): Oh, that girl! Don't talk about her! She'll be the death of me! She's that thick, you honestly wouldn't believe it possible.

LILY (*smiling*): Why, what did she do now?

MRS. MILLER: Oh, nothing. She means all right.

LILY: Anything else I can do, Essie?

MRS. MILLER: Well, she's got the table all wrong. We'll have to reset it. But you're always helping me. It isn't fair to ask you—in your vacation. You need your rest after teaching a pack of wild Indians of kids all year.

LILY (*beginning to help with the table*): You know I love to help. It makes me feel I'm some use in this house instead of just sponging—

MRS. MILLER (*indignantly*): Sponging! You pay, don't you?

LILY: Almost nothing. And you and Nat only take that little to make me feel better about living with you. (*Forcing a smile*) I don't see how you stand me—having a cranky old maid around all the time.

MRS. MILLER: What nonsense you talk! As if Nat and I weren't only too tickled to death to have you! Lily Miller, I've no patience with you when you go on like that. We've been over this a thousand times before, and still you go on! Crazy, that's what it is! (*She changes the subject abruptly*) What time's it getting to be?

LILY (*looking at her watch*): Quarter past six.

MRS. MILLER: I do hope those men folks aren't going to be late for dinner. (*She sighs*) But I suppose with that darned Sachem Club picnic it's more likely than not. (LILY *looks worried, and sighs.* MRS. MILLER *gives her a quick side glance*) I see you've got your new dress on.

LILY (*embarrassedly*): Yes, I thought—if Sid's taking me to the fireworks—I ought to spruce up a little.

MRS. MILLER (*looking away*): Hmm. (*A pause—then she says with an effort to be casual*) You mustn't mind if Sid comes home feeling a bit—gay. I expect Nat to—

and we'll have to listen to all those old stories of his about when he was a boy. You know what those picnics are, and Sid'd be running into all his old friends.

LILY (*agitatedly*): I don't think he will—this time—not after his promise.

MRS. MILLER (*avoiding looking at her*): I know. But men are weak. (*Then quickly*) That was a good notion of Nat's, getting Sid the job on the Waterbury *Standard*. All he ever needed was to get away from the rut he was in here. He's the kind that's the victim of his friends. He's easily led—but there's no real harm in him, you know that. (LILY *keeps silent, her eyes downcast.* MRS. MILLER *goes on meaningly*) He's making good money in Waterbury, too—thirty-five a week. He's in a better position to get married than he ever was.

LILY (*stiffly*): Well, I hope he finds a woman who's will-ing—though after he's through with his betting on horse races, and dice, and playing Kelly pool, there won't be much left for a wife—even if there was nothing else he spent his money on.

MRS. MILLER: Oh, he'd give up all that—for the right woman. (*Suddenly she comes directly to the point*) Lily, why don't you change your mind and marry Sid and reform him? You love him and always have—

LILY (*stiffly*): I can't love a man who drinks.

MRS. MILLER: You can't fool me. I know darned well you love him. And he loves you and always has.

LILY: Never enough to stop drinking for. (*Cutting off* MRS. MILLER's *reply*) No, it's no good in your talking, Essie. We've been over this a thousand times before and I'll always feel the same as long as Sid's the same. If he gave me proof he'd—but even then I don't believe I could. It's sixteen years since I broke off our engagement, but what made me break it off is as clear to me today as it was then. It was what he'd be liable to do now to anyone who married him—his taking up with bad women.

MRS. MILLER (*protests half-heartedly*): But he's always sworn he got raked into that party and never had anything to do with those harlots.

LILY: Well, I don't believe him—didn't then and don't now. I do believe he didn't deliberately plan to, but—Oh, it's no good talking, Essie. What's done is done. But you know how much I like Sid—in spite of everything. I know he was just born to be what he is—irresponsible, never meaning to harm but harming in spite of himself. But don't talk to me about marrying him—because I never could.

MRS. MILLER (*angrily*): He's a dumb fool—a stupid dumb fool, that's what he is!

LILY (*quietly*): No. He's just Sid.

MRS. MILLER: It's a shame for you—a measly shame—you that would have made such a wonderful wife for any man—that ought to have your own home and children!

LILY (*winces but puts her arm around her affectionately—gently*): Now don't you go feeling sorry for me. I won't have that. Here I am, thanks to your and Nat's kindness, with the best home in the world; and as for the children, I feel the same love for yours as if they were mine, and I didn't have the pain of bearing them. And then there are all the boys and girls I teach every year. I like to feel I'm a sort of second mother to them and helping them to grow up to be good men and women. So I don't feel such a useless old maid, after all.

MRS. MILLER (*kisses her impulsively—her voice husky*): You're a good woman, Lily—too good for the rest of us. (*She turns away, wiping a tear furtively—then abruptly*

changing the subject) Good gracious, if I'm not forgetting one of the most important things! I've got to warn
that Tommy against giving me away to Nat about the
fish. He knows, because I had to send him to market
for it, and he's liable to burst out laughing—

LILY: Laughing about what?

MRS. MILLER (*guiltily*): Well, I've never told you, because
it seemed sort of a sneaking trick, but you know how
Nat carries on about not being able to eat bluefish.

LILY: I know he says there's a certain oil in it that poisons him.

MRS. MILLER (*chuckling*): Poisons him, nothing! He's
been eating bluefish for years—only I tell him each time
it's weakfish. We're having it tonight—and I've got to
warn that young imp to keep his face straight.

LILY (*laughing*): Aren't you ashamed, Essie!

MRS. MILLER: Not much, I'm not! I like bluefish! (*She
laughs*) Where is Tommy? In the sitting-room?

LILY: No, Richard's there alone. I think Tommy's out on
the piazza with Mildred. (MRS. MILLER *bustles out
through the back parlor. As soon as she is gone, the
smile fades from* LILY's *lips. Her face grows sad and she
again glances nervously at her watch.* RICHARD *appears
from the back parlor, moving in an aimless way. His
face wears a set expression of bitter gloom; he exudes
tragedy. For* RICHARD, *after his first outburst of grief and
humiliation, has begun to take a masochistic satisfaction in his great sorrow, especially in the concern which
it arouses in the family circle. On seeing his aunt, he
gives her a dark look and turns and is about to stalk
back toward the sitting-room when she speaks to him
pityingly*) Feel any better, Richard?

RICHARD (*somberly*): I'm all right, Aunt Lily. You mustn't worry about me.

LILY (*going to him*): But I do worry about you. I hate to see you so upset.

RICHARD: It doesn't matter. Nothing matters.

LILY (*puts her arm around him sympathetically*): You really mustn't let yourself take it so seriously. You know, something happens and things like that come up, and we think there's no hope—

RICHARD: Things like what come up?

LILY: What's happened between you and Muriel.

RICHARD (*with disdain*): Oh, her! I wasn't even thinking about her. I was thinking about life.

LILY: But then—if we really, *really* love—why, then something else is bound to happen soon that changes everything again, and it's all as it was before the misunderstanding, and everything works out all right in the end. That's the way it is with life.

RICHARD (*with a tragic sneer*): Life! Life is a joke! And everything comes out all wrong in the end!

LILY (*a little shocked*): You mustn't talk that way. But I know you don't mean it.

RICHARD: I do too mean it! You can have your silly optimism, if you like, Aunt Lily. But don't ask me to be so blind. I'm a pessimist! (*Then with an air of cruel cynicism*) As for Muriel, that's all dead and past. I was only kidding her, anyway, just to have a little fun, and she took it seriously, like a fool. (*He forces a cruel smile to his lips*) You know what they say about women and trolley cars, Aunt Lily: there's always another one along in a minute.

LILY (*really shocked this time*): I don't like you when

you say such horrible, cynical things. It isn't nice.

RICHARD: Nice! that's all you women think of! I'm proud to be a cynic. It's the only thing you can be when you really face life. I suppose you think I ought to be heart-broken about Muriel—a little coward that's afraid to say her soul's her own, and keeps tied to her father's apron strings! Well, not for mine! There's plenty of other fish in the sea! (*As he is finishing, his mother comes back through the back parlor.*)

MRS. MILLER: Why, hello. You here, Richard? Getting hungry, I suppose?

RICHARD (*indignantly*): I'm not hungry a bit! That's all you think of, Ma—food!

MRS. MILLER: Well, I must say I've never noticed you to hang back at meal times. (*To* LILY) What's that he was saying about fish in the sea?

LILY (*smiling*): He says he's through with Muriel now.

MRS. MILLER (*tartly—giving her son a rebuking look*): She's through with him, he means! The idea of your sending a nice girl like her things out of those indecent books! (*Deeply offended,* RICHARD *disdains to reply but stalks woundedly to the screen door at left, front, and puts a hand on the knob*) Where are you going?

RICHARD (*quotes from "Candida" in a hollow voice*): "Out, then, into the night with me!" (*He stalks out, slamming the door behind him.*)

MRS. MILLER (*calls*): Well, don't you go far, 'cause din-ner'll be ready in a minute, and I'm not coming running after you! (*She turns to* LILY *with a chuckle*) Goodness, that boy! He ought to be on the stage! (*She mimics*) "Out—into the night"—and it isn't even dark yet! He got that out of one of those books, I suppose. Do you know, I'm actually grateful to old Dave Mc-

Comber for putting an end to his nonsense with Muriel. I never did approve of Richard getting so interested in girls. He's not old enough for such silliness. Why, seems to me it was only yesterday he was still a baby. (*She sighs—then matter-of-factly*) Well, nothing to do now till those men turn up. No use standing here like gawks. We might as well go in the sitting-room and be comfortable.

LILY (*the nervous, worried note in her voice again*): Yes, we might as well. (*They go out through the back parlor. They have no sooner disappeared than the screen door is opened cautiously and* RICHARD *comes back in the room.*)

RICHARD (*stands inside the door, looking after them—quotes bitterly*): "They do not know the secret in the poet's heart." (*He comes nearer the table and surveys it, especially the cut-glass dish containing olives, with contempt and mutters disdainfully*) Food! (*But the dish of olives seems to fascinate him and presently he has approached nearer, and stealthily lifts a couple and crams them into his mouth. He is just reaching out for more when the pantry door is opened slightly and* NORAH *peers in.*)

NORAH: Mister Dick, you thief, lave them olives alone, or the missus'll be swearing it was me at them!

RICHARD (*draws back his hand as if he had been stung—too flustered to be anything but guilty boy for a second*): I—I wasn't eating—

NORAH: Oho, no, of course not, divil fear you, you was only feeling their pulse! (*Then warningly*) Mind what I'm saying now, or I'll have to tell on you to protect me good name! (*She draws back into the pantry, closing the door.* RICHARD *stands, a prey to feelings of bitterest humiliation and seething revolt against everyone and everything. A low whistle comes from just outside the porch door. He starts. Then a masculine voice calls: "Hey, Dick." He goes over to the screen door grumpily— then as he recognizes the owner of the voice, his own as he answers becomes respectful and admiring.)*

RICHARD: Oh, hello, Wint. Come on in. (*He opens the door and* WINT SELBY *enters and stands just inside the door.* SELBY *is nineteen, a classmate of* ARTHUR'S *at Yale. He's a typical, good-looking college boy of the period, not the athletic but the hell-raising sport type. He is tall, blond, dressed in extreme collegiate cut.*)

WINT (*as he enters—warningly, in a low tone*): Keep it quiet, Kid. I don't want the folks to know I'm here. Tell Art I want to see him a second—on the Q.T.

RICHARD: Can't. He's up at the Rands'—won't be home before ten, anyway.

WINT (*irritably*): Damn, I thought he'd be here for dinner. (*More irritably*) Hell, that gums the works for fair!

RICHARD (*ingratiatingly*): What is it, Wint? Can't I help?

WINT (*gives him an appraising glance*): I might tell you, if you can keep your face shut.

RICHARD: I can.

WINT: Well, I ran into a couple of swift babies from New Haven this after. and I dated them up for tonight, thinking I could catch Art. But now it's too late to get anyone else and I'll have to pass it up. I'm nearly broke and I can't afford to blow them both to drinks.

RICHARD (*with shy eagerness*): I've got eleven dollars saved up. I could loan you some.

WINT (*surveys him appreciatively*): Say, you're a good sport. (*Then shaking his head*) Nix, Kid, I don't want to borrow your money. (*Then getting an idea*) But say, have you got anything on for tonight?

RICHARD: No.

WINT: Want to come along with me? (*Then quickly*) I'm not trying to lead you astray, understand. But it'll be a help if you would just sit around with Belle and feed her a few drinks while I'm off with Edith. (*He winks*) See what I mean? You don't have to do anything, not even take a glass of beer—unless you want to.

RICHARD (*boastfully*): Aw, what do you think I am—a rube?

WINT: You mean you're game for anything that's doing?

RICHARD: Sure I am!

WINT: Ever been out with any girls—I mean, real swift ones that there's something doing with, not these dead Janes around here?

RICHARD (*lies boldly*): Aw, what do you think? Sure I have!

WINT: Ever drink anything besides sodas?

RICHARD: Sure. Lots of times. Beer and sloe-gin fizz and —Manhattans.

WINT (*impressed*): Hell, you know more than I thought. (*Then considering*) Can you fix it so your folks won't get wise? I don't want your old man coming after me. You can get back by half-past ten or eleven, though, all right. Think you can cook up some lie to cover that? (*As* RICHARD *hesitates—encouraging him*) Ought to be easy—on the Fourth.

RICHARD: Sure. Don't worry about that.

WINT: But you've got to keep your face closed about this, you hear?—to Art and everybody else. I tell you straight, I wouldn't ask you to come if I wasn't in a hole —and if I didn't know you were coming down to Yale next year, and didn't think you're giving me the straight goods about having been around before. I don't want to lead you astray.

RICHARD (*scornfully*): Aw, I told you that was silly.

WINT: Well, you be at the Pleasant Beach House at half-past nine then. Come in the back room. And don't forget to grab some cloves to take the booze off your breath.

RICHARD: Aw, I know what to do.

WINT: See you later, then. (*He starts out and is just about to close the door when he thinks of something*) And say, I'll say you're a Harvard freshman, and you back me up. They don't know a damn thing about Harvard. I don't want them thinking I'm travelling around with any high-school kid.

RICHARD: Sure. That's easy.

WINT: So long, then. You better beat it right after your dinner while you've got a chance, and hang around until it's time. Watch your step, Kid.

RICHARD: So long. (*The door closes behind* WINT. RICHARD *stands for a moment, a look of bitter, defiant rebellion coming over his face, and mutters to himself*) I'll show her she can't treat me the way she's done! I'll show them all! (*Then the front door is heard slamming, and a moment later* TOMMY *rushes in from the back parlor.*)

TOMMY: Where's Ma?

RICHARD (*surlily*): In the sitting-room. Where did you think, Bonehead?

TOMMY: Pa and Uncle Sid are coming. Mid and I saw them from the front piazza. Gee, I'm glad. I'm awful hungry, ain't you? (*He rushes out through the back parlor, calling*) Ma! They're coming! Let's have dinner quick! (*A moment later* MRS. MILLER *appears from the back parlor accompanied by* TOMMY, *who keeps insisting urgently*) Gee, but I'm awful hungry, Ma!

MRS. MILLER: I know. You always are. You've got a tapeworm, that's what I think.

TOMMY: Have we got lobsters, Ma? Gee, I love lobsters.

MRS. MILLER: Yes, we've got lobsters. And fish. You remember what I told you about that fish. (*He snickers*) Now, do be quiet, Tommy! (*Then with a teasing smile at* RICHARD) Well, I'm glad to see you've got back out of the night, Richard. (*He scowls and turns his back on her.* LILY *appears through the back parlor, nervous and apprehensive. As she does so, from the front yard* SID'S *voice is heard singing "Poor John!"* MRS. MILLER *shakes her head forebodingly—but, so great is the comic spell for her even in her brother's voice, a humorous smile hovers at the corners of her lips*) Mmm! Mmm! Lily, I'm afraid—

LILY (*bitterly*): Yes, I might have known. (MILDRED *runs in through the back parlor. She is laughing to herself a bit shamefacedly. She rushes to her mother.*)

MILDRED: Ma, Uncle Sid's— (*She whispers in her ear.*)

MRS. MILLER: Never mind! You shouldn't notice such things—at your age! And don't you encourage him by laughing at his foolishness, you hear!

TOMMY: You needn't whisper, Mid. Think I don't know? Uncle Sid's soused again.

MRS. MILLER (*shakes him by the arm indignantly*): You be quiet! Did I ever! You're getting too smart! (*Gives him a push*) Go to your place and sit right down and not another word out of you!

TOMMY (*aggrieved—rubbing his arm as he goes to his place*): Aw, Ma!

MRS. MILLER: And you sit down, Richard and Mildred. You better, too, Lily. We'll get him right in here and get some food in him. He'll be all right then. (RICHARD, *preserving the pose of the bitter, disillusioned pessimist, sits down in his place in the chair at right of the two whose backs face front.* MILDRED *takes the other chair facing back, at his left.* TOMMY *has already slid into the end chair at right of those at the rear of table facing front.* LILY *sits in the one of those at left, by the head of the table, leaving the middle one* [SID'S] *vacant. While they are doing this, the front screen door is heard slamming and* NAT'S *and* SID'S *laughing voices, raised as they come in and for a moment after, then suddenly cautiously lowered.* MRS. MILLER *goes to the entrance to the back parlor and calls peremptorily*) You come right in here! Don't stop to wash up or anything. Dinner's coming right on the table.

MILLER'S VOICE (*jovially*): All right, Essie. Here we are! Here we are!

MRS. MILLER (*goes to pantry door, opens it and calls*): All right, Norah. You can bring in the soup. (*She comes back to the back-parlor entrance just as* MILLER *enters. He isn't drunk by any means. He is just mellow and benignly ripened. His face is one large, smiling, happy beam of utter appreciation of life. All's right with the world, so satisfyingly right that he becomes sentimentally moved even to think of it.*)

MILLER: Here we are, Essie! Right on the dot! Here we are! (*He pulls her to him and gives her a smacking kiss on the ear as she jerks her head away.* MILDRED *and* TOMMY *giggle.* RICHARD *holds rigidly aloof and disdainful, his brooding gaze fixed on his plate.* LILY *forces a smile.*)

MRS. MILLER (*pulling away—embarrassedly, almost blushing*): Don't, you Crazy! (*Then recovering herself—tartly*) So I see, you're here! And if I didn't, you've told me four times already!

MILLER (*beamingly*): Now, Essie, don't be critical. Don't be carpingly critical. Good news can stand repeating, can't it? 'Course it can! (*He slaps her jovially on her fat buttocks.* TOMMY *and* MILDRED *roar with glee. And* NORAH, *who has just entered from the pantry with a huge tureen of soup in her hands, almost drops it as she explodes in a merry guffaw.*)

MRS. MILLER (*scandalized*): Nat! Aren't you ashamed!

MILLER: Couldn't resist it! Just simply couldn't resist it! (NORAH, *still standing with the soup tureen held out stiffly in front of her, again guffaws.*)

MRS. MILLER (*turns on her with outraged indignation*): Norah! Bring that soup here this minute! (*She stalks with stiff dignity toward her place at the foot of the table, right.*)

NORAH (*guiltily*): Yes, Mum. (*She brings the soup around the head of the table, passing* MILLER.)

MILLER (*jovially*): Why, hello, Norah!

MRS. MILLER: Nat! (*She sits down stiffly at the foot of the table.*)

NORAH (*rebuking him familiarly*): Arrah now, don't be making me laugh and getting me into trouble!

MRS. MILLER: Norah!

NORAH (*a bit resentfully*): Yes, Mum. Here I am. (*She sets the soup tureen down with a thud in front of* MRS. MILLER *and passes around the other side, squeezing with difficulty between the china closet and the backs of chairs at the rear of the table.*)

MRS. MILLER: Tommy! Stop spinning your napkin ring!

How often have I got to tell you? Mildred! Sit up straight in your chair! Do you want to grow up a humpback? Richard! Take your elbows off the table!

MILLER (*coming to his place at the head of the table, rubbing his hands together genially*): Well, well, well. Well, well, well. It's good to be home again. (NORAH *exits into the pantry and lets the door slam with a bang behind her.*)

MRS. MILLER (*jumps*): Oh! (*Then exasperatedly*) Nat, I do wish you wouldn't encourage that stupid girl by talking to her, when I'm doing my best to train—

MILLER (*beamingly*): All right, Essie. Your word is law! (*Then laughingly*) We did have the darndest fun today! And Sid was the life of that picnic! You ought to have heard him! Honestly, he had that crowd just rolling on the ground and splitting their sides! He ought to be on the stage.

MRS. MILLER (*as* NORAH *comes back with a dish of saltines —begins ladling soup into the stack of plates before her*): He ought to be at this table eating something to sober him up, that's what he ought to be! (*She calls*) Sid! You come right in here! (*Then to* NORAH, *handing her a soup plate*) Here, Norah. (NORAH *begins passing soup*) Sit down, Nat, for goodness sakes. Start eating, everybody. Don't wait for me. You know I've given up soup.

MILLER (*sits down but bends forward to call to his wife in a confidential tone*): Essie—Sid's sort of embarrassed about coming—I mean I'm afraid he's a little bit—not too much, you understand—but he met such a lot of friends and—well, you know, don't be hard on him. Fourth of July is like Christmas—comes but once a year.

Don't pretend to notice, eh? And don't you kids, you hear! And don't you, Lily. He's scared of you.

LILY (*with stiff meekness*): Very well, Nat.

MILLER (*beaming again—calls*): All right, Sid. The coast's clear. (*He begins to absorb his soup ravenously*) Good soup, Essie! Good soup! (*A moment later* SID *makes his entrance from the back parlor. He is in a condition that can best be described as blurry. His movements have a hazy uncertainty about them. His shiny fat face is one broad, blurred, Puckish, naughty-boy grin; his eyes have a blurred, wondering vagueness. As he enters he makes a solemnly intense effort to appear casual and dead, cold sober. He waves his hand aimlessly and speaks with a silly gravity.*)

SID: Good evening. (*They all answer "Good evening," their eyes on their plates. He makes his way vaguely toward his place, continuing his grave effort at conversation*) Beautiful evening. I never remember seeing—more beautiful sunset. (*He bumps vaguely into* LILY's *chair as he attempts to pass behind her—immediately he is all grave politeness*) Sorry—sorry, Lily—deeply sorry.

LILY (*her eyes on her plate—stiffly*): It's all right.

SID (*manages to get into his chair at last—mutters to himself*): Wha' was I sayin'? Oh, sunsets. But why butt in? Hasn't sun—perfect right to set? Mind y'r own business. (*He pauses thoughtfully, considering this—then looks around from face to face, fixing each with a vague, blurred, wondering look, as if some deep puzzle were confronting him. Then suddenly he grins mistily and nods with satisfaction*) And there you are! Am I right?

MILLER (*humoring him*): Right.

SID: Right! (*He is silent, studying his soup plate, as if it were some strange enigma. Finally he looks up and regards his sister and asks with wondering amazement*) Soup?

MRS. MILLER: Of course, it's soup. What did you think it was? And you hurry up and eat it.

SID (*again regards his soup with astonishment*): Well! (*Then suddenly*) Well, all right then! Soup be it! (*He picks up his spoon and begins to eat, but after two tries in which he finds it difficult to locate his mouth, he addresses the spoon plaintively*) Spoon, is this any way to treat a pal? (*Then suddenly comically angry, putting the spoon down with a bang*) Down with spoons! (*He raises his soup plate and declaims*) "We'll drink to the dead already, and hurrah for the next who dies." (*Bowing solemnly to right and left*) Your good health, ladies *and* gents. (*He starts drinking the soup. MILLER guffaws and MILDRED and TOMMY giggle. Even RICHARD forgets his melancholy and snickers, and MRS. MILLER conceals a smile. Only LILY remains stiff and silent.*)

MRS. MILLER (*with forced severity*): Sid!

SID (*peers at her muzzily, lowering the soup plate a little from his lips*): Eh?

MRS. MILLER: Oh, nothing. Never mind.

SID (*solemnly offended*): Are you—publicly rebuking me before assembled—? Isn't soup liquid? Aren't liquids drunk? (*Then considering this to himself*) What if they are drunk? It's a good man's failing. (*He again peers mistily about at the company*) Am I right or wrong?

MRS. MILLER: Hurry up and finish your soup, and stop talking nonsense!

SID (*turning to her—again offendedly*): Oh, no, Essie, if I ever so far forget myself as to drink a leg of lamb, then you might have some—excuse for— Just think of waste effort eating soup with spoons—fifty gruelling lifts per plate—billions of soup-eaters on globe—why, it's simply staggering! (*Then darkly to himself*) No more spoons for me! If I want to develop my biceps, I'll buy Sandow Exerciser! (*He drinks the rest of his soup in a gulp and beams around at the company, suddenly all happiness again*) Am I right, folks?

MILLER (*who has been choking with laughter*): Haw, haw! You're right, Sid.

SID (*peers at him blurredly and shakes his head sadly*): Poor old Nat! Always wrong—but heart of gold, heart of purest gold. And drunk again, I regret to note. Sister, my heart bleeds for you and your poor fatherless chicks!

MRS. MILLER (*restraining a giggle—severely*): Sid! Do shut up for a minute! Pass me your soup plates, everybody. If we wait for that girl to take them, we'll be here all night. (*They all pass their plates, which* MRS. MILLER *stacks up and then puts on the sideboard. As she is doing this,* NORAH *appears from the pantry with a platter of broiled fish. She is just about to place these before* MILLER *when* SID *catches her eye mistily and rises to his feet, making her a deep, uncertain bow.*)

SID (*raptly*): Ah, Sight for Sore Eyes, my beautiful Macushla, my star-eyed Mavourneen—

MRS. MILLER: Sid!

NORAH (*immensely pleased—gives him an arch, flirtatious*

glance): Ah sure, Mister Sid, it's you that have kissed the Blarney Stone, when you've a drop taken!

MRS. MILLER (*outraged*): Norah! Put down that fish!

NORAH (*flusteredly*): Yes, Mum. (*She attempts to put the fish down hastily before* MILLER, *but her eyes are fixed nervously on* MRS. MILLER *and she gives* MILLER *a nasty swipe on the side of the head with the edge of the dish.*)

MILLER: Ouch! (*The children, even* RICHARD, *explode into laughter.*)

NORAH (*almost lets the dish fall*): Oh, glory be to God! Is it hurted you are?

MILLER (*rubbing his head—good-naturedly*): No, no harm done. Only careful, Norah, careful.

NORAH (*gratefully*): Yes, sorr. (*She thumps down the dish in front of him with a sigh of relief.*)

SID (*who is still standing—with drunken gravity*): Careful, Mavourneen, careful! You might have hit him some place besides the head. Always aim at his head, remember—so as not to worry us. (*Again the children explode. Also* NORAH. *Even* LILY *suddenly lets out an hysterical giggle and is furious with herself for doing so.*)

LILY: I'm so sorry, Nat. I didn't mean to laugh. (*Turning on* SID *furiously*) Will you please sit down and stop making a fool of yourself? (SID *gives her a hurt, mournful look and then sinks meekly down on his chair.*)

NORAH (*grinning cheerfully, gives* LILY *a reassuring pat on the back*): Ah, Miss Lily, don't mind him. He's only under the influence. Sure, there's no harm in him at all.

MRS. MILLER: Norah! (NORAH *exits hastily into the pantry, letting the door slam with a crash behind her.*

There is silence for a moment as MILLER *serves the fish and it is passed around.* NORAH *comes back with the vegetables and disappears again, and these are dished out.*)

MILLER (*is about to take his first bite—stops suddenly and asks his wife*): This isn't, by any chance, bluefish, is it, my dear?

MRS. MILLER (*with a warning glance at* TOMMY): Of course not. You know we never have bluefish, on account of you.

MILLER (*addressing the table now with the gravity of a man confessing his strange peculiarities*): Yes, I regret to say, there's a certain peculiar oil in bluefish that invariably poisons me. (*At this,* TOMMY *cannot stand it any more but explodes into laughter.* MRS. MILLER, *after a helpless glance at him, follows suit; then* LILY *goes off into uncontrollable, hysterical laughter, and* RICHARD *and* MILDRED *are caught in the contagion.* MILLER *looks around at them with a weak smile, his dignity now ruffled a bit*) Well, I must say I don't see what's so darned funny about my being poisoned.

SID (*peers around him—then with drunken cunning*): Aha! Nat, I suspect—plot! This fish looks blue to me—very blue—in fact despondent, desperate, and— (*He points his fork dramatically at* MRS. MILLER) See how guilty she looks a ver—veritable Lucretia Georgia! Can it be this woman has been slowly poisoning you all these years? And how well—you've stood it! What an iron constitution! Even now, when you are invariably at death's door, I can't believe— (*Everyone goes off into uncontrollable laughter.*)

MILLER (*grumpily*): Oh, give us a rest, you darned fool!

A joke's a joke, but— (*He addresses his wife in a wounded tone*) Is this true, Essie?

MRS. MILLER (*wiping the tears from her eyes—defiantly*): Yes, it is true, if you must know, and you'd never have suspected it, if it weren't for that darned Tommy, and Sid poking his nose in. You've eaten bluefish for years and thrived on it and it's all nonsense about that peculiar oil.

MILLER (*deeply offended*): Kindly allow me to know my own constitution! Now I think of it, I've felt upset afterwards every damned time we've had fish! (*He pushes his plate away from him with proud renunciation*) I can't eat this.

MRS. MILLER (*insultingly matter-of-fact*): Well, don't then. There's lots of lobster coming and you can fill up on that. (RICHARD *suddenly bursts out laughing again.*)

MILLER (*turns to him caustically*): You seem in a merry mood, Richard. I thought you were the original of the Heart Bowed Down today.

SID (*with mock condolence*): Never mind, Dick. Let them—scoff! What can they understand about girls whose hair sizzchels, whose lips are fireworks, whose eyes are red-hot sparks—

MILDRED (*laughing*): Is that what he wrote to Muriel? (*Turning to her brother*) You silly goat, you!

RICHARD (*surlily*): Aw, shut up, Mid. What do I care about her? I'll show all of you how much I care!

MRS. MILLER: Pass your plates as soon as you're through, everybody. I've rung for the lobster. And that's all. You don't get any dessert or tea after lobster, you know. (NORAH *appears bearing a platter of cold boiled lobsters which she sets before* MILLER, *and disappears.*)

TOMMY: Gee, I love lobster! (MILLER *puts one on each plate, and they are passed around and everyone starts in pulling the cracked shells apart.*)

MILLER (*feeling more cheerful after a couple of mouthfuls—determining to give the conversation another turn, says to his daughter*): Have a good time at the beach, Mildred?

MILDRED: Oh, fine, Pa, thanks. The water was wonderful and warm.

MILLER: Swim far?

MILDRED: Yes, for me. But that isn't so awful far.

MILLER: Well, you ought to be a good swimmer, if you take after me. I used to be a regular water rat when I was a boy. I'll have to go down to the beach with you one of these days—though I'd be rusty, not having been in in all these years. (*The reminiscent look comes into his eyes of one about to embark on an oft-told tale of childhood adventure*) You know, speaking of swimming, I never go down to that beach but what it calls to mind the day I and Red Sisk went in swimming there and I saved his life. (*By this time the family are beginning to exchange amused, guilty glances. They all know what is coming.*)

SID (*with a sly, blurry wink around*): Ha! Now we—have it again!

MILLER (*turning on him*): Have what?

SID: Nothing—go on with your swimming—don't mind me.

MILLER (*glares at him—but immediately is overcome by the reminiscent mood again*): Red Sisk—his father kept a blacksmith shop where the Union Market is now—we kids called him Red because he had the darndest reddest crop of hair—

SID (*as if he were talking to his plate*): Remarkable!—
the curious imagination—of little children.

MRS. MILLER (*as she sees* MILLER *about to explode—interposes tactfully*): Sid! Eat your lobster and shut up! Go on, Nat.

MILLER (*gives* SID *a withering look—then is off again*):
Well, as I was saying, Red and I went swimming that
day. Must have been—let me see—Red was fourteen,
bigger and older than me, I was only twelve—forty-
five years ago—wasn't a single house down there then—
but there was a stake out where the whistling buoy is
now, about a mile out. (TOMMY, *who has been having
difficulty restraining himself, lets out a stifled giggle.*
MILLER *bends a frowning gaze on him*) One more
sound out of you, young man, and you'll leave the table!

MRS. MILLER (*quickly interposing, trying to stave off the
story*): Do eat your lobster, Nat. You didn't have any
fish, you know.

MILLER (*not liking the reminder—pettishly*): Well, if I'm
going to be interrupted every second anyway— (*He
turns to his lobster and chews in silence for a moment.*)

MRS. MILLER (*trying to switch the subject*): How's Anne's
mother's rheumatism, Mildred?

MILDRED: Oh, she's much better, Ma. She was in wading
today. She says salt water's the only thing that really
helps her bunion.

MRS. MILLER: Mildred! Where are your manners? At the
table's no place to speak of—

MILLER (*fallen into the reminiscent obsession again*):
Well, as I was saying, there was I and Red, and he
dared me to race him out to the stake and back. Well, I

didn't let anyone dare me in those days. I was a spunky kid. So I said all right and we started out. We swam and swam and were pretty evenly matched; though, as I've said, he was bigger and older than me, but finally I drew ahead. I was going along easy, with lots in reserve, not a bit tired, when suddenly I heard a sort of gasp from behind me—like this—"Help." (*He imitates. Everyone's eyes are firmly fixed on his plate, except* SID's) And I turned and there was Red, his face all pinched and white, and he says weakly: "Help, Nat! I got a cramp in my leg!" Well, I don't mind telling you I got mighty scared. I didn't know what to do. Then suddenly I thought of the pile. If I could pull him to that, I could hang on to him till someone'd notice us. But the pile was still—well, I calculate it must have been two hundred feet away.

SID: Two hundred and fifty!

MILLER (*in confusion*): What's that?

SID: Two hundred *and* fifty! I've taken down the distance every time you've saved Red's life for thirty years and the mean average to that pile is two hundred and fifty feet! (*There is a burst of laughter from around the table.* SID *continues complainingly*) Why didn't you let that Red drown, anyway, Nat? I never knew him but I know I'd never have liked him.

MILLER (*really hurt, forces a feeble smile to his lips and pretends to be a good sport about it*): Well, guess you're right, Sid. Guess I have told that one too many times and bored everyone. But it's a good true story for kids because it illustrates the danger of being foolhardy in the water—

MRS. MILLER (*sensing the hurt in his tone, comes to his*

rescue): Of course it's a good story—and you tell it whenever you've a mind to. And you, Sid, if you were in any responsible state, I'd give you a good piece of my mind for teasing Nat like that.

MILLER (*with a sad, self-pitying smile at his wife*): Getting old, I guess, Mother—getting to repeat myself. Someone ought to stop me.

MRS. MILLER: No such thing! You're as young as you ever were. (*She turns on* SID *again angrily*) You eat your lobster and maybe it'll keep your mouth shut!

SID (*after a few chews—irrepressibly*): Lobster! Did you know, Tommy, your Uncle Sid is the man invented lobster? Fact! One day—when I was building the Pyramids—took a day off and just dashed off lobster. He was bigger'n' older than me and he had the darndest reddest crop of hair but I dashed him off just the same! Am I right, Nat? (*Then suddenly in the tones of a side-show barker*) Ladies *and* Gents—

MRS. MILLER: Mercy sakes! Can't you shut up?

SID: In this cage you see the lobster. You will not believe me, ladies *and* gents, but it's a fact that this interesting bivalve only makes love to his mate once in every thousand years—but, dearie me, how he does enjoy it! (*The children roar.* LILY *and* MRS. MILLER *laugh in spite of themselves—then look embarrassed.* MILLER *guffaws —then suddenly grows shocked.*)

MILLER: Careful, Sid, careful. Remember you're at home.

TOMMY (*suddenly in a hoarse whisper to his mother, with an awed glance of admiration at his uncle*): Ma! Look at him! He's eating that claw, shells and all!

MRS. MILLER (*horrified*): Sid, do you want to kill yourself? Take it away from him, Lily!

SID (*with great dignity*): But I prefer the shells. All famous epicures prefer the shells—to the less delicate, coarser meat. It's the same with clams. Unless I eat the shells there is a certain, peculiar oil that invariably poisons— Am I right, Nat?

MILLER (*good-naturedly*): You seem to be getting a lot of fun kidding me. Go ahead, then. I don't mind.

MRS. MILLER: He better go right up to bed for a while, that's what he better do.

SID (*considering this owlishly*): Bed? Yes, maybe you're right. (*He gets to his feet*) I am not at all well—in very delicate condition—we are praying for a boy. Am I right, Nat? Nat, I kept telling you all day I was in delicate condition and yet you kept forcing demon chowder on me, although you knew full well—even if you were full—that there is a certain, peculiar oil in chowder that invariably— (*They are again all laughing—*LILY, *hysterically.*)

MRS. MILLER: *Will* you get to bed, you idiot!

SID (*mutters graciously*): Immediately—if not sooner. (*He turns to pass behind* LILY, *then stops, staring down at her*) But wait. There is still a duty I must perform. No day is complete without it. Lily, answer once and for all, will you marry me?

LILY (*with an hysterical giggle*): No, I won't—never!

SID (*nodding his head*): Right! And perhaps it's all for the best. For how could I forget the pre-precepts taught me at mother's dying knee. "Sidney," she said, "never marry a woman who drinks! Lips that touch liquor shall never touch yours!" (*Gazing at her mournfully*) Too bad! So fine a woman once—and now such a slave to rum! (*Turning to* NAT) What can we do to save her,

Nat? (*In a hoarse, confidential whisper*) Better put her in institution where she'll be removed from temptation! The mere smell of it seems to drive her frantic!

MRS. MILLER (*struggling with her laughter*): You leave Lily alone, and go to bed!

SID: Right! (*He comes around behind* LILY's *chair and moves toward the entrance to the back parlor—then suddenly turns and says with a bow*) Good night, ladies—*and* gents. We will meet—bye and bye! (*He gives an imitation of a Salvation Army drum*) Boom! Boom! Boom! Come and be saved, Brothers! (*He starts to sing the old Army hymn*)

> *"In the sweet*
> *Bye and bye*
> *We will meet on that beautiful shore."*

(*He turns and marches solemnly out through the back parlor, singing*)

> *"Work and pray*
> *While you may.*
> *We will meet in the sky bye and bye."*

(MILLER *and his wife and the children are all roaring with laughter.* LILY *giggles hysterically.*)

MILLER (*subsiding at last*): Haw, haw. He's a case, if ever there was one! Darned if you can help laughing at him—even when he's poking fun at you!

MRS. MILLER: Goodness, but he's a caution! Oh, my sides ache, I declare! I was trying so hard not to—but you can't help it, he's so silly! But I suppose we really shouldn't. It only encourages him. But, my lands—!

LILY (*suddenly gets up from her chair and stands*

rigidly, her face working—jerkily): That's just it—
you shouldn't—even I laughed—it does encourage—
that's been his downfall—everyone always laughing,
everyone always saying what a card he is, what a case,
what a caution, so funny—and he's gone on—and we're
all responsible—making it easy for him—we're all to
blame—and all we do is laugh!

MILLER (*worriedly*): Now, Lily, now, you mustn't take
on so. It isn't as serious as all that.

LILY (*bitterly*): Maybe—it is—to me. Or was—once.
(*Then contritely*) I'm sorry, Nat. I'm sorry, Essie. I
didn't mean to—I'm not feeling myself tonight. If you'll
excuse me, I'll go in the front parlor and lie down on
the sofa awhile.

MRS. MILLER: Of course, Lily. You do whatever you've a
mind to. (LILY *goes out.*)

MILLER (*frowning—a little shamefaced*): Hmm. I suppose she's right. Never knew Lily to come out with
things that way before. Anything special happened, Essie?

MRS. MILLER: Nothing I know—except he'd promised to
take her to the fireworks.

MILLER: That's so. Well, supposing I take her? I don't
want her to feel disappointed.

MRS. MILLER (*shaking her head*): Wild horses couldn't
drag her there now.

MILLER: Hmm. I thought she'd got completely over her
foolishness about him long ago.

MRS. MILLER: She never will.

MILLER: She'd better. He's got fired out of that Waterbury job—told me at the picnic after he'd got enough
Dutch courage in him.

MRS. MILLER: Oh, dear! Isn't he the fool!

MILLER: I knew something was wrong when he came home. Well, I'll find a place for him on my paper again, of course. He always was the best news-getter this town ever had. But I'll tell him he's got to stop his damn nonsense.

MRS. MILLER (*doubtfully*): Yes.

MILLER: Well, no use sitting here mourning over spilt milk. (*He gets up, and* RICHARD, MILDRED, TOMMY *and* MRS. MILLER *follow his example, the children quiet and a bit awed*) You kids go out in the yard and try to keep quiet for a while, so's your Uncle Sid'll get to sleep and your Aunt Lily can rest.

TOMMY (*mournfully*): Ain't we going to set off the sky-rockets and Roman candles, Pa?

MILLER: Later, Son, later. It isn't dark enough for them yet anyway.

MILDRED: Come on, Tommy. I'll see he keeps quiet, Pa.

MILLER: That's a good girl. (MILDRED *and* TOMMY *go out through the screen door.* RICHARD *remains standing, sunk in bitter, gloomy thoughts.* MILLER *glances at him —then irritably*) Well, Melancholy Dane, what are you doing?

RICHARD (*darkly*): I'm going out—for a while. (*Then suddenly*) Do you know what I think? It's Aunt Lily's fault, Uncle Sid's going to ruin. It's all because he loves her, and she keeps him dangling after her, and eggs him on and ruins his life—like all women love to ruin men's lives! I don't blame him for drinking himself to death! What does he care if he dies, after the way she's treated him! I'd do the same thing myself if I were in his boots!

MRS. MILLER (*indignantly*): Richard! You stop that talk!

RICHARD (*quotes bitterly*)

"Drink! for you know not whence you come nor why.
Drink! for you know not why you go nor where!"

MILLER *(losing his temper—harshly)*: Listen here, young
man! I've had about all I can stand of your nonsense
for one day! You're growing a lot too big for your size,
seems to me! You keep that damn fool talk to yourself,
you hear me—or you're going to regret it! Mind now!
(He strides angrily away through the back parlor.)

MRS. MILLER *(still indignant)*: Richard, I'm ashamed of
you, that's what I am. *(She follows her husband. RICH-
ARD stands for a second, bitter, humiliated, wronged,
even his father turned enemy, his face growing more
and more rebellious. Then he forces a scornful smile to
his lips.)*

RICHARD: Aw, what the hell do I care? I'll show them!
(He turns and goes out the screen door.)

Curtain

ACT THREE
Scene I

SCENE—*The back room of a bar in a small hotel—a small, dingy room, dimly lighted by two fly-specked globes in a fly-specked gilt chandelier suspended from the middle of the ceiling. At left, front, is the swinging door leading to the bar. At rear of door, against the wall, is a nickel-in-the-slot player-piano. In the rear wall, right, is a door leading to the "Family Entrance" and the stairway to the upstairs rooms. In the middle of the right wall is a window with closed shutters. Three tables with stained tops, four chairs around each table, are placed at center, front, at right, toward rear, and at rear, center. A brass cuspidor is on the floor by each table. The floor is unswept, littered with cigarette and cigar butts. The hideous saffron-colored wall-paper is blotched and spotted.*

It is about 10 o'clock the same night. RICHARD *and* BELLE *are discovered sitting at the table at center,* BELLE *at left of it,* RICHARD *in the next chair at the middle of table, rear, facing front.*

BELLE *is twenty, a rather pretty peroxide blonde, a typical college "tart" of the period, and of the cheaper variety, dressed with tawdry flashiness. But she is a fairly recent recruit to the ranks, and is still a bit remorseful behind her make-up and defiantly careless manner.*

BELLE *has an empty gin-rickey glass before her,* RICHARD *a half-empty glass of beer. He looks horribly timid, embarrassed and guilty, but at the same time thrilled and proud of at last mingling with the pace that kills.*

The player-piano is grinding out "Bedelia." The BAR-TENDER, *a stocky young Irishman with a foxily cunning, stupid face and a cynically wise grin, stands just inside the bar entrance, watching them over the swinging door.*

BELLE (*with an impatient glance at her escort—rattling the ice in her empty glass*): Drink up your beer, why don't you? It's getting flat.

RICHARD (*embarrassedly*): I let it get that way on purpose. I like it better when it's flat. (*But he hastily gulps down the rest of his glass, as if it were some nasty-tasting medicine. The* BARTENDER *chuckles audibly.* BELLE *glances at him.*)

BELLE (*nodding at the player-piano scornfully*): Say, George, is "Bedelia" the latest to hit this hick burg? Well, it's only a couple of years old! You'll catch up in time! Why don't you get a new roll for that old box?

BARTENDER (*with a grin*): Complain to the boss, not me. We're not used to having Candy Kiddoes like you around—or maybe we'd get up to date.

BELLE (*with a professionally arch grin at him*): Don't kid me, please. I can't bear it. (*Then she sings to the music from the piano, her eyes now on* RICHARD) "Bedelia, I'd like to feel yer." (*The* BARTENDER *laughs. She smirks at* RICHARD) Ever hear those words to it, Kid?

RICHARD (*who has heard them but is shocked at hearing a girl say them—putting on a blasé air*): Sure, lots of times. That's old.

BELLE (*edging her chair closer and putting a hand over one of his*): Then why don't you act as if you knew what they were all about?

RICHARD (*terribly flustered*): Sure, I've heard that old parody lots of times. What do you think I am?

BELLE: I don't know, Kid. Honest to God, you've got me guessing.

BARTENDER (*with a mocking chuckle*): He's a hot sport, can't you tell it? I never seen such a spender. My head's dizzy bringing you in drinks!

BELLE (*laughs irritably—to* RICHARD): Don't let him kid you. You show him. Loosen up and buy another drink, what say?

RICHARD (*humiliated—manfully*): Sure. Excuse me. I was thinking of something else. Have anything you like. (*He turns to the* BARTENDER *who has entered from the bar*) See what the lady will have—and have one on me yourself.

BARTENDER (*coming to the table—with a wink at* BELLE): That's talking! Didn't I say you were a sport? I'll take a cigar on you. (*To* BELLE) What's yours, Kiddo—the same?

BELLE: Yes. And forget the house rules this time and remember a rickey is supposed to have gin in it.

BARTENDER (*grinning*): I'll try to—seeing it's you. (*Then to* RICHARD) What's yours—another beer?

RICHARD (*shyly*): A small one, please. I'm not thirsty.

BELLE (*calculatedly taunting*): Say, honest, are things that slow up at Harvard? If they had you down at New Haven, they'd put you in a kindergarten! Don't be such a dead one! Filling up on beer will only make you sleepy. Have a man's drink!

RICHARD (*shamefacedly*): All right. I was going to. Bring me a sloe-gin fizz.

BELLE (*to* BARTENDER): And make it a real one.

BARTENDER (*with a wink*): I get you. Something that'll warm him up, eh? (*He goes into the bar, chuckling.*)

BELLE (*looks around the room—irritably*): Christ, what

a dump! (RICHARD *is startled and shocked by this curse and looks down at the table*) If this isn't the deadest burg I ever struck! Bet they take the sidewalks in after nine o'clock! (*Then turning on him*) Say, honestly, Kid, does your mother know you're out?

RICHARD (*defensively*): Aw, cut it out, why don't you— trying to kid me!

BELLE (*glances at him—then resolves on a new tack—patting his hand*) All right. I didn't mean to, Dearie. Please don't get sore at me.

RICHARD: I'm not sore.

BELLE (*seductively*): You see, it's this way with me. I think you're one of the sweetest kids I've ever met— and I could like you such a lot if you'd give me half a chance—instead of acting so cold and indifferent.

RICHARD: I'm not cold and indifferent. (*Then solemnly tragic*) It's only that I've got—a weight on my mind.

BELLE (*impatiently*): Well, get it off your mind and give something else a chance to work. (*The* BARTENDER *comes in, bringing the drinks.*)

BARTENDER (*setting them down—with a wink at* BELLE): This'll warm him for you. Forty cents, that is—with the cigar.

RICHARD (*pulls out his roll and hands a dollar bill over— with exaggerated carelessness*): Keep the change. (BELLE *emits a gasp and seems about to protest, then thinks better of it. The* BARTENDER *cannot believe his luck for a moment—then pockets the bill hastily, as if afraid* RICHARD *will change his mind.*)

BARTENDER (*respect in his voice*): Thank you, sir.

RICHARD (*grandly*): Don't mention it.

BARTENDER: I hope you like the drink. I took special pains with it. (*The voice of the* SALESMAN, *who has just come* in the bar, calls *"Hey! Anybody here?" and a coin is rapped on the bar*) I'm coming. (*The* BARTENDER *goes out.*)

BELLE (*remonstrating gently, a new appreciation for her escort's possibilities in her voice*): You shouldn't be so generous, Dearie. Gets him in bad habits. A dime would have been plenty.

RICHARD: Ah, that's all right. I'm no tightwad.

BELLE: That's the talk I like to hear. (*With a quick look toward the bar, she stealthily pulls up her dress—to* RICHARD's *shocked fascination—and takes a package of cheap cigarettes from her stocking*) Keep an eye out for that bartender, Kid, and tell me if you see him coming. Girls are only allowed to smoke upstairs in the rooms, he said.

RICHARD (*embarrassedly*): All right. I'll watch.

BELLE (*having lighted her cigarette and inhaled deeply, holds the package out to him*): Have a Sweet? You smoke, don't you?

RICHARD (*taking one*): Sure! I've been smoking for the last two years—on the sly. But next year I'll be allowed —that is, pipes and cigars. (*He lights his cigarette with elaborate nonchalance, puffs, but does not inhale— then, watching her, with shocked concern*) Say, you oughtn't to inhale like that! Smoking's awful bad for girls, anyway, even if they don't—

BELLE (*cynically amused*): Afraid it will stunt my growth? Gee, Kid, you are a scream! You'll grow up to be a minister yet! (RICHARD *looks shamefaced. She scans him impatiently—then holds up her drink*) Well, here's how! Bottoms up, now! Show me you really know how to drink. It'll take that load off your mind. (RICHARD *follows her example and they both drink the whole con-*

tents of their glasses before setting them down) There! That's something like! Feel better?

RICHARD (*proud of himself—with a shy smile*): You bet.

BELLE: Well, you'll feel still better in a minute—and then maybe you won't be so distant and unfriendly, eh?

RICHARD: I'm not.

BELLE: Yes, you are. I think you just don't like me.

RICHARD (*more manfully*): I do too like you.

BELLE: How much? A lot?

RICHARD: Yes, a lot.

BELLE: Show me how much! (*Then as he fidgets embarrassedly*) Want me to come sit on your lap?

RICHARD: Yes—I—(*She comes and sits on his lap. He looks desperately uncomfortable, but the gin is rising to his head and he feels proud of himself and devilish, too.*)

BELLE: Why don't you put your arm around me? (*He does so awkwardly*) No, not that dead way. Hold me tight. You needn't be afraid of hurting me. I like to be held tight, don't you?

RICHARD: Sure I do.

BELLE: 'Specially when it's by a nice handsome kid like you. (*Ruffling his hair*) Gee, you've got pretty hair, do you know it? Honest, I'm awfully strong for you! Why can't you be about me? I'm not so awfully ugly, am I?

RICHARD: No, you're—you're pretty.

BELLE: You don't say it as if you meant it.

RICHARD: I do mean it—honest.

BELLE: Then why don't you kiss me? (*She bends down her lips toward his. He hesitates, then kisses her and at once shrinks back*) Call that kissing? Here. (*She holds his head and fastens her lips on his and holds them there. He starts and struggles. She laughs*) What's the matter, Honey Boy? Haven't you ever kissed like that before?

RICHARD: Sure. Lots of times.

BELLE: Then why did you jump as if I'd bitten you? (*Squirming around on his lap*) Gee, I'm getting just crazy about you! What shall we do about it, eh? Tell me.

RICHARD: I—don't know. (*Then boldly*) I—I'm crazy about you, too.

BELLE (*kissing him again*): Just think of the wonderful time Edith and your friend, Wint, are having upstairs —while we sit down here like two dead ones. A room only costs two dollars. And, seeing I like you so much, I'd only take five dollars—from you. I'd do it for nothing—for you—only I've got to live and I owe my room rent in New Haven—and you know how it is. I get ten dollars from everyone else. Honest! (*She kisses him again, then gets up from his lap—briskly*) Come on. Go out and tell the bartender you want a room. And hurry. Honest, I'm so strong for you I can hardly wait to get you upstairs!

RICHARD (*starts automatically for the door to the bar— then hesitates, a great struggle going on in his mind— timidity, disgust at the money element, shocked modesty, and the guilty thought of* MURIEL, *fighting it out with the growing tipsiness that makes him want to be a hell of a fellow and go in for all forbidden fruit, and makes this tart a romantic, evil vampire in his eyes. Finally, he stops and mutters in confusion*) I can't.

BELLE: What, are you too bashful to ask for a room? Let me do it, then. (*She starts for the door.*)

RICHARD (*desperately*): No—I don't want you to—I don't want to.

BELLE (*surveying him, anger coming into her eyes*) Well, if you aren't the lousiest cheap skate!

RICHARD: I'm not a cheap skate!

BELLE: Keep me around here all night fooling with you when I might be out with some real live one—if there is such a thing in this burg!—and now you quit on me! Don't be such a piker! You've got five dollars! I seen it when you paid for the drinks, so don't hand me any lies!

RICHARD: I— Who said I hadn't? And I'm not a piker. If you need the five dollars so bad—for your room rent —you can have it without—I mean, I'll be glad to give —(*He has been fumbling in his pocket and pulls out his nine-dollar roll and holds out the five to her.*)

BELLE (*hardly able to believe her eyes, almost snatches it from his hand—then laughs and immediately becomes sentimentally grateful*): Thanks, Kid. Gee—oh, thanks —Gee, forgive me for losing my temper and bawling you out, will you? Gee, you're a regular peach! You're the nicest kid I've ever met! (*She kisses him and he grins proudly, a hero to himself now on many counts*) Gee, you're a peach! Thanks, again!

RICHARD (*grandly—and quite tipsily*): It's—nothing— only too glad. (*Then boldly*) Here—give me another kiss, and that'll pay me back.

BELLE (*kissing him*): I'll give you a thousand, if you want 'em. Come on, let's sit down, and we'll have another drink—and this time I'll blow you just to show my appreciation. (*She calls*) Hey, George! bring us another round—the same!

RICHARD (*a remnant of caution coming to him*): I don't know as I ought to—

BELLE: Oh, another won't hurt you. And I want to blow you, see. (*They sit down in their former places.*)

RICHARD (*boldly draws his chair closer and puts an arm around her—tipsily*): I like you a lot—now I'm getting to know you. You're a darned nice girl.

BELLE: Nice is good! Tell me another! Well, if I'm so nice, why didn't you want to take me upstairs? That's what I don't get.

RICHARD (*lying boldly*): I did want to—only I— (*Then he adds solemnly*) I've sworn off. (*The* BARTENDER *enters with the drinks.*)

BARTENDER (*setting them on the table*): Here's your pleasure. (*Then regarding* RICHARD's *arm about her waist*) Ho-ho, we're coming on, I see. (RICHARD *grins at him muzzily.*)

BELLE (*digs into her stocking and gives him a dollar*): Here. This is mine. (*He gives her change and she tips him a dime, and he goes out. She puts the five* RICHARD *had given her in her stocking and picks up her glass*) Here's how—and thanks again. (*She sips.*)

RICHARD (*boisterously*): Bottoms up! Bottoms up! (*He drinks all of his down and sighs with exaggerated satisfaction*) Gee, that's good stuff, all right. (*Hugging her*) Give me another kiss, Belle.

BELLE (*kisses him*): What did you mean a minute ago when you said you'd sworn off?

RICHARD (*solemnly*): I took an oath I'd be faithful.

BELLE (*bristling*): I'm not good enough to talk about her, I suppose?

RICHARD: I didn't—mean that. You're all right. (*Then*

with tipsy gravity) Only you oughtn't to lead this kind of life. It isn't right—for a nice girl like you. Why don't you reform?

BELLE (*sharply*): Nix on that line of talk! Can it, you hear! You can do a lot with me for five dollars—but you can't reform me, see. Mind your own business, Kid, and don't butt in where you're not wanted!

RICHARD: I—I didn't mean to hurt your feelings.

BELLE: I know you didn't mean. You're only like a lot of people who mean well, to hear them tell it. (*Changing the subject*) So you're faithful to your one love, eh? (*With an ugly sneer*) And how about her? Bet you she's out with a guy under some bush this minute, giving him all he wants. Don't be a sucker, Kid! Even the little flies do it!

RICHARD (*starting up his chair again—angrily*): Don't you say that! Don't you dare!

BELLE (*unimpressed—with a cynical shrug of her shoulders*): All right. Have it your own way and be a sucker! It cuts no ice with me.

RICHARD: You don't know her or—

BELLE: And don't want to. Shut up about her, can't you? (*She stares before her bitterly.* RICHARD *subsides into scowling gloom. He is becoming perceptibly more intoxicated with each moment now. The* BARTENDER *and the* SALESMAN *appear just inside the swinging door. The* BARTENDER *nods toward* BELLE, *giving the* SALESMAN *a wink. The* SALESMAN *grins and comes into the room, carrying his highball in his hand. He is a stout, jowly-faced man in his late thirties, dressed with cheap nattiness, with the professional breeziness and jocular, kid-'em-along manner of his kind.* BELLE *looks up as he*

enters and he and she exchange a glance of complete
recognition. She knows his type by heart and he knows
hers.)

SALESMAN (*passes by her to the table at right—grinning
genially*): Good evening.

BELLE: Good evening.

SALESMAN (*sitting down*): Hope I'm not butting in on
your party—but my dogs were giving out standing at
that bar.

BELLE: All right with me. (*Giving* RICHARD *a rather con-
temptuous look*) I've got no party on.

SALESMAN: That sounds hopeful.

RICHARD (*suddenly recites sentimentally*)

"But I wouldn't do such, 'cause I loved her too much,
But I learned about women from her."

(*Turns to scowl at the* SALESMAN—*then to* BELLE) Let's
have 'nother drink!

BELLE: You've had enough. (RICHARD *subsides, muttering
to himself.*)

SALESMAN: What is it—a child poet or a child actor?

BELLE: Don't know. Got me guessing.

SALESMAN: Well, if you could shake the cradle-robbing
act, maybe we could do a little business.

BELLE: That's easy. I just pull my freight. (*She shakes*
RICHARD *by the arm*) Listen, Kid. Here's an old friend
of mine, Mr. Smith of New Haven, just come in. I'm
going over and sit at his table for a while, see. And you
better go home.

RICHARD (*blinking at her and scowling*): I'm never going
home! I'll show them!

BELLE: Have it your own way—only let me up. (*She*

takes his arm from around her and goes to sit by the
SALESMAN. RICHARD *stares after her offendedly*.)

RICHARD: Go on. What do I care what you do? (*He recites scornfully*) "For a woman's only a woman, but a
good cigar's a smoke."

SALESMAN (*as* BELLE *sits beside him*): Well, what kind of
beer will you have, Sister?

BELLE: Mine's a gin rickey.

SALESMAN: You've got extravagant tastes, I'm sorry to
see.

RICHARD (*begins to recite sepulchrally*)

> "Yet each man kills the thing he loves,
> By each let this be heard."

SALESMAN (*grinning*): Say, this is rich! (*He calls encouragement*) That's swell dope, young feller. Give us
some more.

RICHARD (*ignoring him—goes on more rhetorically*)

> "Some do it with a bitter look,
> Some with a flattering word,
> The coward does it with a kiss,
> The brave man with a sword!"

(*He stares at* BELLE *gloomily and mutters tragically*) I
did it with a kiss! I'm a coward.

SALESMAN: That's the old stuff, Kid. You've got something on the ball, all right, all right! Give us another—
right over the old pan, now!

BELLE (*with a laugh*): Get the hook!

RICHARD (*glowering at her—tragically*)

" 'Oho,' they cried, 'the world is wide,
  But fettered limbs go lame!
  And once, or twice, to throw the dice
  Is a gentlemanly game,
  But he does not win who plays with Sin
  In the secret House of Shame!' "

BELLE (*angrily*): Aw, can it! Give us a rest from that bunk!

SALESMAN (*mockingly*): This gal of yours don't appreciate poetry. She's a lowbrow. But I'm the kid that eats it up. My middle name is Kelly and Sheets! Give us some more of the same! Do you know "The Lobster and the Wise Guy"? (*Turns to* BELLE *seriously*) No kidding, that's a peacherino. I heard a guy recite it at Poli's. Maybe this nut knows it. Do you, Kid? (*But* RICHARD *only glowers at him gloomily without answering.*)

BELLE (*surveying* RICHARD *contemptuously*): He's copped a fine skinful—and gee, he's hardly had anything.

RICHARD (*suddenly—with a dire emphasis*): "And then—at ten o'clock—Eilert Lovborg will come—with vine leaves in his hair!"

BELLE: And bats in his belfry, if he's you!

RICHARD (*regards her bitterly—then starts to his feet bellicosely—to the* SALESMAN): I don't believe you ever knew her in New Haven at all! You just picked her up now! You leave her alone, you hear! You won't do anything to her—not while I'm here to protect her!

BELLE (*laughing*): Oh, my God! Listen to it!

SALESMAN: Ssshh! This is a scream! Wait! (*He addresses* RICHARD *in tones of exaggerated melodrama*) Curse you, Jack Dalton, if I won't unhand her, what then?

RICHARD (*threateningly*): I'll give you a good punch in

the snoot, that's what! (*He moves toward their table.*)

SALESMAN (*with mock terror—screams in falsetto*): Help! Help! (*The* BARTENDER *comes in irritably.*)

BARTENDER: Hey, Cut out the noise. What the hell's up with you?

RICHARD (*tipsily*): He's too—damn fresh!

SALESMAN (*with a wink*): He's going to murder me. (*Then gets a bright idea for eliminating* RICHARD— *seriously to the* BARTENDER) It's none of my business, Brother, but if I were in your boots I'd give this young souse the gate. He's under age; any fool can see that.

BARTENDER (*guiltily*): He told me he was over eighteen.

SALESMAN: Yes, and I tell you I'm the Pope—but you don't have to believe me. If you're not looking for trouble, I'd advise you to get him started for some other gin mill and let them do the lying, if anything comes up.

BARTENDER: Hmm. (*He turns to* RICHARD *angrily and gives him a push*): Come on, now. On your way! You'll start no trouble in here! Beat it now!

RICHARD: I will not beat it!

BARTENDER: Oho, won't you? (*He gives him another push that almost sends him sprawling.*)

BELLE (*callously*): Give him the bum's rush! I'm sick of his bull! (RICHARD *turns furiously and tries to punch the* BARTENDER.)

BARTENDER (*avoids the punch*): Oho, you would, would you! (*He grabs* RICHARD *by the back of the neck and the seat of the pants and marches him ignominiously toward the swinging door.*)

RICHARD: Leggo of me, you dirty coward!

BARTENDER: Quiet now—or I'll pin a Mary Ann on your jaw that'll quiet you! (*He rushes him through the screen door and a moment later the outer doors are heard swinging back and forth.*)

SALESMAN (*with a chuckle*): Hand it to me, Kid. How was that for a slick way of getting rid of him?

BELLE (*suddenly sentimental*): Poor kid. I hope he makes home all right. I liked him—before he got soused.

SALESMAN: Who is he?

BELLE: The boy who's upstairs with my friend told me, but I didn't pay much attention. Name's Miller. His old man runs a paper in this one-horse burg, I think he said.

SALESMAN (*with a whistle*): Phew! He must be Nat Miller's kid, then.

BARTENDER (*coming back from the bar*): Well, he's on his way—with a good boot in the tail to help him!

SALESMAN (*with a malicious chuckle*): Yes? Well, maybe that boot will cost you a job, Brother. Know Nat Miller who runs the *Globe*? That's his kid.

BARTENDER (*his face falling*): The hell he is! Who said so?

SALESMAN: This baby doll. (*Getting up*) Say, I'll go keep cases on him—see he gets on the trolley all right, anyway. Nat Miller's a good scout. (*He hurries out.*)

BARTENDER (*viciously*): God damn the luck! If he ever finds out I served his kid, he'll run me out of town. (*He turns on* BELLE *furiously*) Why didn't you put me wise, you lousy tramp, you!

BELLE: Hey! I don't stand for that kind of talk—not from no hick beer-squirter like you, see!

BARTENDER (*furiously*): You don't, don't you? Who was it but you told me to hand him dynamite in that fizz? (*He gives her chair a push that almost throws her to the floor*) Beat it, you—and beat it quick—or I'll call Sullivan from the corner and have you run in for street-walking! (*He gives her a push that lands her against the family-entrance door*) Get the hell out of here—and no long waits!

BELLE (*opens the door and goes out—turns and calls back viciously*): I'll fix you for this, you thick Mick, if I have to go to jail for it. (*She goes out and slams the door.*)

BARTENDER (*looks after her worriedly for a second—then shrugs his shoulders*): That's only her bull. (*Then with a sigh as he returns to the bar*) Them lousy tramps is always getting this dump in Dutch!

Curtain

ACT THREE
Scene II

SCENE—*Same as Act one—Sitting-room of the Miller home —about 11 o'clock the same night.*

MILLER *is sitting in his favorite rocking-chair at left of table, front. He has discarded collar and tie, coat and shoes, and wears an old, worn, brown dressing-gown and disreputable-looking carpet slippers. He has his reading specs on and is running over items in a newspaper. But his mind is plainly preoccupied and worried, and he is not paying much attention to what he reads.*

MRS. MILLER *sits by the table at right, front. She also has on her specs. A sewing basket is on her lap and she is trying hard to keep her attention fixed on the doily she is doing. But, as in the case of her husband, but much* more apparently, her mind is preoccupied, and she is obviously on tenterhooks of nervous uneasiness.

LILY is sitting in the armchair by the table at rear, facing right. She is pretending to read a novel, but her attention wanders, too, and her expression is sad, although now it has lost all its bitterness and become submissive and resigned again.

MILDRED sits at the desk at right, front, writing two words over and over again, stopping each time to survey the result critically, biting her tongue, intensely concentrated on her work.

TOMMY sits on the sofa at left, front. He has had a hard day and is terribly sleepy but will not acknowledge it. His eyes blink shut on him, his head begins to nod, but he isn't giving up, and every time he senses any of the family glancing in his direction, he goads himself into a bright-eyed wakefulness.

MILDRED (*finally surveys the two words she has been writing and is satisfied with them*): There. (*She takes the paper over to her mother*) Look, Ma. I've been practising a new way of writing my name. Don't look at the others, only the last one. Don't you think it's the real goods?

MRS. MILLER (*pulled out of her preoccupation*): Don't talk that horrible slang. It's bad enough for boys, but for a young girl supposed to have manners—my goodness, when I was your age, if my mother'd ever heard me—

MILDRED: Well, don't you think it's nice, then?

MRS. MILLER (*sinks back into preoccupation—scanning the paper—vaguely*): Yes, very nice, Mildred—very nice, indeed. (*Hands the paper back mechanically.*)

MILDRED (*is a little piqued, but smiles*): Absent-minded! I don't believe you even saw it. (*She passes around the table to show her* AUNT LILY. MILLER *gives an uneasy glance at his wife and then, as if afraid of meeting her eye, looks quickly back at his paper again.*)

MRS. MILLER (*staring before her—sighs worriedly*): Oh, I do wish Richard would come home!

MILLER: There now, Essie. He'll be in any minute now. Don't you worry about him.

MRS. MILLER: But I do worry about him!

LILY (*surveying* MILDRED'S *handiwork—smiling*): This is fine, Mildred. Your penmanship is improving wonderfully. But don't you think that maybe you've got a little too many flourishes?

MILDRED (*disappointedly*): But, Aunt Lily, that's just what I was practising hardest on.

MRS. MILLER (*with another sigh*): What time is it now, Nat?

MILLER (*adopting a joking tone*): I'm going to buy a clock for in here. You have me reaching for my watch every couple of minutes. (*He has pulled his watch out of his vest pocket—with forced carelessness*) Only a little past ten.

MRS. MILLER: Why, you said it was that an hour ago! Nat Miller, you're telling me a fib, so's not to worry me. You let me see that watch!

MILLER (*guiltily*): Well, it's quarter to eleven—but that's not so late—when you remember it's Fourth of July.

MRS. MILLER: If you don't stop talking Fourth of July—! To hear you go on, you'd think that was an excuse for anything from murder to picking pockets!

MILDRED (*has brought her paper around to her father and now shoves it under his nose*): Look, Pa.

MILLER (*seizes on this interruption with relief*): Let's see. Hmm. Seems to me you've been inventing a new signature every week lately. What are you in training for—writing checks? You must be planning to catch a rich husband.

MILDRED (*with an arch toss of her head*): No wedding bells for me! But how do you like it, Pa?

MILLER: It's overpowering—no other word for it, overpowering! You could put it on the Declaration of Independence and not feel ashamed.

MRS. MILLER (*desolately, almost on the verge of tears*): It's all right for you to laugh and joke with Mildred! I'm the only one in this house seems to care—(*Her lips tremble.*)

MILDRED (*a bit disgustedly*): Ah, Ma, Dick only sneaked off to the fireworks at the beach, you wait and see.

MRS. MILLER: Those fireworks were over long ago. If he had, he'd be home.

LILY (*soothingly*): He probably couldn't get a seat, the trolleys are so jammed, and he had to walk home.

MILLER (*seizing on this with relief*): Yes, I never thought of that, but I'll bet that's it.

MILDRED: Ah, don't let him worry you, Ma. He just wants to show off he's heartbroken about that silly Muriel—and get everyone fussing over him and wondering if he hasn't drowned himself or something.

MRS. MILLER (*snappily*): You be quiet! The way you talk at times, I really believe you're that hard-hearted you haven't got a heart in you! (*With an accusing glance at her husband*) One thing I know, you don't get that from me! (*He meets her eye and avoids it guiltily. She sniffs and looks away from him around the room.* TOMMY, *who is nodding and blinking is afraid her eye is on him. He straightens alertly and speaks in a voice that, in spite of his effort, is dripping with drowsiness.*

TOMMY: Let me see what you wrote, Mid.

MILDRED (*cruelly mocking*): You? You're so sleepy you couldn't see it.

TOMMY (*valiantly*): I am not sleepy!

MRS. MILLER (*has fixed her eye on him*): My gracious, I was forgetting you were still up! You run up to bed this minute! It's hours past your bedtime!

TOMMY: But it's the Fourth of July. Ain't it, Pa?

MRS. MILLER (*gives her hubsand an accusing stare*): There! You see what you've done? You might know he'd copy your excuses! (*Then sharply to* TOMMY) You heard what I said, Young Man!

TOMMY: Aw, Ma, can't I stay up a *little* longer?

MRS. MILLER: I said, no! You obey me and no more arguing about it!

TOMMY (*drags himself to his feet*): Aw! I should think I could stay up till Dick—

MILLER (*kindly but firmly*): You heard your ma say no more arguing. When she says git, you better git. (TOMMY *accepts his fate resignedly and starts around kissing them all good night.*)

TOMMY (*kissing her*): Good night, Aunt Lily.

LILY: Good night, dear. Sleep well.

TOMMY (*pecking at* MILDRED): Good night, you.

MILDRED: Good night, you.

TOMMY (*kissing him*): Good night, Pa.

MILLER: Good night, Son. Sleep tight.

TOMMY (*kissing her*): Good night, Ma.

MRS. MILLER: Good night. Here! You look feverish. Let me feel of your head. No, you're all right. Hurry up, now. And don't forget your prayers.

(TOMMY *goes slowly to the doorway—then turns suddenly, the discovery of another excuse lighting up his face.*)

TOMMY: Here's another thing, Ma. When I was up to the water closet last—

MRS. MILLER. (*sharply*): When you were *where*?

TOMMY: The bathroom.

MRS. MILLER: That's better.

TOMMY: Uncle Sid was snoring like a fog horn—and he's right next to my room. How can I ever get to sleep while he's—(*He is overcome by a jaw-cracking yawn.*)

MRS. MILLER: I guess you'd get to sleep all right if you were inside a fog horn. You run along now. (TOMMY *gives up, grins sleepily, and moves off to bed. As soon as he is off her mind, all her former uneasiness comes back on* MRS. MILLER *tenfold. She sighs, moves restlessly, then finally asks*) What time is it now, Nat?

MILLER: Now, Essie, I just told you a minute ago.

MRS. MILLER (*resentfully*): I don't see how you can take it so calm! Here it's midnight, you might say, and our Richard still out, and we don't even know where he is.

MILDRED: I hear someone on the piazza. Bet that's him now, Ma.

MRS. MILLER (*her anxiety immediately turning to relieved anger*): You give him a good piece of your mind, Nat, you hear me! You're too easy with him, that's the whole trouble! The idea of him daring to stay out like this! (*The front door is heard being opened and shut,* and someone whistling "*Waltz Me Around Again, Willie.*")

MILDRED: No, that isn't Dick. It's Art.

MRS. MILLER (*her face falling*): Oh. (*A moment later* ARTHUR *enters through the front parlor, whistling softly, half under his breath, looking complacently pleased with himself.*)

MILLER (*surveys him over his glasses, not with enthusiasm—shortly*): So you're back, eh? We thought it was Richard.

ARTHUR: Is he still out? Where'd he go to?

MILLER: That's just what we'd like to know. You didn't run into him anywhere, did you?

ARTHUR: No. I've been at the Rands' ever since dinner. (*He sits down in the armchair at left of table, rear*) I suppose he sneaked off to the beach to watch the fireworks.

MILLER (*pretending an assurance he is far from feeling*): Of course. That's what we've been trying to tell your mother, but she insists on worrying her head off.

MRS. MILLER: But if he was going to the fireworks, why wouldn't he say so? He knew we'd let him.

ARTHUR (*with calm wisdom*): That's easy, Ma. (*He grins superiorly*) Didn't you hear him this morning showing off bawling out the Fourth like an anarchist? He wouldn't want to reneg on that to you—but he'd want to see the old fireworks just the same. (*He adds complacently*) I know. He's at the foolish age.

MILLER (*stares at* ARTHUR *with ill-concealed astonishment, then grins*): Well, Arthur, by gosh, you make me feel as if I owed you an apology when you talk horse sense like that. (*He turns to his wife, greatly relieved*) Arthur's hit the nail right on the head, I think, Essie.

That was what I couldn't figure out—why he—but now it's clear as day.

MRS. MILLER. (*with a sigh*): Well, I hope you're right. But I wish he was home.

ARTHUR (*takes out his pipe and fills and lights it with solemn gravity*): He oughtn't to be allowed out this late at his age. I wasn't, Fourth or no Fourth—if I remember.

MILLER (*a twinkle in his eyes*): Don't tax your memory trying to recall those ancient days of your youth. (MIL-DRED *laughs and* ARTHUR *looks sheepish. But he soon regains his aplomb.*)

ARTHUR (*importantly*): We had a corking dinner at the Rands'. We had sweetbreads on toast.

MRS. MILLER (*arising momentarily from her depression*): Just like the Rands to put on airs before you! I never could see anything to sweetbreads. Always taste like soap to me. And no real nourishment to them. I wouldn't have the pesky things on my table! (ARTHUR *again feels sat upon.*)

MILDRED (*teasingly*): Did you kiss Elsie good night?

ARTHUR: Stop trying to be so darn funny all the time! You give me a pain in the ear!

MILDRED: And that's where she gives me a pain, the stuck-up thing!—think she's the whole cheese!

MILLER (*irritably*): And that's where your everlasting wrangling gives me a pain, you two! Give us a rest! (*There is silence for a moment.*)

MRS. MILLER (*sighs worriedly again*): I do wish that boy would get home!

MILLER (*glances at her uneasily, peeks surreptitiously at his watch—then has an inspiration and turns to* ARTHUR): Arthur, what's this I hear about your having such a good singing voice? Rand was telling me he liked nothing better than to hear you sing—said you did every night you were up there. Why don't you ever give us folks at home here a treat?

ARTHUR (*pleased, but still nursing wounded dignity*): I thought you'd only sit on me.

MRS. MILLER (*perking up—proudly*): Arthur has a real nice voice. He practises when you're not at home. I didn't know you cared for singing, Nat.

MILLER: Well, I do—nothing better—and when I was a boy I had a fine voice myself and folks used to say I'd ought—(*Then abruptly, mindful of his painful experience with reminiscence at dinner, looking about him guiltily*) Hmm. But don't hide your light under a bushel, Arthur. Why not give us a song or two now? You can play for him, can't you, Mildred?

MILDRED (*with a toss of her head*): I can play as well as Elsie Rand, at least!

ARTHUR (*ignoring her—clearing his throat importantly*): I've been singing a lot tonight. I don't know if my voice—

MILDRED (*forgetting her grudge, grabs her brother's hand and tugs at it*): Come on. Don't play modest. You know you're just dying to show off. (*This puts* ARTHUR *off it at once. He snatches his hand away from her angrily.*)

ARTHUR: Let go of me, you! (*Then with surly dignity*) I don't feel like singing tonight, Pa. I will some other time.

MILLER: You let him alone, Mildred! (*He winks at* AR-THUR, *indicating with his eyes and a nod of his head* MRS. MILLER, *who has again sunk into worried brood-*

*ing. He makes it plain by this pantomime that he wants
him to sing to distract his mother's mind.*)

ARTHUR (*puts aside his pipe and gets up promptly*): Oh—
sure, I'll do the best I can. (*He follows* MILDRED *into the
front parlor, where he switches on the lights.*)

MILLER (*to his wife*): It won't keep Tommy awake.
Nothing could. And Sid, he'd sleep through an earth-
quake. (*Then suddenly, looking through the front parlor—grumpily*) Darn it, speak of the devil, here he
comes. Well, he's had a good sleep and he'd ought to be
sobered up. (LILY *gets up from her chair and looks
around her huntedly, as if for a place to hide.* MILLER
says soothingly) Lily, you just sit down and read your
book and don't pay any attention to him. (*She sits
down again and bends over her book tensely. From the
front parlor comes the tinkling of a piano as* MILDRED
runs over the scales. In the midst of this, SID *enters
through the front parlor. All the effervescence of his
jag has worn off and he is now suffering from a bad
case of hangover—nervous, sick, a prey to gloomy re-
morse and bitter feelings of self-loathing and self-pity.
His eyes are bloodshot and puffed, his face bloated, the
fringe of hair around his baldness tousled and tufty. He
sidles into the room guiltily, his eyes shifting about,
avoiding looking at anyone.*)

SID (*forcing a sickly, twitching smile*): Hello.

MILLER (*considerately casual*): Hello, Sid. Had a good
nap? (*Then, as* SID *swallows hard and is about to break
into further speech,* MILDRED'S *voice comes from the
front parlor,* "I haven't played that in ever so long, but
I'll try," *and she starts an accompaniment.* MILLER *motions* SID *to be quiet*) Ssshh! Arthur's going to sing for
us. (SID *flattens himself against the edge of the bookcase*

at center, rear, miserably self-conscious and ill-at-ease there but nervously afraid to move anywhere else. AR- THUR *begins to sing. He has a fairly decent voice but his method is untrained sentimentality to a dripping degree. He sings that old sentimental favorite, "Then You'll Remember Me." The effect on his audience is in- stant.* MILLER *gazes before him with a ruminating mel- ancholy, his face seeming to become gently sorrowful and old.* MRS. MILLER *stares before her, her expression becoming more and more doleful.* LILY *forgets to pre- tend to read her book but looks over it, her face grow- ing tragically sad. As for* SID, *he is moved to his re- morseful, guilt-stricken depths. His mouth pulls down at the corners and he seems about to cry. The song comes to an end.* MILLER *starts, then claps his hands en- thusiastically and calls*) Well done, Arthur—well done! Why, you've got a splendid voice! Give us some more! You liked that, didn't you, Essie?

MRS. MILLER (*dolefully*): Yes—but it's sad—terrible sad.

SID (*after swallowing hard, suddenly blurts out*): Nat and Essie—and Lily—I—I want to apologize—for com- ing home—the way I did—there's no excuse—but I didn't mean—

MILLER (*sympathetically*): Of course, Sid. It's all forgot- ten.

MRS. MILLER (*rousing herself—affectionately pitying*): Don't be a goose, Sid. We know how it is with picnics. You forget it. (*His face lights up a bit but his gaze shifts to* LILY *with a mute appeal, hoping for a word from her which is not forthcoming. Her eyes are fixed on her book, her body tense and rigid.*)

SID (*finally blurts out desperately*): Lily—I'm sorry— about the fireworks. Can you—forgive me? (*But* LILY *remains implacably silent. A stricken look comes over* SID's *face. In the front parlor* MILDRED *is heard saying* "But I only know the chorus"—*and she starts another accompaniment.*)

MILLER (*comes to* SID's *rescue*): Ssshh! We're going to have another song. Sit down, Sid. (SID, *hanging his head, flees to the farthest corner, left, front, and sits at the end of the sofa, facing front, hunched up, elbows on knees, face in hands, his round eyes childishly wounded and woe-begone.* ARTHUR *sings the popular* "Dearie," *playing up its sentimental values for all he is worth. The effect on his audience is that of the previous song, intensified—especially upon* SID. *As he finishes,* MILLER *again starts and applauds*) Mighty fine, Arthur! You sang that darned well! Didn't he, Essie?

MRS. MILLER (*dolefully*): Yes—But I wish he wouldn't sing such sad songs. (*Then, her lips trembling*) Richard's always whistling that.

MILLER (*hastily—calls*): Give us something cheery, next one, Arthur. You know, just for variety's sake.

SID (*suddenly turns toward* LILY—*his voice choked with tears—in a passion of self-denunciation*): You're right, Lily!—right not to forgive me!—I'm no good and never will be!—I'm a no-good drunken bum!—you shouldn't even wipe your feet on me!—I'm a dirty, rotten drunk!—no good to myself or anybody else!—if I had any guts I'd kill myself, and good riddance!—but I haven't!—I'm yellow, too!—a yellow, drunken bum! (*He hides his face in his hands and begins to sob like a sick little boy. This is too much for* LILY. *All her bitter hurt and steely resolve to ignore and punish him vanish in a flash, swamped by a pitying love for him. She runs*

*and puts her arm around him—even kisses him ten-
derly and impulsively on his bald head, and soothes
him as if he were a little boy.* MRS. MILLER, *almost
equally moved, has half risen to go to her brother, too,
but* MILLER *winks and shakes his head vigorously and
motions her to sit down.*)

LILY: There! Don't cry, Sid! I can't bear it! Of course, I
forgive you! Haven't I always forgiven you? I know
you're not to blame—So don't, Sid!

SID (*lifts a tearful, humbly grateful, pathetic face to her—
but a face that the dawn of a cleansed conscience is already beginning to restore to its natural Puckish expression*): Do you really forgive me—I know I don't
deserve it—can you really—?

LILY (*gently*): I told you I did, Sid—and I do.

SID (*kisses her hand humbly, like a big puppy licking it*):
Thanks, Lily. I can't tell you— (*In the front parlor,*
ARTHUR *begins to sing rollickingly "Waiting at the
Church," and after the first line or two* MILDRED *joins
in.* SID'S *face lights up with appreciation and, automatically, he begins to tap one foot in time, still holding fast to* LILY'S *hand. When they come to "sent
around a note, this is what she wrote," he can no
longer resist, but joins in a shaky bawl*): "Can't get
away to marry you today, My wife won't let me!" (*As
the song finishes, the two in the other room laugh.*
MILLER *and* SID *laugh.* LILY *smiles at* SID'S *laughter. Only*
MRS. MILLER *remains dolefully preoccupied, as if she
hadn't heard.*)

MILLER: That's fine, Arthur and Mildred. That's darned
good.

SID (*turning to* LILY *enthusiastically*): You ought to hear

Vesta Victoria sing that! Gosh, she's great! I heard her at Hammerstein's Victoria—you remember, that trip I made to New York.

LILY (*her face suddenly tired and sad again—for her memory of certain aspects of that trip is the opposite from what he would like her to recall at this moment— gently disengaging her hand from his—with a hopeless sigh*): Yes, I remember, Sid. (*He is overcome momentarily by guilty confusion. She goes quietly and sits down in her chair again. In the front parlor, from now on,* MILDRED *keeps starting to run over popular tunes but always gets stuck and turns to another.*)

MRS. MILLER (*suddenly*): What time is it now, Nat? (*Then without giving him a chance to answer*) Oh, I'm getting worried something dreadful, Nat! You don't know what might have happened to Richard! You read in the papers every day about boys getting run over by automobiles.

LILY: Oh, don't say that, Essie!

MILLER (*sharply, to conceal his own reawakened apprehension*): Don't get to imagining things, now!

MRS. MILLER: Well, why couldn't it happen, with everyone that owns one out tonight, and lots of those driving, drunk? Or he might have gone down to the beach dock, and fallen overboard! (*On the verge of hysteria*) Oh, I know something dreadful's happened! And you can sit there listening to songs and laughing as if— Why don't you do something? Why don't you go out and find him? (*She bursts into tears.*)

LILY (*comes to her quickly and puts her arm around her*): Essie, you mustn't worry so! You'll make yourself sick! Richard's all right. I've got a feeling in my bones he's all right.

MILDRED (*comes hurrying in from the front parlor*): What's the trouble? (ARTHUR *appears in the doorway beside her. She goes to her mother and also puts an arm around her*) Ah, don't cry, Ma! Dick'll turn up in a minute or two, wait and see!

ARTHUR: Sure, he will!

MILLER (*has gotten to his feet, frowning—soberly*): I was going out to look—if he wasn't back by twelve sharp. That'd be the time it'd take him to walk from the beach if he left after the last car. But I'll go now, if it'll ease your mind. I'll take the auto and drive out the beach road—and likely pick him up on the way. (*He has taken his collar and tie from where they hang from one corner of the bookcase at rear, center, and is starting to put them on*) You better come with me, Arthur.

ARTHUR: Sure thing, Pa. (*Suddenly he listens and says*) Ssshh! There's someone on the piazza now—coming around to this door, too. That must be him. No one else would—

MRS. MILLER: Oh, thank God, thank God!

MILLER (*with a sheepish smile*): Darn him! I've a notion to give him hell for worrying us all like this. (*The screen door is pushed violently open and* RICHARD *lurches in and stands swaying a little, blinking his eyes in the light. His face is a pasty pallor, shining with perspiration, and his eyes are glassy. The knees of his trousers are dirty, one of them torn from the sprawl on the sidewalk he had taken, following the* BARTENDER'S *kick. They all gape at him, too paralyzed for a moment to say anything.*)

MRS. MILLER: Oh, God, what's happened to him! He's gone crazy! Richard!

SID (*the first to regain presence of mind—with a grin*): Crazy, nothing. He's only soused!

ARTHUR: He's drunk, that's what! (*Then shocked and condemning*) You've got your nerve! You fresh kid! We'll take that out of you when we get you down to Yale!

RICHARD (*with a wild gesture of defiance—maudlinly dramatic*)

> "Yesterday this Day's Madness did prepare
> Tomorrow's Silence, Triumph, or Despair.
> Drink! for—"

MILLER (*his face grown stern and angry, takes a threatening step toward him*): Richard! How dare—!

MRS. MILLER (*hysterically*): Don't you strike him, Nat! Don't you—!

SID (*grabbing his arm*): Steady, Nat! Keep your temper! No good bawling him out now! He don't know what he's doing!

MILLER (*controlling himself and looking a bit ashamed*): All right—you're right, Sid.

RICHARD (*drunkenly glorying in the sensation he is creating—recites with dramatic emphasis*): "And then—I will come—with vine leaves in my hair!" (*He laughs with a double-dyed sardonicism.*)

MRS. MILLER (*staring at him as if she couldn't believe her eyes*): Richard! You're intoxicated!—you bad, wicked boy, you!

RICHARD (*forces a wicked leer to his lips and quotes with ponderous mockery*): "Fancy that, Hedda!" (*Then suddenly his whole expression changes, his pallor takes on a greenish, sea-sick tinge, his eyes seem to be turned inward uneasily—and, all pose gone, he calls to his*

mother appealingly, like a sick little boy) Ma! I feel—
rotten! (MRS. MILLER *gives a cry and starts to go to him,
but* SID *steps in her way.*)

SID: You let me take care of him, Essie. I know this
game backwards.

MILLER (*putting his arm around his wife*): Yes, you
leave him to Sid.

SID (*his arm around* RICHARD—*leading him off through
the front parlor*): Come on, Old Sport! Upstairs we
go! Your old Uncle Sid'll fix you up. He's the kid that
wrote the book!

MRS. MILLER (*staring after them—still aghast*): Oh, it's
too terrible! Imagine our Richard! And did you hear
him talking about some Hedda? Oh, I know he's been
with one of those bad women, I know he has—my
Richard! (*She hides her face on* MILLER'S *shoulder and
sobs heartbrokenly.*)

MILLER (*a tired, harassed, deeply worried look on his
face—soothing her*): Now, now, you mustn't get to
imagining such things! You mustn't, Essie! (LILY *and*
MILDRED *and* ARTHUR *are standing about awkwardly
with awed, shocked faces.*)

Curtain

ACT FOUR
Scene I

SCENE—*The same—Sitting-room of the Miller house— about one o'clock in the afternoon of the following day.*

As the curtain rises, the family, with the exception of RICHARD, *are discovered coming in through the back parlor from dinner in the dining-room.* MILLER *and his wife come first. His face is set in an expression of frowning severity.* MRS. MILLER'S *face is drawn and worried. She has evidently had no rest yet from a sleepless, tearful night.* SID *is himself again, his expression as innocent as if nothing had occurred the previous day that remotely concerned him. And, outside of eyes that are bloodshot and nerves that are shaky, he shows no aftereffects except that he is terribly sleepy.* LILY *is gently sad and depressed.* ARTHUR *is self-consciously a virtuous young man against whom nothing can be said.* MILDRED *and* TOMMY *are subdued, covertly watching their father.*

They file into the sitting-room in silence and then stand around uncertainly, as if each were afraid to be the first to sit down. The atmosphere is as stiltedly grave as if they were attending a funeral service. Their eyes keep fixed on the head of the house, who has gone to the window at right and is staring out frowningly, savagely chewing a toothpick.

MILLER (*finally—irritably*): Damn it, I'd ought to be back at the office putting in some good licks! I've a whole pile of things that have got to be done today!

MRS. MILLER (*accusingly*): You don't mean to tell me

you're going back without seeing him? It's your *duty—!*

MILLER (*exasperatedly*): 'Course I'm not! I wish you'd stop jumping to conclusions! What else did I come home for, I'd like to know? Do I usually come way back here for dinner on a busy day? I was only wishing this hadn't come up—just at this particular time. (*He ends up very lamely and is irritably conscious of the fact.*)

TOMMY (*who has been fidgeting restlessly—unable to bear the suspense a moment longer*): What is it Dick done? Why is everyone scared to tell me?

MILLER (*seizes this as an escape valve—turns and fixes his youngest son with a stern forbidding eye*): Young man, I've never spanked you yet, but that don't mean I never will! Seems to me that you've been just itching for it lately! You keep your mouth shut till you're spoken to—or I warn you something's going to happen!

MRS. MILLER: Yes, Tommy, you keep still and don't bother your pa. (*Then warningly to her husband*) Careful what you say, Nat. Little pitchers have big ears.

MILLER (*peremptorily*): You kids skedaddle—all of you. Why are you always hanging around the house? Go out and play in the yard, or take a walk, and get some fresh air. (MILDRED *takes* TOMMY's *hand and leads him out through the front parlor.* ARTHUR *hangs back, as if the designation "kids" couldn't possibly apply to him. His father notices this—impatiently*) You, too, Arthur. (AR-THUR *goes out with a stiff, wounded dignity.*)

LILY (*tactfully*): I think I'll go for a walk, too. (*She goes out through the front parlor.* SID *makes a movement as if to follow her.*)

MILLER: I'd like you to stay, Sid—for a while, anyway.

SID: Sure (*He sits down in the rocking-chair at right, rear, of table and immediately yawns*) Gosh, I'm dead. Don't know what's the matter with me today. Can't seem to keep awake.

MILLER (*with caustic sarcasm*): Maybe that demon chowder you drank at the picnic poisoned you! (SID *looks sheepish and forces a grin. Then* MILLER *turns to his wife with the air of one who determinedly faces the unpleasant*) Where is Richard?

MRS. MILLER (*flusteredly*): He's still in bed. I made him stay in bed to punish him—and I thought he ought to, anyway, after being so sick. But he says he feels all right.

SID (*with another yawn*): 'Course he does. When you're young you can stand anything without it fazing you. Why, I remember when I could come down on the morning after, fresh as a daisy, and eat a breakfast of pork chops and fried onions and— (*He stops guiltily.*)

MILLER (*bitingly*): I suppose that was before eating lobster shells had ruined your iron constitution!

MRS. MILLER (*regards her brother severely*): If I was in your shoes, I'd keep still! (*Then turning to her husband*) Richard must be feeling better. He ate all the dinner I sent up, Norah says.

MILLER: I thought you weren't going to give him any dinner—to punish him.

MRS. MILLER (*guiltily*): Well—in his weakened condition —I thought it best— (*Then defensively*) But you needn't think I haven't punished him. I've given him pieces of my mind he won't forget in a hurry. And I've kept reminding him his real punishment was still to come—that you were coming home to dinner on purpose—and then he'd learn that you could be terrible stern when he did such awful things.

MILLER (*stirs uncomfortably*): Hmm!

MRS. MILLER: And that's just what it's your duty to do— punish him good and hard! The idea of him daring— (*Then hastily*) But you be careful how you go about it, Nat. Remember he's like you inside—too sensitive for his own good. And he never would have done it, I know, if it hadn't been for that darned little dunce, Muriel, and her numbskull father—and then all of us teasing him and hurting his feelings all day—and then you lost your temper and were so sharp with him right after dinner before he went out.

MILLER (*resentfully*): I see this is going to work round to where it's all my fault!

MRS. MILLER: Now, I didn't say that, did I? Don't go losing your temper again. And here's another thing. You know as well as I, Richard would never have done such a thing alone. Why, he wouldn't know how! He must have been influenced and led by someone.

MILLER: Yes, I believe that. Did you worm out of him who it was? (*Then angrily*) By God, I'll make whoever it was regret it!

MRS. MILLER: No, he wouldn't admit there was anyone. (*Then triumphantly*) But there is one thing I did worm out of him—and I can tell you it relieved my mind more'n anything. You know, I was afraid he'd been with one of those bad women. Well, turns out there wasn't any Hedda. She was just out of those books he's been reading. He swears he's never known a Hedda in his life. And I believe him. Why, he seemed disgusted with me for having such a notion. (*Then lamely*) So somehow—I can't kind of feel it's all as bad as I thought it was. (*Then quickly and indignantly*) But it's bad enough, goodness knows—and you punish him good just the same. The idea of a boy his age—! Shall I go up now and tell him to get dressed, you want to see him?

MILLER (*helplessly—and irritably*): Yes! I can't waste all day listening to you!

MRS. MILLER (*worriedly*): Now you keep your temper, Nat, remember! (*She goes out through the front parlor.*)

MILLER: Darn women, anyway! They always get you mixed up. Their minds simply don't know what logic is! (*Then he notices that* SID *is dozing—sharply*) Sid!

SID (*blinking—mechanically*): I'll take the same. (*Then hurriedly*) What'd you say, Nat?

MILLER (*caustically*): What I didn't say was what'll you have. (*Irritably*) Do you want to be of some help, or don't you? Then keep awake and try and use your brains! This is a damned sight more serious than Essie has any idea! She thinks there weren't any girls mixed up with Richard's spree last night—but I happen to know there were! (*He takes a letter from his pocket*) Here's a note a woman left with one of the boys downstairs at the office this morning—didn't ask to see me, just said give me this. He'd never seen her before—said she looked like a tart. (*He has opened the letter and reads*) "Your son got the booze he drank last night at the Pleasant Beach House. The bartender there knew he was under age but served him just the same. He thought it was a good joke to get him soused. If you have any guts you will run that bastard out of town." Well, what do you think of that? It's a woman's handwriting—not signed, of course.

SID: She's one of the babies, all right—judging from her elegant language.

MILLER: See if you recognize the handwriting.

SID (*with a reproachful look*): Nat, I resent the implication that I correspond with all the tramps around this town. (*Looking at the letter*) No, I don't know who this one could be. (*Handing the letter back*) But I deduce that the lady had a run-in with the barkeep and wants revenge.

MILLER (*grimly*): And I deduce that before that she must have picked up Richard—or how would she know who he was?—and took him to this dive.

SID: Maybe. The Pleasant Beach House is nothing but a bed house—(*Quickly*) At least, so I've been told.

MILLER: That's just the sort of damned fool thing he might do to spite Muriel, in the state of mind he was in—pick up some tart. And she'd try to get him drunk so—

SID: Yes, it might have happened like that—and it might not. How're we ever going to prove it? Everyone at the Pleasant Beach will lie their heads off.

MILLER (*simply and proudly*): Richard won't lie.

SID: Well, don't blame him if he don't remember everything that happened last night. (*Then sincerely concerned*) I hope you're wrong, Nat. That kind of baby is dangerous for a kid like Dick—in more ways than one. You know what I mean.

MILLER (*frowningly*): Yep—and that's just what's got me worried. Damn it, I've got to have a straight talk with him—about women and all those things. I ought to have long ago.

SID: Yes. You ought.

MILLER: I've tried to a couple of times. I did it all right with Wilbur and Lawrence and Arthur, when it came time—but, hell, with Richard I always get sort of ashamed of myself and can't get started right. You feel, in spite of all his bold talk out of books, that he's so darned innocent inside.

SID: I know. I wouldn't like the job. (*Then after a pause —curiously*) How were you figuring to punish him for his sins?

MILLER (*frowning*): To be honest with you, Sid, I'm damned if I know. All depends on what I feel about what he feels when I first size him up—and then it'll be like shooting in the dark.

SID: If I didn't know you so well, I'd say don't be too hard on him. (*He smiles a little bitterly*) If you remember, I was always getting punished—and see what a lot of good it did me!

MILLER (*kindly*): Oh, there's lots worse than you around, so don't take to boasting. (*Then, at a sound from the front parlor—with a sigh*) Well, here comes the Bad Man, I guess.

SID (*getting up*): I'll beat it. (*But it is* MRS. MILLER *who appears in the doorway, looking guilty and defensive.* SID *sits down again.*)

MRS. MILLER: I'm sorry, Nat—but he was sound asleep and I didn't have the heart to wake him. I waited for him to wake up but he didn't.

MILLER (*concealing a relief of which he is ashamed— exasperatedly*): Well, I'll be double damned! If you're not the—

MRS. MILLER (*defensively aggressive*): Now don't lose your temper at me, Nat Miller! You know as well as I do he needs all the sleep he can get today—after last night's ructions! Do you want him to be taken down sick? And what difference does it make to you anyway? You can see him when you come home for supper, can't you? My goodness, I never saw you so savage-tempered! You'd think you couldn't bear waiting to punish him!

MILLER (*outraged*): Well, I'll be eternally —(*Then suddenly he laughs*) No use talking, you certainly take the cake! But you know darned well I told you I'm not coming home to supper tonight. I've got a date with Jack Lawson that may mean a lot of new advertising and it's important.

MRS. MILLER: Then you can see him when you do come home.

MILLER (*covering his evident relief at this respite with a fuming manner*): All right! All right! I give up! I'm going back to the office. (*He starts for the front parlor*) Bring a man all the way back here on a busy day and then you— No consideration— (*He disappears, and a moment later the front door is heard shutting behind him.*)

MRS. MILLER: Well! I never saw Nat so bad-tempered.

SID (*with a chuckle*): Bad temper, nothing. He's so tickled to get out of it for a while he can't see straight!

MRS. MILLER (*with a sniff*): I hope I know him better than you. (*Then fussing about the room, setting this and that in place, while* SID *yawns drowsily and blinks his eyes*) Sleeping like a baby—so innocent-looking. You'd think butter wouldn't melt in his mouth. It all goes to show you never can tell by appearances—not even when it's your own child. The idea!

SID (*drowsily*): Oh, Dick's all right, Essie. Stop worrying.

MRS. MILLER (*with a sniff*): Of course, you'd say that. I suppose you'll have him out with you painting the town red the next thing! (*As she is talking,* RICHARD *appears in the doorway from the sitting-room. He shows no ill effects from his experience the night before. In fact, he looks surprisingly healthy. He is dressed in old clothes that look as if they had been hurriedly flung on. His expression is one of hang-dog guilt mingled with a defensive defiance.*)

RICHARD (*with self-conscious unconcern, ignoring his mother*): Hello, Sid.

MRS. MILLER (*whirls on him*): What are you doing here, Young Man? I thought you were asleep! Seems to me you woke up pretty quick—just after your pa left the house!

RICHARD (*sulkily*): I wasn't asleep. I heard you in the room.

MRS. MILLER (*outraged*): Do you mean to say you were deliberately deceiving—

RICHARD: I wasn't deceiving. You didn't ask if I was asleep.

MRS. MILLER: It amounts to the same thing and you know it! It isn't enough your wickedness last night, but now you have to take to lying!

RICHARD: I wasn't lying, Ma. If you'd asked if I was asleep I'd have said no.

MRS. MILLER: I've a good mind to send you straight back to bed and make you stay there!

RICHARD: Ah, what for, Ma? It was only giving me a headache, lying there.

MRS. MILLER: If you've got a headache, I guess you know it doesn't come from that! And imagine me standing there, and feeling sorry for you, like a fool—even having a run-in with your pa because—But you wait till he comes back tonight! If you don't catch it!

RICHARD (*sulkily*): I don't care.

MRS. MILLER: You don't care? You talk as if you weren't sorry for what you did last night!

RICHARD (*defiantly*): I'm not sorry.

MRS. MILLER: Richard! You ought to be ashamed! I'm beginning to think you're hardened in wickedness, that's what!

RICHARD (*with bitter despondency*): I'm not sorry because I don't care a darn what I did, or what's done to me, or anything about anything! I won't do it again—

MRS. MILLER (*seizing on this to relent a bit*): Well, I'm glad to hear you say that, anyway!

RICHARD: But that's not because I think it was wicked or any such old-fogy moral notion, but because it wasn't any fun. It didn't make me happy and funny like it does Uncle Sid—

SID (*drowsily*): What's that? Who's funny?

RICHARD (*ignoring him*): It only made me sadder—and sick—so I don't see any sense in it.

MRS. MILLER: Now you're talking sense! That's a good boy.

RICHARD: But I'm not sorry I tried it once—curing the soul by means of the senses, as Oscar Wilde says. (*Then with despairing pessimism*) But what does it matter what I do or don't do? Life is all a stupid farce! I'm through with it! (*With a sinister smile*) It's lucky there aren't any of General Gabler's pistols around—or you'd see if I'd stand it much longer!

MRS. MILLER (*worriedly impressed by this threat—but pretending scorn*): I don't know anything about General Gabler—I suppose that's more of those darned books—but you're a silly gabbler yourself when you talk that way!

RICHARD (*darkly*): That's how little you know about me.

MRS. MILLER (*giving in to her worry*): I wish you wouldn't say those terrible things—about life and pistols! You don't want to worry me to death, do you?

RICHARD (*reassuringly stoical now*): You needn't worry, Ma. It was only my despair talking. But I'm not a coward. I'll face—my fate.

MRS. MILLER (*stands looking at him puzzledly—then gives it up with a sigh*): Well, all I can say is you're the queerest boy I ever did hear of! (*Then solicitously, putting her hand on his forehead*) How's your headache? Do you want me to get you some Bromo Seltzer?

RICHARD (*taken down—disgustedly*): No, I don't! Aw, Ma, you don't understand anything!

MRS. MILLER: Well, I understand this much: It's your liver, that's what! You'll take a good dose of salts tomorrow morning, and no nonsense about it! (*Then suddenly*) My goodness, I wonder what time it's getting to be. I've got to go upstreet. (*She goes to the front-parlor doorway—then turns*) You stay here, Richard, you hear? Remember, you're not allowed out today—for a punishment. (*She hurries away.* RICHARD *sits in tragic gloom.* SID, *without opening his eyes, speaks to him drowsily.*)

SID: Well, how's my fellow Rum Pot, as good old Dowie calls us? Got a head?

RICHARD (*startled—sheepishly*): Aw, don't go dragging that up, Uncle Sid. I'm never going to be such a fool again, I tell you.

SID (*with drowsy cynicism—not unmixed with bitterness at the end*): Seems to me I've heard someone say that before. Who could it have been, I wonder? Why, if it wasn't Sid Davis! Yes, sir, I've heard him say that very thing a thousand times, must be. But then he's always fooling; you can't take a word he says seriously; he's a card, that Sid is!

RICHARD (*darkly*): I was desperate, Uncle—even if she wasn't worth it. I was wounded to the heart.

SID: I like to the quick better myself—more stylish. (*Then sadly*) But you're right. Love is hell on a poor sucker. Don't I know it? (RICHARD *is disgusted and disdains to reply.* SID's *chin sinks on his chest and he begins to breathe noisily, fast asleep.* RICHARD *glances at him with aversion. There is a sound of someone on the porch and the screen door is opened and* MILDRED *enters. She smiles on seeing her uncle, then gives a start on seeing* RICHARD.)

MILDRED: Hello! Are you allowed up?

RICHARD: Of course, I'm allowed up.

MILDRED (*comes and sits in her father's chair at right, front, of table*): How did Pa punish you?

RICHARD: He didn't. He went back to the office without seeing me.

MILDRED: Well, you'll catch it later. (*Then rebukingly*) And you ought to. If you'd ever seen how awful you looked last night!

RICHARD: Ah, forget it, can't you?

MILDRED: Well, are you ever going to do it again, that's what I want to know.

RICHARD: What's that to you?

MILDRED (*with suppressed excitement*): Well, if you don't solemnly swear you won't—then I won't give you something I've got for you.

RICHARD: Don't try to kid me. You haven't got anything.

MILDRED: I have, too.

RICHARD: What?

MILDRED: Wouldn't you like to know! I'll give you three guesses.

RICHARD (*with disdainful dignity*): Don't bother me. I'm in no mood to play riddles with kids!

MILDRED: Oh, well, if you're going to get snippy! Anyway you haven't promised yet.

RICHARD (*a prey to keen curiosity now*): I promise. What is it?

MILDRED: What would you like best in the world?

RICHARD: I don't know. What?

MILDRED: And you pretend to be in love! If I told Muriel that!

RICHARD (*breathlessly*): Is it—from her?

MILDRED (*laughing*): Well, I guess it's a shame to keep you guessing. Yes. It is from her. I was walking past her place just now when I saw her waving from their parlor window, and I went up and she said give this to Dick, and she didn't have a chance to say anything else because her mother called her and said she wasn't allowed to have company. So I took it—and here it is. (*She gives him a letter folded many times into a tiny square.* RICHARD *opens it with a trembling eagerness and reads.* MILDRED *watches him curiously—then sighs affectedly*) Gee, it must be nice to be in love like you are—all with one person.

RICHARD (*his eyes shining*): Gee, Mid, do you know what she says—that she didn't mean a word in that other letter. Her old man made her write it. And she loves me and only me and always will, no matter how they punish her!

MILDRED: My! I'd never think she had that much spunk.

RICHARD: Huh! You don't know her! Think I could fall in love with a girl that was afraid to say her soul's her own? I should say not! (*Then more gleefully still*) And she's going to try and sneak out and meet me tonight. She says she thinks she can do it. (*Then suddenly feeling this enthusiasm before* MILDRED *is entirely the wrong note for a cynical pessimist—with an affected bitter laugh*) Ha! I knew darned well she couldn't hold out—that she'd ask to see me again. (*He misquotes cynically*) "Women never know when the curtain has fallen. They always want another act."

MILDRED: Is that so, Smarty?

RICHARD (*as if he were weighing the matter*): I don't know whether I'll consent to keep this date or not.

MILDRED: Well, I know! You're not allowed out, you silly! So you can't!

RICHARD (*dropping all pretense—defiantly*): Can't I, though! You wait and see if I can't! I'll see her tonight if it's the last thing I ever do! I don't care how I'm punished after!

MILDRED (*admiringly*): Goodness! I never thought you had such nerve!

RICHARD: You promise to keep your face shut, Mid— until after I've left—then you can tell Pa and Ma where I've gone—I mean, if they're worrying I'm off like last night.

MILDRED: All right. Only you've got to do something for me when I ask.

RICHARD: 'Course I will. (*Then excitedly*) And say, Mid! Right now's the best chance for me to get away—while everyone's out! Ma'll be coming back soon and she'll keep watching me like a cat— (*He starts for the back parlor*) I'm going. I'll sneak out the back.

MILDRED (*excitedly*): But what'll you do till nighttime? It's ages to wait.

RICHARD: What do I care how long I wait! (*Intensely sincere now*) I'll think of her—and dream! I'd wait a million years and never mind it—for her! (*He gives his sister a superior scornful glance*) The trouble with you is, you don't understand what love means! (*He disappears through the back parlor.* MILDRED *looks after him admiringly.* SID *puffs and begins to snore peacefully.*)

Curtain

ACT FOUR
Scene II

SCENE—*A strip of beach along the harbor. At left, a bank of dark earth, running half-diagonally back along the beach, marking the line where the sand of the beach ends and fertile land begins. The top of the bank is grassy and the trailing boughs of willow trees extend out over it and over a part of the beach. At left, front, is a path leading up the bank, between the willows. On the beach, at center, front, a white, flat-bottomed rowboat is drawn up, its bow about touching the bank, the painter trailing up the bank, evidently made fast to the trunk of a willow. Halfway down the sky, at rear, left, the crescent of the new moon casts a soft, mysterious, caressing light over everything. The sand of the beach shimmers palely. The forward half (left of center) of the rowboat is in the deep shadow cast by the willow, the stern section is in moon-*

light. In the distance, the orchestra of a summer hotel can be heard very faintly at intervals.

RICHARD *is discovered sitting sideways on the gunwale of the rowboat near the stern. He is facing left, watching the path. He is in a great state of anxious expectancy, squirming about uncomfortably on the narrow gunwale, kicking at the sand restlessly, twirling his straw hat, with a bright-colored band in stripes, around on his finger.*

RICHARD *(thinking aloud)*: Must be nearly nine. . . . I can hear the Town Hall clock strike, it's so still tonight . . . Gee, I'll bet Ma had a fit when she found out I'd sneaked out . . . I'll catch hell when I get back, but it'll be worth it . . . if only Muriel turns up . . . she didn't say for certain she could . . . gosh, I wish she'd come! . . . am I sure she wrote nine? . . . *(He puts the straw hat on the seat amidships and pulls the folded letter out of his pocket and peers at it in the moonlight)* Yes, it's nine, all right. *(He starts to put the note back in his pocket, then stops and kisses it—then shoves it away hastily, sheepish, looking around him shamefacedly, as if afraid he were being observed)* Aw, that's silly . . . no, it isn't either . . . not when you're really in love. . . . *(He jumps to his feet restlessly)* Darn it, I wish she'd show up! . . . think of something else . . . that'll make the time pass quicker . . . where was I this time last night? . . . waiting outside the Pleasant Beach House . . . Belle . . . ah, forget her! . . . now, when Muriel's coming . . . that's a fine time to think of—! . . . but you hugged and kissed her . . . not until I was drunk, I didn't . . . and then it was all showing off . . . darned fool! . . . and I didn't go upstairs with her . . . even if she was pretty . . . aw, she wasn't pretty . . . she was all painted up . . . she was just a whore . . . she was everything dirty . . . Muriel's a million times prettier anyway . . . Muriel and I will go upstairs . . . when we're married . . . but that will be beautiful . . . but I oughtn't even to think of that yet . . . it's not right . . . I'd never—now . . . and she'd never . . . she's a decent girl . . . I couldn't love her if she wasn't . . . but after we're married. . . . (*He gives a little shiver of passionate longing—then resolutely turns his mind away from these improper, almost desecrating thoughts*) That damned barkeep kicking me . . . I'll bet you if I hadn't been drunk I'd have given him one good punch in the nose, even if he could have licked me after! . . . (*Then with a shiver of shamefaced revulsion and self-disgust*) Aw, you deserved a kick in the pants . . . making such a darned slob of yourself . . . reciting the Ballad of Reading Gaol to those lowbrows! . . . you must have been a fine sight when you got home . . . having to be put to bed and getting sick! . . . Phaw! . . . (*He squirms disgustedly*) Think of something else, can't you? . . . recite something . . . see if you remember . . .

> "*Nay, let us walk from fire unto fire*
> *From passionate pain to deadlier delight—*
> *I am too young to live without desire,*
> *Too young art thou to waste this summernight—*"

. . . gee, that's a peach! . . . I'll have to memorize the rest and recite it to Muriel the next time. . . . I wish I could write poetry . . . about her and me. . . . (*He sighs and stares around him at the night*) Gee, it's beautiful tonight . . . as if it was a special night . . .

for me and Muriel. . . . Gee, I love tonight. . . . I love the sand, and the trees, and the grass, and the water and the sky, and the moon . . . it's all in me and I'm in it . . . God, it's so beautiful! (*He stands staring at the moon with a rapt face. From the distance the Town Hall clock begins to strike. This brings him back to earth with a start*) There's nine now. . . . (*He peers at the path apprehensively*) I don't see her . . . she must have got caught. . . . (*Almost tearfully*) Gee, I hate to go home and catch hell . . . without having seen her! . . . (*Then calling a manly cynicism to his aid*) Aw, who ever heard of a woman ever being on time. . . . I ought to know enough about life by this time not to expect . . . (*Then with sudden excitement*) There she comes now. . . . Gosh! (*He heaves a huge sigh of relief—then recites dramatically to himself, his eyes on the approaching figure*)

> *"And lo my love, mine own soul's heart, more dear*
> *Than mine own soul, more beautiful than God,*
> *Who hath my being between the hands of her—"*

(*Then hastily*) Mustn't let her know I'm so tickled. . . . I ought to be mad about that first letter, anyway . . . if women are too sure of you, they treat you like slaves . . . let her suffer, for a change. . . . (*He starts to stroll around with exaggerated carelessness, turning his back on the path, hands in pockets, whistling with insouciance "Waiting at the Church."*

(MURIEL MC COMBER *enters from down the path, left front. She is fifteen, going on sixteen. She is a pretty girl with a plump, graceful little figure, fluffy, light-brown hair, big naïve wondering dark eyes, a round dimpled face, a melting drawly voice. Just now she is in a great thrilled state of timid adventurousness. She hesitates in the shadow at the foot of the path, waiting for* RICHARD *to see her; but he resolutely goes on whistling with back turned, and she has to call him.*)

MURIEL: Oh, Dick.

RICHARD (*turns around with an elaborate simulation of being disturbed in the midst of profound meditation*): Oh, hello. Is it nine already? Gosh, time passes—when you're thinking.

MURIEL (*coming toward him as far as the edge of the shadow—disappointedly*): I thought you'd be waiting right here at the end of the path. I'll bet you'd forgotten I was even coming.

RICHARD (*strolling a little toward her but not too far— carelessly*): No, I hadn't forgotten, honest. But got to thinking about life.

MURIEL: You might think of me for a change, after all the risk I've run to see you! (*Hesitating timidly on the edge of the shadow*) Dick! You come here to me. I'm afraid to go out in that bright moonlight where anyone might see me.

RICHARD (*coming toward her—scornfully*): Aw, there you go again—always scared of life!

MURIEL (*indignantly*): Dick Miller, I do think you've got an awful nerve to say that after all the risks I've run making this date and then sneaking out! You didn't take the trouble to sneak any letter to me, I notice!

RICHARD: No, because after your first letter, I thought everything was dead and past between us.

MURIEL: And I'll bet you didn't care one little bit! (*On the verge of humiliated tears*) Oh, I was a fool ever to come here! I've got a good notion to go right home and never speak to you again! (*She half turns back toward the path.*)

RICHARD (*frightened—immediately becomes terribly sincere—grabbing her hand*): Aw, don't go, Muriel! Please! I didn't mean anything like that, honest, I didn't! Gee, if you knew how broken-hearted I was by that first letter, and how darned happy your second letter made me—!

MURIEL (*happily relieved—but appreciates she has the upper hand now and doesn't relent at once*): I don't believe you.

RICHARD: You ask Mid how happy I was. She can prove it.

MURIEL: She'd say anything you told her to. I don't care anything about what she'd say. It's you. You've got to swear to me—

RICHARD: I swear!

MURIEL (*demurely*): Well then, all right. I'll believe you.

RICHARD (*his eyes on her face lovingly—genuine adoration in his voice*): Gosh, you're pretty tonight, Muriel! It seems ages since we've been together! If you knew how I've suffered—!

MURIEL: I did, too.

RICHARD (*unable to resist falling into his tragic literary pose for a moment*): The despair in my soul— (*He recites dramatically*) "Something was dead in each of us, And what was dead was Hope!" That was me! My hope of happiness was dead! (*Then with sincere boyish fervor*) Gosh, Muriel, it sure is wonderful to be with you again! (*He puts a timid arm around her awkwardly.*)

MURIEL (*shyly*): I'm glad—it makes you happy. I'm happy, too.

RICHARD: Can't I—won't you let me kiss you—now? Please! (*He bends his face toward hers.*)

MURIEL (*ducking her head away—timidly*): No. You mustn't. Don't—

RICHARD: Aw, why can't I?

MURIEL: Because—I'm afraid.

RICHARD (*discomfited—taking his arm from around her —a bit sulky and impatient with her*): Aw, that's what you always say! You're always so afraid! Aren't you ever going to let me?

MURIEL: I will—sometime.

RICHARD: When?

MURIEL: Soon, maybe.

RICHARD: Tonight, will you?

MURIEL (*coyly*): I'll see.

RICHARD: Promise?

MURIEL: I promise—maybe.

RICHARD: All right. You remember you've promised. (*Then coaxingly*) Aw, don't let's stand here. Come on out and we can sit down in the boat.

MURIEL (*hesitantly*): It's so bright out there.

RICHARD: No one'll see. You know there's never anyone around here at night.

MURIEL (*illogically*): I know there isn't. That's why I thought it would be the best place. But there might be someone.

RICHARD (*taking her hand and tugging at it gently*): There isn't a soul. (MURIEL *steps out a little and looks up and down fearfully.* RICHARD *goes on insistently*) Aw, what's the use of a moon if you can't see it!

MURIEL: But it's only a new moon. That's not much to look at.

RICHARD: But I want to see you. I can't here in the shadow. I want to—drink in—all your beauty.

MURIEL (*can't resist this*): Well, all right—only I can't stay only a few minutes. (*She lets him lead her toward the stern of the boat.*)

RICHARD (*pleadingly*): Aw, you can stay a little while, can't you? Please! (*He helps her in and she settles herself in the stern seat of the boat, facing diagonally left front.*)

MURIEL: A little while. (*He sits beside her*) But I've got to be home in bed again pretending to be asleep by ten o'clock. That's the time Pa and Ma come up to bed, as regular as clock work, and Ma always looks into my room.

RICHARD: But you'll have oodles of time to do that.

MURIEL (*excitedly*): Dick, you have no idea what I went through to get here tonight! My, but it was exciting! You know Pa's punishing me by sending me to bed at eight sharp, and I had to get all undressed and into bed 'cause at half-past he sends Ma up to make sure I've obeyed, and she came up, and I pretended to be asleep, and she went down again, and I got up and dressed in such a hurry—I must look a sight, don't I?

RICHARD: You do not! You look wonderful!

MURIEL: And then I sneaked down the back stairs. And the pesky old stairs squeaked, and my heart was in my mouth, I was so scared, and then I sneaked out through the back yard, keeping in the dark under the trees, and— My, but it was exciting! Dick, you don't realize how I've been punished for your sake. Pa's been so mean and nasty, I've almost hated him!

RICHARD: And you don't realize what I've been through

for you—and what I'm in for—for sneaking out— (*Then darkly*) And for what I did last night—what your letter made me do!

MURIEL (*made terribly curious by his ominous tone*): What did my letter make you do?

RICHARD (*beginning to glory in this*): It's too long a story —and let the dead past bury its dead. (*Then with real feeling*) Only it isn't past, I can tell you! What I'll catch when Pa gets hold of me!

MURIEL: Tell me, Dick! Begin at the beginning and tell me!

RICHARD (*tragically*): Well, after your old—your father left our place I caught holy hell from Pa.

MURIEL: Dick! You mustn't swear!

RICHARD (*somberly*): Hell is the only word that can describe it. And on top of that, to torture me more, he gave me your letter. After I'd read that I didn't want to live any more. Life seemed like a tragic farce.

MURIEL: I'm so awful sorry, Dick—honest I am! But you might have known I'd never write that unless—

RICHARD: I thought your love for me was dead. I thought you'd never loved me, that you'd only been cruelly mocking me—to torture me!

MURIEL: Dick! I'd never! You know I'd never!

RICHARD: I wanted to die. I sat and brooded about death. Finally I made up my mind I'd kill myself.

MURIEL (*excitedly*): Dick! You didn't!

RICHARD: I did, too! If there'd been one of Hedda Gabler's pistols around, you'd have seen if I wouldn't have done it beautifully! I thought, when I'm dead, she'll be sorry she ruined my life!

MURIEL (*cuddling up a little to him*): If you ever had! I'd have died, too! Honest, I would!

RICHARD: But suicide is the act of a coward. That's what stopped me. (*Then with a bitter change of tone*) And anyway, I thought to myself, she isn't worth it.

MURIEL (*huffily*): That's a nice thing to say!

RICHARD: Well, if you meant what was in the letter, you wouldn't have been worth it, would you?

MURIEL: But I've told you Pa—

RICHARD: So I said to myself, I'm through with women; they're all alike!

MURIEL: I'm not.

RICHARD: And I thought, what difference does it make what I do now? I might as well forget her and lead the pace that kills, and drown my sorrows! You know I had eleven dollars saved up to buy you something for your birthday, but I thought, she's dead to me now and why shouldn't I throw it away? (*Then hastily*) I've still got almost five left, Muriel, and I can get you something nice with that.

MURIEL (*excitedly*): What do I care about your old presents? You tell me what you did!

RICHARD (*darkly again*): After it was dark, I sneaked out and went to a low dive I know about.

MURIEL: Dick Miller, I don't believe you ever!

RICHARD: You ask them at the Pleasant Beach House if I didn't! They won't forget me in a hurry!

MURIEL (*impressed and horrified*): You went there? Why, that's a terrible place! Pa says it ought to be closed by the police!

RICHARD (*darkly*): I said it was a dive, didn't I? It's a "secret house of shame." And they let me into a secret room behind the barroom. There wasn't anyone there but a Princeton Senior I know—he belongs to Tiger Inn and he's fullback on the football team—and he had two chorus girls from New York with him, and they were all drinking champagne.

MURIEL (*disturbed by the entrance of the chorus girls*): Dick Miller! I hope you didn't notice—

RICHARD (*carelessly*): I had a highball by myself and then I noticed one of the girls—the one that wasn't with the fullback—looking at me. She had strange-looking eyes. And then she asked me if I wouldn't drink champagne with them and come and sit with her.

MURIEL: She must have been a nice thing! (*Then a bit falteringly*) And did—you?

RICHARD (*with tragic bitterness*): Why shouldn't I, when you'd told me in that letter you'd never see me again?

MURIEL (*almost tearfully*): But you ought to have known Pa made me—

RICHARD: I didn't know that then. (*Then rubbing it in*) Her name was Belle. She had yellow hair—the kind that burns and stings you!

MURIEL: I'll bet it was dyed!

RICHARD: She kept smoking one cigarette after another —but that's nothing for a chorus girl.

MURIEL (*indignantly*): She was low and bad, that's what she was or she couldn't be a chorus girl, and her smoking cigarettes proves it! (*Then falteringly again*) And then what happened?

RICHARD (*carelessly*): Oh, we just kept drinking champagne—I bought a round—and then I had a fight with the barkeep and knocked him down because he'd insulted her. He was a great big thug but—

MURIEL (*huffily*): I don't see how he could—insult that kind! And why did you fight for her? Why didn't the

Princeton fullback who'd brought them there? He must have been bigger than you.

RICHARD (*stopped for a moment—then quickly*): He was too drunk by that time.

MURIEL: And were you drunk?

RICHARD: Only a little then. I was worse later. (*Proudly*) You ought to have seen me when I got home! I was on the verge of delirium tremens!

MURIEL: I'm glad I didn't see you. You must have been awful. I hate people who get drunk. I'd have hated you!

RICHARD: Well, it was all your fault, wasn't it? If you hadn't written that letter—

MURIEL: But I've told you I didn't mean— (*Then faltering but fascinated*) But what happened with that Belle —after—before you went home?

RICHARD: Oh, we kept drinking champagne and she said she'd fallen in love with me at first sight and she came and sat on my lap and kissed me.

MURIEL (*stiffening*): Oh!

RICHARD (*quickly, afraid he has gone too far*): But it was only all in fun, and then we just kept on drinking champagne, and finally I said good night and came home.

MURIEL: And did you kiss her?

RICHARD: No, I didn't.

MURIEL (*distractedly*): You did, too! You're lying and you know it. You did, too! (*Then tearfully*) And there I was right at that time lying in bed not able to sleep, wondering how I was ever going to see you again and crying my eyes out, while you—! (*She suddenly jumps to her feet in a tearful fury*) I hate you! I wish you

were dead! I'm going home this minute! I never want
to lay eyes on you again! And this time I mean it!
(*She tries to jump out of the boat but he holds her
back. All the pose has dropped from him now and he
is in a frightened state of contrition.*)

RICHARD (*imploringly*): Muriel! Wait! Listen!

MURIEL: I don't want to listen! Let me go! If you don't
I'll bite your hand!

RICHARD: I won't let you go! You've got to let me explain! I never—! Ouch! (*For* MURIEL *has bitten his
hand and it hurts, and, stung by the pain, he lets go
instinctively, and she jumps quickly out of the boat and
starts running toward the path.* RICHARD *calls after her
with bitter despair and hurt*) All right! Go if you want
to—if you haven't the decency to let me explain! I hate
you, too! I'll go and see Belle!

MURIEL (*seeing he isn't following her, stops at the foot of
the path—defiantly*): Well, go and see her—if that's the
kind of girl you like! What do I care? (*Then as he
only stares before him broodingly, sitting dejectedly in
the stern of the boat, a pathetic figure of injured grief*)
You can't explain! What can you explain! You owned
up you kissed her!

RICHARD: I did not. I said she kissed me.

MURIEL (*scornfully, but drifting back a step in his direction*): And I suppose you just sat and let yourself be
kissed! Tell that to the Marines!

RICHARD (*injuredly*): All right! If you're going to call
me a liar every word I say—

MURIEL (*drifting back another step*): I didn't call you a
liar. I only meant—it sounds fishy. Don't you know it
does?

RICHARD: I don't know anything. I only know I wish I was dead!

MURIEL (*gently reproving*): You oughtn't to say that. It's wicked. (*Then after a pause*) And I suppose you'll tell me you didn't fall in love with her?

RICHARD (*scornfully*): I should say not! Fall in love with that kind of girl! What do you take me for?

MURIEL (*practically*): How do you know what you did if you drank so much champagne?

RICHARD: I kept my head—with her. I'm not a sucker, no matter what you think!

MURIEL (*drifting nearer*): Then you didn't—love her?

RICHARD: I hated her! She wasn't even pretty! And I had a fight with her before I left, she got so fresh. I told her I loved you and never could love anyone else, and for her to leave me alone.

MURIEL: But you said just now you were going to see her—

RICHARD: That was only bluff. I wouldn't—unless you left me. Then I wouldn't care what I did—any more than I did last night. (*Then suddenly defiant*) And what if I did kiss her once or twice? I only did it to get back at you!

MURIEL: Dick!

RICHARD: You're a fine one to blame me—when it was all your fault! Why can't you be fair? Didn't I think you were out of my life forever? Hadn't you written me you were? Answer me that!

MURIEL: But I've told you a million times that Pa—

RICHARD: Why didn't you have more sense than to let him make you write it? Was it my fault you didn't?

MURIEL: It was your fault for being so stupid! You ought

to have known he stood right over me and told me
each word to write. If I'd refused, it would only have
made everything worse. I had to pretend, so I'd get a
chance to see you. Don't you see, Silly? And I had
sand enough to sneak out to meet you tonight, didn't
I? (*He doesn't answer. She moves nearer*) Still I can
see how you felt the way you did—and maybe I am to
blame for that. So I'll forgive and forget, Dick—if you'll
swear to me you didn't even think of loving that—

RICHARD (*eagerly*): I didn't! I swear, Muriel. I couldn't.
I love you!

MURIEL: Well, then—I still love you.

RICHARD: Then come back here, why don't you?

MURIEL (*coyly*): It's getting late.

RICHARD: It's not near half-past yet.

MURIEL (*comes back and sits down by him shyly*): All
right—only I'll have to go soon, Dick. (*He puts his
arm around her. She cuddles up close to him*) I'm
sorry—I hurt your hand.

RICHARD: That was nothing. It felt wonderful—even to
have you bite!

MURIEL (*impulsively takes his hand and kisses it*):
There! That'll cure it. (*She is overcome by confusion
at her boldness.*)

RICHARD: You shouldn't—waste that—on my hand. (*Then
tremblingly*) You said—you'd let me—

MURIEL: I said, maybe.

RICHARD: Please, Muriel. You know—I want it so!

MURIEL: Will it wash off—her kisses—make you forget
you ever—for always?

RICHARD: I should say so! I'd never remember—anything
but it—never want anything but it—ever again.

MURIEL (*shyly lifting her lips*): Then—all right—Dick.

(*He kisses her tremblingly and for a moment their lips remain together. Then she lets her head sink on his shoulder and sighs softly*) The moon *is* beautiful, isn't it?

RICHARD (*kissing her hair*): Not as beautiful as you! Nothing is! (*Then after a pause*) Won't it be wonderful when we're married?

MURIEL: Yes—but it's so long to wait.

RICHARD: Perhaps I needn't go to Yale. Perhaps Pa will give me a job. Then I'd soon be making enough to—

MURIEL: You better do what your pa thinks best—and I'd like you to be at Yale. (*Then patting his face*) Poor you! Do you think he'll punish you awful?

RICHARD (*intensely*): I don't know and I don't care! Nothing would have kept me from seeing you tonight —not if I'd had to crawl over red-hot coals! (*Then falling back on Swinburne—but with passionate sincerity*) You have my being between the hands of you! You are "my love, mine own soul's heart, more dear than mine own soul, more beautiful than God!"

MURIEL (*shocked and delighted*): Ssshh! It's wrong to say that.

RICHARD (*adoringly*): Gosh, but I love you! Gosh, I love you— Darling!

MURIEL: I love you, too—Sweetheart! (*They kiss. Then she lets her head sink on his shoulder again and they both sit in a rapt trance, staring at the moon. After a pause—dreamily*) Where'll we go on our honeymoon, Dick? To Niagara Falls?

RICHARD (*scornfully*): That dump where all the silly fools go? I should say not! (*With passionate romanticism*) No, we'll go to some far-off wonderful place! (*He calls on Kipling to help him*) Somewhere out on the Long Trail—the trail that is always new—on the road to Mandalay! We'll watch the dawn come up like thunder out of China!

MURIEL (*hazily but happily*): That'll be wonderful, won't it?

Curtain

ACT FOUR
Scene III

SCENE—*The sitting-room of the Miller house again—about 10 o'clock the same night.* MILLER *is sitting in his rocker at left, front, of table, his wife in the rocker at right, front, of table. Moonlight shines through the screen door at right, rear. Only the green-shaded reading lamp is lit and by its light* MILLER, *his specs on, is reading a book while his wife, sewing basket in lap, is working industriously on a doily.* MRS. MILLER's *face wears an expression of unworried content.* MILLER's *face has also lost its look of harassed preoccupation, although he still is a prey to certain misgivings, when he allows himself to think of them. Several books are piled on the table by his elbow, the books that have been confiscated from* RICHARD.

MILLER (*chuckles at something he reads—then closes the book and puts it on the table.* MRS. MILLER *looks up from her sewing*): This Shaw's a comical cuss—even if his ideas are so crazy they oughtn't to allow them to be printed. And that Swinburne's got a fine swing to his poetry—if he'd only choose some other subjects besides loose women.

MRS. MILLER (*smiling teasingly*): I can see where you're becoming corrupted by those books, too—pretending to read them out of duty to Richard, when your nose has been glued to the page!

MILLER: No, no—but I've got to be honest. There's something to them. That Rubaiyat of Omar Khayyam, now. I read that over again and liked it even better than I had before—parts of it, that is, where it isn't all about boozing.

MRS. MILLER (*has been busy with her own thoughts during this last—with a deep sigh of relief*): My, but I'm glad Mildred told me where Richard went off to. I'd have worried my heart out if she hadn't. But now, it's all right.

MILLER (*frowning a little*): I'd hardly go so far as to say that. Just because we know he's all right tonight doesn't mean last night is wiped out. He's still got to be punished for that.

MRS. MILLER (*defensively*): Well, if you ask me, I think after the way I punished him all day, and the way I know he's punished himself, he's had about all he deserves. I've told you how sorry he was, and how he said he'd never touch liquor again. It didn't make him feel happy like Sid, but only sad and sick, so he didn't see anything in it for him.

MILLER: Well, if he's really got that view of it driven into his skull, I don't know but I'm glad it all happened. That'll protect him more than a thousand lectures— just horse sense about himself. (*Then frowning again*) Still, I can't let him do such things and go scot-free.

And then; besides, there's another side to it— (*He stops abruptly.*)

MRS. MILLER (*uneasily*): What do you mean, another side?

MILLER (*hastily*): I mean, discipline. There's got to be some discipline in a family. I don't want him to get the idea he's got a stuffed shirt at the head of the table. No, he's got to be punished, if only to make the lesson stick in his mind, and I'm going to tell him he can't go to Yale, seeing he's so undependable.

MRS. MILLER (*up in arms at once*): Not go to Yale! I guess he can go to Yale! Every man of your means in town is sending his boys to college! What would folks think of you? You let Wilbur go, and you'd have let Lawrence, only he didn't want to, and you're letting Arthur! If our other children can get the benefit of a college education, you're not going to pick on Richard—

MILLER: Hush up, for God's sake! If you'd let me finish what I started to say! I said I'd *tell* him that now—bluff —then later on I'll change my mind, if he behaves himself.

MRS. MILLER: Oh, well, if that's all— (*Then defensively again*) But it's your duty to give him every benefit. He's got an exceptional brain, that boy has! He's proved it by the way he likes to read all those deep plays and books and poetry.

MILLER: But I thought you —(*He stops, grinning helplessly.*)

MRS. MILLER: You thought I what?

MILLER: Never mind.

MRS. MILLER (*sniffs, but thinks it better to let this pass*): You mark my words, that boy's going to turn out to be a great lawyer, or a great doctor, or a great writer, or—

MILLER (*grinning*): You agree he's going to be great, anyway.

MRS. MILLER: Yes, I most certainly have a lot of faith in Richard.

MILLER: Well, so have I, as far as that goes.

MRS. MILLER (*after a pause—judicially*): And as for his being in love with Muriel, I don't see but what it might work out real well. Richard could do worse.

MILLER: But I thought you had no use for her, thought she was stupid.

MRS. MILLER: Well, so I did, but if she's good for Richard and he wants her— (*Then inconsequentially*) Ma used to say you weren't overbright, but she changed her mind when she saw I didn't care if you were or not.

MILLER (*not exactly pleased by this*): Well, I've been bright enough to—

MRS. MILLER (*going on as if he had not spoken*): And Muriel's real cute-looking, I have to admit that. Takes after her mother. Alice Briggs was the prettiest girl before she married.

MILLER: Yes, and Muriel will get big as a house after she's married, the same as her mother did. That's the trouble. A man never can tell what he's letting himself in for— (*He stops, feeling his wife's eyes fixed on him with indignant suspicion.*)

MRS. MILLER (*sharply*): I'm not too fat and don't you say it!

MILLER: Who was talking about you?

MRS. MILLER: And I'd rather have some flesh on my bones than be built like a string bean and bore a hole in a chair every time I sat down—like some people!

MILLER (*ignoring the insult—flatteringly*): Why, no

one'd ever call you fat, Essie. You're only plump, like a good figure ought to be.

MRS. MILLER (*childishly pleased—gratefully giving tit for tat*): Well, you're not skinny, either—only slender—and I think you've been putting on weight lately, too. (*Having thus squared matters she takes up her sewing again. A pause. Then* MILLER *asks incredulously.*)

MILLER: You don't mean to tell me you're actually taking this Muriel crush of Richard's seriously, do you? I know it's a good thing to encourage right now but—pshaw, why, Richard'll probably forget all about her before he's away six months, and she'll have forgotten him.

MRS. MILLER: Don't be so cynical. (*Then, after a pause, thoughtfully*) Well, anyway, he'll always have it to remember—no matter what happens after—and that's something.

MILLER: You bet that's something. (*Then with a grin*) You surprise me at times with your deep wisdom.

MRS. MILLER: You don't give me credit for ever having common sense, that's why. (*She goes back to her sewing.*)

MILLER (*after a pause*): Where'd you say Sid and Lily had gone off to?

MRS. MILLER: To the beach to listen to the band. (*She sighs sympathetically*) Poor Lily! Sid'll never change, and she'll never marry him. But she seems to get some queer satisfaction out of fussing over him like a hen that's hatched a duck—though Lord knows I wouldn't in her shoes!

MILLER: Arthur's up with Elsie Rand, I suppose?

MRS. MILLER: Of course.

MILLER: Where's Mildred?

MRS. MILLER: Out walking with her latest. I've forgot who it is. I can't keep track of them. (*She smiles.*)

MILLER (*smiling*): Then, from all reports, we seem to be completely surrounded by love!

MRS. MILLER: Well, we've had our share, haven't we? We don't have to begrudge it to our children. (*Then has a sudden thought*) But I've done all this talking about Muriel and Richard and clean forgot how wild old McComber was against it. But he'll get over that, I suppose.

MILLER (*with a chuckle*): He has already. I ran into him upstreet this afternoon and he was meek as pie. He backed water and said he guessed I was right. Richard had just copied stuff out of books, and kids would be kids, and so on. So I came off my high horse a bit—but not too far—and I guess all that won't bother anyone any more. (*Then rubbing his hands together—with a boyish grin of pleasure*) And I told you about getting that business from Lawson, didn't I? It's been a good day, Essie—a darned good day! (*From the hall beyond the front parlor the sound of the front door being opened and shut is heard. MRS. MILLER leans forward to look, pushing her specs up.*)

MRS. MILLER (*in a whisper*): It's Richard.

MILLER (*immediately assuming an expression of becoming gravity*) Hmm. (*He takes off his spectacles and puts them back in their case and straightens himself in his chair. RICHARD comes slowly in from the front parlor. He walks like one in a trance, his eyes shining with a dreamy happiness, his spirit still too exalted to be conscious of his surroundings, or to remember the threatened punishment. He carries his straw hat dangling in his hand, quite unaware of its existence.*)

Ah, Wilderness!

RICHARD (*dreamily, like a ghost addressing fellow shades*):
Hello.

MRS. MILLER (*staring at him worriedly*): Hello, Richard.

MILLER (*sizing him up shrewdly*): Hello, Son.

(RICHARD *moves past his mother and comes to the far
corner, left front, where the light is dimmest, and sits
down on the sofa, and stares before him, his hat
dangling in his hand.*)

MRS. MILLER (*with frightened suspicion now*): Goodness, he acts queer! Nat, you don't suppose he's been—?

MILLER (*with a reassuring smile*): No. It's love, not
liquor, this time.

MRS. MILLER (*only partly reassured—sharply*): Richard!
What's the matter with you? (*He comes to himself
with a start. She goes on scoldingly*) How many times
have I told you to hang up your hat in the hall when
you come in! (*He looks at his hat as if he were surprised at its existence. She gets up fussily and goes to
him*) Here. Give it to me. I'll hang it up for you this
once. And what are you sitting over here in the dark
for? Don't forget your father's been waiting to talk to
you! (*She comes back to the table and he follows her,
still half in a dream, and stands by his father's chair.
MRS. MILLER starts for the hall with his hat.*)

MILLER (*quietly but firmly now*): You better leave
Richard and me alone for a while, Essie.

MRS. MILLER (*turns to stare at him apprehensively*): Well
—all right. I'll go sit on the piazza. Call me if you want
me. (*Then a bit pleadingly*) But you'll remember all I
said, Nat, won't you? (MILLER *nods reassuringly. She
disappears through the front parlor.* RICHARD, *keenly
conscious of himself as the about-to-be-sentenced crim-
inal by this time, looks guilty and a bit defiant, searches*

*his father's expressionless face with uneasy side glances,
and steels himself for what is coming.*)

MILLER (*casually, indicating* MRS. MILLER'S *rocker*): Sit
down, Richard. (RICHARD *slumps awkwardly into the
chair and sits in a self-conscious, unnatural position.*
MILLER *sizes him up keenly—then suddenly smiles and
asks with quiet mockery*) Well, how are the vine leaves
in your hair this evening?

RICHARD (*totally unprepared for this approach—shamefacedly mutters*): I don't know, Pa.

MILLER: Turned out to be poison ivy, didn't they?
(*Then kindly*) But you needn't look so alarmed. I'm
not going to read you any temperance lecture. That'd
bore me more than it would you. And, in spite of your
damn foolishness last night, I'm still giving you credit
for having brains. So I'm pretty sure anything I could
say to you you've already said to yourself.

RICHARD (*his head down—humbly*): I know I was a
darned fool.

MILLER (*thinking it well to rub in this aspect—disgustedly*): You sure were—not only a fool but a down-
right, stupid, disgusting fool! (RICHARD *squirms, his head
still lower*) It was bad enough for you to let me and
Arthur see you, but to appear like that before your
mother and Mildred—! And I wonder if Muriel would
think you were so fine if she ever saw you as you
looked and acted then. I think she'd give you your
walking papers for keeps. And you couldn't blame her.
No nice girl wants to give her love to a stupid drunk!

RICHARD (*writhing*): I know, Pa.

MILLER (*after a pause—quietly*): All right. Then that settles—the booze end of it. (*He sizes* RICHARD *up searchingly—then suddenly speaks sharply*) But there is an-

other thing that's more serious. How about that tart you went to bed with at the Pleasant Beach House?

RICHARD (*flabbergasted—stammers*): You know—? But I didn't! If they've told you about her down there, they must have told you I didn't! She wanted me to—but I wouldn't. I gave her the five dollars just so she'd let me out of it. Honest, Pa, I didn't! She made everything seem rotten and dirty—and—I didn't want to do a thing like that to Muriel—no matter how bad I thought she'd treated me—even after I felt drunk, I didn't. Honest!

MILLER: How'd you happen to meet this lady, anyway?

RICHARD: I can't tell that, Pa. I'd have to snitch on someone—and you wouldn't want me to do that.

MILLER (*a bit taken aback*): No. I suppose I wouldn't. Hmm. Well, I believe you—and I guess that settles that. (*Then, after a quick furtive glance at* RICHARD, *he nerves himself for the ordeal and begins with a shamefaced, self-conscious solemnity*) But listen here, Richard, it's about time you and I had a serious talk about— hmm—certain matters pertaining to—and now that the subject's come up of its own accord, it's a good time—I mean, there's no use in procrastinating further—so, here goes. (*But it doesn't go smoothly and as he goes on he becomes more and more guiltily embarrassed and self-conscious and his expressions more stilted.* RICARD *sedulously avoids even glancing at him, his own embarrassment made tenfold more painful by his father's*) Richard, you have now come to the age when— Well, you're a fully developed man, in a way, and it's only natural for you to have certain desires of the flesh, to put it that way— I mean, pertaining to the opposite sex—certain natural feelings and temptations—that'll want to be gratified—and you'll want to gratify them. Hmm— well, human society being organized as it is, there's only one outlet for—unless you're a scoundrel and go around ruining decent girls—which you're not, of course. Well, there are a certain class of women—always have been and always will be as long as human nature is what it is— It's wrong, maybe, but what can you do about it? I mean, girls like that one you—girls there's something doing with—and lots of 'em are pretty, and it's human nature if you— But that doesn't mean to ever get mixed up with them seriously! You just have what you want and pay 'em and forget it. I know that sounds hard and unfeeling, but we're talking facts and— But don't think I'm encouraging you to— If you can stay away from 'em, all the better—but if—why— hmm— Here's what I'm driving at, Richard. They're apt to be whited sepulchres— I mean, your whole life might be ruined if—so, darn it, you've got to know how to—I mean, there are ways and means— (*Suddenly he can go no farther and winds up helplessly*) But, hell, I suppose you boys talk all this over among yourselves and you know more about it than I do. I'll admit I'm no authority. I never had anything to do with such women, and it'll be a hell of a lot better for you if you never do!

RICHARD (*without looking at him*): I'm never going to, Pa. (*Then shocked indignation coming into his voice*) I don't see how you could think I could—now—when you know I love Muriel and am going to marry her. I'd die before I'd—!

MILLER (*immensely relieved—enthusiastically*): That's the

talk! By God, I'm proud of you when you talk like that! (*Then hastily*) And now that's all of that. There's nothing more to say and we'll forget it, eh?

RICHARD (*after a pause*): How are you going to punish me, Pa?

MILLER: I was sort of forgetting that, wasn't I? Well, I'd thought of telling you you couldn't go to Yale—

RICHARD (*eagerly*): Don't I have to go? Gee, that's great! Muriel thought you'd want me to. I was telling her I'd rather you gave me a job on the paper because then she and I could get married sooner. (*Then with a boyish grin*) Gee, Pa, you picked a lemon. That isn't any punishment. You'll have to do something besides that.

MILLER (*grimly—but only half concealing an answering grin*): Then you'll go to Yale and you'll stay there till you graduate, that's the answer to that! Muriel's got good sense and you haven't! (RICHARD *accepts this philosophically*) And now we're finished, you better call your mother. (RICHARD *opens the screen door and calls* "Ma," *and a moment later she comes in. She glances quickly from son to husband and immediately knows that all is well and tactfully refrains from all questions.*)

MRS. MILLER: My, it's a beautiful night. The moon's way down low—almost setting. (*She sits in her chair and sighs contentedly.* RICHARD *remains standing by the door, staring out at the moon, his face pale in the moonlight.*)

MILLER (*with a nod at* RICHARD, *winking at his wife*): Yes, I don't believe I've hardly ever seen such a beautiful night—with such a wonderful moon. Have you, Richard?

RICHARD (*turning to them—enthusiastically*): No! It was wonderful—down at the beach— (*He stops abruptly, smiling shyly.*)

MILLER (*watching his son—after a pause—quietly*): I can only remember a few nights that were as beautiful as this—and they were so long ago, when your mother and I were young and planning to get married.

RICHARD (*stares at him wonderingly for a moment, then quickly from his father to his mother and back again, strangely, as if he'd never seen them before—then he looks almost disgusted and swallows as if an acrid taste had come into his mouth—but then suddenly his face is transfigured by a smile of shy understanding and sympathy. He speaks shyly*): Yes, I'll bet those must have been wonderful nights, too. You sort of forget the moon was the same way back then—and everything.

MILLER (*huskily*): You're all right, Richard. (*He gets up and blows his nose.*)

MRS. MILLER (*fondly*): You're a good boy, Richard. (RICHARD *looks dreadfully shy and embarrassed at this. His father comes to his rescue.*)

MILLER: Better get to bed early tonight, Son, hadn't you?

RICHARD: I couldn't sleep. Can't I go out on the piazza and sit for a while—until the moon sets?

MILLER: All right. Then you better say good night now. I don't know about your mother, but I'm going to bed right away. I'm dead tired.

MRS. MILLER: So am I.

RICHARD (*goes to her and kisses her*): Good night, Ma.

MRS. MILLER: Good night. Don't you stay up till all hours now.

RICHARD (*comes to his father and stands awkwardly before him*): Good night, Pa.

MILLER (*puts his arm around him and gives him a hug*): Good night, Richard. (RICHARD *turns impulsively and kisses him—then hurries out the screen door.* MILLER *stares after him—then says huskily*) First time he's done that in years. I don't believe in kissing between fathers and sons after a certain age—seems mushy and silly—but that meant something! And I don't think we'll ever have to worry about his being safe—from himself—again. And I guess no matter what life will do to him, he can take care of it now. (*He sighs with satisfaction and, sitting down in his chair, begins to unlace his shoes*) My darned feet are giving me fits!

MRS. MILLER (*laughing*): Why do you bother unlacing your shoes now, you big goose—when we're going right up to bed?

MILLER (*as if he hadn't thought of that before, stops*): Guess you're right. (*Then getting to his feet—with a grin*) Mind if I don't say my prayers tonight, Essie? I'm certain God knows I'm too darned tired.

MRS. MILLER: Don't talk that way. It's real sinful. (*She gets up—then laughing fondly*) If that isn't you all over! Always looking for an excuse to— You're worse than Tommy! But all right. I suppose tonight you needn't. You've had a hard day. (*She puts her hand on the reading-lamp switch*) I'm going to turn out the light. All ready?

MILLER: Yep. Let her go, Gallagher. (*She turns out the lamp. In the ensuing darkness the faint moonlight shines full in through the screen door. Walking together toward the front parlor they stand full in it for a moment, looking out.* MILLER *puts his arm around her. He says in a low voice*) There he is—like a statue of Love's Young Dream. (*Then he sighs and speaks with a gentle nostalgic melancholy*) What's it that Rubaiyat says:

"Yet Ah, that Spring should vanish with the Rose!
That Youth's sweet-scented manuscript should close!"

(*Then throwing off his melancholy, with a loving smile at her*) Well, Spring isn't everything, is it, Essie? There's a lot to be said for Autumn. That's got beauty, too. And Winter—if you're together.

MRS. MILLER (*simply*): Yes, Nat. (*She kisses him and they move quietly out of the moonlight, back into the darkness of the front parlor.*)

Curtain

All God's Chillun

Got Wings

❁

A PLAY IN TWO ACTS

CHARACTERS

JIM HARRIS

MRS. HARRIS, *his mother*

HATTIE, *his sister*

ELLA DOWNEY

SHORTY

JOE

MICKEY

Whites and Negroes.

SCENES

ACT ONE
Scene I

A CORNER *in lower New York, at the edge of a colored district. Three narrow streets converge. A triangular building in the rear, red brick, four-storied, its ground floor a grocery. Four-story tenements stretch away down the skyline of the two streets. The fire escapes are crowded with people. In the street leading left, the faces are all white; in the street leading right, all black. It is hot Spring. On the sidewalk are eight children, four boys and four girls. Two of each sex are white, two black. They are playing marbles. One of the black boys is* JIM HARRIS. *The little blonde girl, her complexion rose and white, who sits behind his elbow and holds his marbles is* ELLA DOWNEY. *She is eight. They play the game with concentrated attention for a while. People pass, black and white, the Negroes frankly participants in the spirit of Spring, the whites laughing constrainedly, awkward in natural emotion. Their words are lost. One hears only their laughter. It expresses the difference in race. There are street noises—the clattering roar of the Elevated, the puff of its locomotives, the ruminative lazy sound of a horsecar, the hooves of its team clacking on the cobbles. From the street of the whites a high-pitched, nasal tenor sings the chorus of "Only a Bird in a Gilded Cage." On the street of the blacks a Negro strikes up the chorus of: "I Guess I'll Have to Telegraph My Baby." As this singing ends, there is laughter, distinctive in quality, from both streets. Then silence. The light in the street begins to grow brilliant with the glow of the setting sun. The game of marbles goes on.*

WHITE GIRL (*tugging at the elbow of her brother*): Come on, Mickey!

HER BROTHER (*roughly*): Aw, gwan, youse!

WHITE GIRL: Aw right den. You kin git a lickin' if you wanter. (*Gets up to move off.*)

HER BROTHER: Aw, git off de eart'!

WHITE GIRL: De old woman'll be madder'n hell!

HER BROTHER (*worried now*): I'm comin', ain't I? Hold your horses.

BLACK GIRL (*to a black boy*): Come on, you Joe. We gwine git frailed too, you don't hurry.

JOE: Go long!

MICKEY: Bust up de game, huh? I gotta run! (*Jumps to his feet.*)

OTHER WHITE BOY: Me, too! (*Jumps up.*)

OTHER BLACK GIRL: Lawdy, it's late!

JOE: Me for grub!

MICKEY (*to* JIM HARRIS): You's de winner, Jim Crow. Yeh gotta play tomorrer.

JIM (*readily*): Sure t'ing, Mick. Come one, come all! (*He laughs.*)

OTHER WHITE BOY: Me, too! I gotta git back at yuh.

JIM: Aw right, Shorty.

LITTLE GIRLS: Hurry! Come on, come on! (*The six start off together. Then they notice that* JIM *and* ELLA *are hesitating, standing awkwardly and shyly together. They turn to mock.*)

JOE: Look at dat Jim Crow! Land sakes, he got a gal! (*He laughs. They all laugh.*)

JIM (*ashamed*): Ne'er mind, you Chocolate!

MICKEY: Look at de two softies, will yeh! Mush! Mush! (*He and the two other boys take this up.*)

LITTLE GIRLS (*pointing their fingers at* ELLA): Shame! Shame! Everybody knows your name! Painty Face! Painty Face!

ELLA (*hanging her head*): Shut up!

LITTLE WHITE GIRL: He's been carrying her books!

COLORED GIRL: Can't you find nuffin' better'n him, Ella? Look at de big feet he got! (*She laughs. They all laugh.* JIM *puts one foot on top of the other, looking at* ELLA.)

ELLA: Mind yer own business, see! (*She strides toward them angrily. They jump up and dance in an ecstasy, screaming and laughing.*)

ALL: Found yeh! Found yeh out!

MICKEY: Mush-head! Jim Crow de Sissy! Stuck on Painty Face!

JOE: Will Painty Face let you hold her doll, boy?

SHORTY: Sissy! Softy! (ELLA *suddenly begins to cry. At this they all howl.*)

ALL: Cry-baby! Cry-baby! Look at her! Painty Face!

JIM (*suddenly rushing at them, with clenched fists, furiously*): Shut yo' moufs! I kin lick de hull of you! (*They all run away, laughing, shouting, and jeering, quite triumphant now that they have made him, too, lose his temper. He comes back to* ELLA, *and stands beside her sheepishly, stepping on one foot after the other. Suddenly he blurts out*) Don't bawl no more, I done chased 'em.

ELLA (*comforted, politely*): T'anks.

JIM (*swelling out*): It was a cinch. I kin wipe up de street wid any one of dem. (*He stretches out his arms, trying to bulge out his biceps.*) Feel dat muscle!

ELLA (*does so gingerly—then with admiration*): My!

JIM (*protectingly*): You mustn't never be scared when I'm hanging round, Painty Face.

ELLA: Don't call me that, Jim—please!

JIM (*contritely*): I didn't mean nuffin'. I didn't know you'd mind.

ELLA: I do—more'n anything.

JIM: You oughtn't to mind. Dey's jealous, dat's what.

ELLA: Jealous? Of what?

JIM (*pointing to her face*): Of dat. Red 'n' white. It's purty.

ELLA: I hate it!

JIM: It's purty. Yes, it's—it's purty. It's—outa sight!

ELLA: I hate it. I wish I was black like you.

JIM (*sort of shrinking*): No you don't. Dey'd call you Crow, den—or Chocolate—or Smoke.

ELLA: I wouldn't mind.

JIM (*somberly*): Dey'd call you nigger sometimes, too.

ELLA: I wouldn't mind.

JIM (*humbly*): You wouldn't mind?

ELLA: No, I wouldn't mind. (*An awkward pause.*)

JIM (*suddenly*): You know what, Ella? Since I been tuckin' yo' books to school and back, I been drinkin' lots o' chalk 'n' water tree times a day. Dat Tom, de barber, he tole me dat make me white, if I drink enough. (*Pleadingly*) Does I look whiter?

ELLA (*comfortingly*): Yes—maybe—a little bit—

JIM (*trying a careless tone*): Reckon dat Tom's a liar, an' de joke's on me! Dat chalk only makes me feel kinder sick inside.

ELLA (*wonderingly*): Why do you want to be white?

JIM: Because—just because—I lak dat better.

ELLA: I wouldn't. I like black. Let's you and me swap.

I'd like to be black. (*Clapping her hands*) Gee, that'd be fun, if we only could!

JIM (*hesitatingly*): Yes—maybe—

ELLA: Then they'd call me Crow, and you'd be Painty Face!

JIM: They wouldn't never dast call you nigger, you bet I'd kill em! (*A long pause. Finally she takes his hand shyly. They both keep looking as far away from each other as possible.*)

ELLA: I like you.

JIM: I like you.

ELLA: Do you want to be my feller?

JIM: Yes.

ELLA: Then I'm your girl.

JIM: Yes. (*Then grandly*) You kin bet none o' de gang gwine call you Painty Face from dis out! I lam' 'em good! (*The sun has set. Twilight has fallen on the street. An organ grinder comes up to the corner and plays "Annie Rooney." They stand hand-in-hand and listen. He goes away. It is growing dark.*)

ELLA (*suddenly*): Golly, it's late! I'll get a lickin'!

JIM: Me, too.

ELLA: I won't mind it much.

JIM: Me nuther.

ELLA: See you going to school tomorrow?

JIM: Sure.

ELLA: I gotta skip now.

JIM: Me, too.

ELLA: I like you, Jim.

JIM: I like you.

ELLA: Don't forget.

JIM: Don't you.

ELLA: Good-by.

JIM: So long. (*They run away from each other—then stop abruptly, and turn as at a signal.*)

ELLA: Don't forget.

JIM: I won't, you bet!

ELLA: Here! (*She kisses her hand at him, then runs off in frantic embarrassment.*)

JIM (*overcome*): Gee! (*Then he turns and darts away as the curtain falls.*)

ACT ONE
Scene II

THE *same corner. Nine years have passed. It is again late Spring at a time in the evening which immediately follows the hour of Scene One. Nothing has changed much. One street is still all white, the other all black. The fire escapes are laden with drooping human beings. The grocery store is still at the corner. The street noises are now more rhythmically mechanical, electricity having taken the place of horse and steam. People pass, white and black. They laugh as in Scene 1. From the street of the whites the high-pitched nasal tenor sings: "Gee, I Wish I Had a Girl," and the Negro replies with "All I Got Was Sympathy." The singing is followed again by laughter from both streets. Then silence. The dusk grows darker. With a spluttering flare the arc-lamp at the corner is lit and sheds a pale glare over the street. Two young roughs slouch up to the corner, as tough in manner as they can make themselves. One is the* SHORTY *of*

Scene One; the other the Negro, JOE. *They stand loafing.
A boy of seventeen or so passes by, escorting a girl of
about the same age. Both are dressed in their best, the boy
in black with stiff collar, the girl in white.*

SHORTY (*scornfully*): Hully cripes! Pipe who's here. (*To
the girl, sneeringly*) What's matter, Liz? Don't yer rec-
ernize yer old fr'ens?

GIRL (*frightenedly*): Hello, Shorty.

SHORTY: Why de glad rags? Goin' to graduation? (*He
tries to obstruct their way, but, edging away from him,
they turn and run.*)

JOE: Har-har! Look at dem scoot, will you! (SHORTY *grins
with satisfaction.*)

SHORTY (*looking down other street*): Here comes Mickey.

JOE: He won de semi-final last night easy?

SHORTY: Knocked de bloke out in de thoid.

JOE: Dat boy's suah a-comin'! He'll be de champeen
yit.

SHORTY (*judicially*): Got a good chanct—if he leaves de
broads alone. Dat's where he's wide open. (MICKEY
*comes in from the left. He is dressed loudly, a straw
hat with a gaudy band cocked over one cauliflower
ear. He has acquired a typical "pug's" face, with the
added viciousness of a natural bully. One of his eyes is
puffed, almost closed, as a result of his battle the night
before. He swaggers up.*)

BOTH: Hello, Mickey.

MICKEY: Hello.

JOE: Hear you knocked him col'.

MICKEY: Sure. I knocked his block off. (*Changing the
subject*) Say. Seen 'em goin' past to de graduation
racket?

SHORTY (*with a wink*): Why, you int'rested?

JOE (*chuckling*): Mickey's gwine roun' git a good conduct medal.

MICKEY: Sure. Dey kin pin it on de seat o' me pants. (*They laugh*) Listen. Seen Ella Downey goin'?

SHORTY: Painty Face? No, she ain't been along.

MICKEY (*with authority*): Can dat name, see! Want a bunch o' fives in yer kisser? Den nix! She's me goil, understan'?

JOE (*venturing to joke*): Which one? Yo' number ten?

MICKEY (*flattered*): Sure. De real K.O. one.

SHORTY (*pointing right—sneeringly*): Gee! Pipe Jim Crow all dolled up for de racket.

JOE (*with disgusted resentment*): You mean tell me dat nigger's graduatin'?

SHORTY: Ask him. (JIM HARRIS *comes in. He is dressed in black, stiff white collar, etc.—a quiet-mannered Negro boy with a queerly baffled, sensitive face.*)

JIM (*pleasantly*): Hello, fellows. (*They grunt in reply, looking over him scornfully.*)

JOE (*staring resentfully*): Is you graduatin' tonight?

JIM: Yes.

JOE (*spitting disgustedly*): Fo' Gawd's sake! You *is* gittin' high-falutin'!

JIM (*smiling deprecatingly*): This is my second try. I didn't pass last year.

JOE: What de hell does it git you, huh? Whatever is you gwine do wid it now you gits it? Live lazy on yo' ol' woman?

JIM (*assertively*): I'm going to study and become a lawyer.

JOE (*with a snort*): Fo' Chris' sake, nigger!

JIM (*fiercely*): Don't you call me that—not before them!

JOE (*pugnaciously*): Does you deny you's a nigger? I shows you—

MICKEY (*gives them both a push—truculently*): Cut it out, see! I'm runnin' dis corner. (*Turning to* JIM *insultingly*) Say you! Painty Face's gittin' her ticket tonight, ain't she?

JIM: You mean Ella—

MICKEY: Painty Face Downey, dat's who I mean! I don't have to be perlite wit' her. She's me goil!

JIM (*glumly*): Yes, she's graduating.

SHORTY (*winks at* MICKEY): Smart, huh?

MICKEY (*winks back—meaningly*): Willin' to loin, take it from me! (JIM *stands tensely as if a struggle were going on in him.*)

JIM (*finally blurts out*): I want to speak to you, Mickey —alone.

MICKEY (*surprised—insultingly*): Aw, what de hell—!

JIM (*excitedly*): It's important, I tell you!

MICKEY: Huh? (*Stares at him inquisitively—then motions the others back carelessly and follows* JIM *down front.*)

SHORTY: Some noive!

JOE (*vengefully*): I gits dat Jim alone, you wait!

MICKEY: Well, spill de big news. I ain't got all night. I got a date.

JIM: With—Ella?

MICKEY: What's dat to you?

JIM (*the words tumbling out*): What—I wanted to say! I know—I've heard—all the stories—what you've been doing around the ward—with other girls—it's none of my business, with them—but she—Ella it's different— she's not that kind—

MICKEY (*insultingly*): Who told yuh so, huh?

JIM (*draws back his fist threateningly*): Don't you dare—! (MICKEY *is so paralyzed by this effrontery that he actually steps back.*)

MICKEY: Say, cut de comedy! (*Beginning to feel insulted*) Listen, you Jim Crow! Ain't you wise I could give yuh one poke dat'd knock yuh into next week?

JIM: I'm only asking you to act square, Mickey.

MICKEY: What's it to yuh? Why, yuh lousy goat, she wouldn't spit on yuh even! She hates de sight of a coon.

JIM (*in agony*): I—I know—but once she didn't mind —we were kids together—

MICKEY: Aw, ferget dat! Dis is *now!*

JIM: And I'm still her friend always—even if she don't like colored people—

MICKEY: Coons, why don't yuh say it right! De trouble wit' you is yuh're gittin' stuck up, dat's what! Stay where yeh belong, see! Yer old man made coin at de truckin' game and yuh're tryin' to buy yerself white— graduatin' and law, for Christ sake! Yuh're gittin' yerself in Dutch wit' everyone in de ward—and it ain't cause yer a coon neider. Don't de gang all train wit' Joe dere and lots of others? But yuh're tryin' to buy white and it won't git yuh no place, see!

JIM (*trembling*): Some day—I'll show you—

MICKEY (*turning away*): Aw, gwan!

JIM: D'you think I'd change—be you—your dirty white—!

MICKEY (*whirling about*): What's dat?

JIM (*with hysterical vehemence*): You act square with her—or I'll show you up—I'll report you—I'll write to the papers—the sporting writers—I'll let them know how white you are!

MICKEY (*infuriated*): Yuh damn nigger, I'll bust yer jaw in! (*Assuming his ring pose he weaves toward* JIM, *his face set in a cruel scowl.* JIM *waits helplessly but with a certain dignity.*)

SHORTY: Cheese it! A couple bulls! And here's de Downey skoit comin', too.

MICKEY: I'll get yuh de next time! (ELLA DOWNEY *enters from the right. She is seventeen, still has the same rose and white complexion, is pretty but with a rather repelling bold air about her.*)

ELLA (*smiles with pleasure when she sees* MICKEY): Hello, Mick. Am I late? Say, I'm so glad you won last night. (*She glances from one to the other as she feels something in the air*) Hello! What's up?

MICKEY: Dis boob. (*He indicates* JIM *scornfully.*)

JIM (*diffidently*): Hello, Ella.

ELLA (*shortly, turning away*): Hello. (*Then to* MICKEY) Come on, Mick. Walk down with me. I got to hurry.

JIM (*blurts out*): Wait—just a second. (*Painfully*) Ella, do you hate—colored people?

MICKEY: Aw, shut up!

JIM: Please answer.

ELLA (*forcing a laugh*): Say! What is this—another exam?

JIM (*doggedly*): Please answer.

ELLA (*irritably*): Of course I don't! Haven't I been brought up alongside—why, some of my oldest—the girls I've been to public school the longest with—

JIM: Do you hate me, Ella?

ELLA (*confusedly and more irritably*): Say, is he drunk? Why should I? I don't hate anyone.

JIM: Then why haven't you ever hardly spoken to me—for years?

ELLA (*resentfully*): What would I speak about? You and me've got nothing in common any more.

JIM (*desperately*): Maybe not any more—but—right on this corner—do you remember once—?

ELLA: I don't remember nothing! (*Angrily*) Say! What's got into you to be butting into my business all of a sudden like this? Because you finally managed to graduate, has it gone to your head?

JIM: No, I—only want to help you, Ella.

ELLA: Of all the nerve! You're certainly forgetting your place! Who's asking you for help, I'd like to know? Shut up and stop bothering me!

JIM (*insistently*): If you ever need a friend—a true friend—

ELLA: I've got lots of friends among my own—kind, I can tell you. (*Exasperatedly*) You make me sick! Go to the devil! (*She flounces off. The three men laugh.* MICKEY *follows her.* JIM *is stricken. He goes and sinks down limply on a box in front of the grocery store.*)

SHORTY: I'm going to shoot a drink. Come on, Joe, and I'll blow yuh.

JOE (*who has never ceased to follow every move of* JIM's *with angry, resentful eyes*): Go long. I'se gwine stay here a secon'. I got a lil' argument. (*He points to* JIM.)

SHORTY: Suit yerself. Do a good job. See yuh later. (*He goes, whistling.*)

JOE (*stands for a while glaring at* JIM, *his fierce little eyes peering out of his black face. Then he spits on his hands aggressively and strides up to the oblivious* JIM. *he stands in front of him, gradually working himself into a fury at the other's seeming indifference to his words*): Listen to me, nigger: I got a heap to whisper in yo' ear! Who is you, anyhow? Who does you think you is? Don't yo' old man and mine work on de docks togidder befo' yo' old man gits his own truckin' business? Yo' ol' man swallers his nickels, my ol' man buys him beer wid dem and swallers dat—dat's the on'y dif'rence. Don't you 'n' me drag up togidder?

JIM (*dully*): I'm your friend, Joe.

JOE: No, you isn't! I ain't no fren' o' yourn! I don't even know who you is! What's all dis schoolin' you doin'? What's all dis dressin' up and graduatin' an' sayin' you gwine study be a lawyer? What's all dis fakin' an' pretendin' and swellin' out grand an' talkin' soft and perlite? What's all dis denyin' you's a nigger—an' wid de white boys listenin' to you say it! Is you aimin' to buy white wid yo' ol' man's dough like Mickey say? What is you? (*In a rage at the other's silence*) You don't talk? Den I takes it out o' yo' hide! (*He grabs* JIM *by the throat with one hand and draws the other fist back*) Tell me befo' I wrecks yo' face in! Is you a nigger or isn't you? (*Shaking him*) Is you a nigger, Nigger? Nigger, is you a nigger?

JIM (*looking into his eyes—quietly*): Yes. I'm a nigger. We're both niggers. (*They look at each other for a moment.* JOE's *rage vanishes. He slumps onto a box beside* JIM's. *He offers him a cigarette.* JIM *takes it.* JOE *scratches a match and lights both their cigarettes.*)

JOE (*after a puff, with full satisfaction*): Man, why didn't you 'splain dat in de fust place?

JIM: We're both niggers. (*The same hand-organ man of Scene One comes to the corner. He plays the chorus of "Bon-bon Buddie The Chocolate Drop." They both stare straight ahead listening. Then the organ man goes away. A silence.* JOE *gets to his feet.*)

JOE: I'll go get me a cold beer. (*He starts to move off—*

then turns) Time you was graduatin', ain't it? (*He goes.* JIM *remains sitting on his box staring straight before him as the curtain falls.*)

ACT ONE
Scene III

THE *same corner five years later. Nothing has changed much. It is a night in Spring. The arc-lamp discovers faces with a favorless cruelty. The street noises are the same but more intermittent and dulled with a quality of fatigue. Two people pass, one black and one white. They are tired. They both yawn, but neither laughs. There is no laughter from the two streets. From the street of the whites the tenor, more nasal than ever and a bit drunken, wails in high barbershop falsetto the last half of the chorus of "When I Lost You." The Negro voice, a bit maudlin in turn, replies with the last half of "Waitin' for the Robert E. Lee." Silence.* SHORTY *enters. He looks tougher than ever, the typical gangster. He stands waiting, singing a bit drunkenly, peering down the street.*

SHORTY (*indignantly*): Yuh bum! Ain't yuh ever comin'? (*He begins to sing: "And sewed up in her yellow kimono, She had a blue-barreled forty-five gun, For to get her man Who'd done her wrong." Then he comments scornfully*) Not her, dough! No gat for her. She ain't got de noive. A little sugar. Dat'll fix her. (ELLA *enters. She is dressed poorly, her face is pale and hollow-eyed, her voice cold and tired.*)

SHORTY: Yuh got de message?

ELLA: Here I am.

SHORTY: How yuh been?

ELLA: All right. (*A pause. He looks at her puzzledly*).

SHORTY (*a bit embarrassedly*): Well, I s'pose yuh'd like me to give yuh some dope on Mickey, huh?

ELLA: No.

SHORTY: Mean to say yuh don't wanter know where he is or what he's doin'?

ELLA: No.

SHORTY: Since when?

ELLA: A long time.

SHORTY (*after a pause—with a rat-like viciousness*): Between you'n me, kid, you'll get even soon—you'n all de odder dames he's tossed. I'm on de inside. I've watched him trainin'. His next scrap, watch it! He'll go! It won't be de odder guy. It'll be all youse dames he's kidded—and de ones what's kidded him. Youse'll all be in de odder guy's corner. He won't need no odder seconds. Youse'll trow water on him, and sponge his face, and take de kinks out of his socker—and Mickey'll catch it on de button—and he won't be able to take it no more—'cause all your weight—you and de odders—'ll be behind dat punch. Ha, ha! (*He laughs an evil laugh*) And Mickey'll go—down to his knees first—(*He sinks to his knees in the attitude of a groggy boxer.*)

ELLA: I'd like to see him on his knees!

SHORTY: And den—flat on his pan—dead to de woild—de boidies singin' in de trees—ten—out! (*He suits his action to the words, sinking flat on the pavement, then rise and laughs the same evil laugh.*)

ELLA: He's been out—for me—a long time. (*A pause*)
   Why did you send for me?

SHORTY: He sent me.

ELLA: Why?

SHORTY: To slip you dis wad o' dough. (*He reluctantly
   takes a roll of bills from his pocket and holds it out to
   her.*)

ELLA (*looks at the money indifferently*): What for?

SHORTY: For you.

ELLA: No.

SHORTY: For de kid den.

ELLA: The kid's dead. He took diphtheria.

SHORTY: Hell yuh say! When?

ELLA: A long time.

SHORTY: Why didn't you write Mickey—?

ELLA: Why should I? He'd only be glad.

SHORTY (*after a pause*): Well—it's better.

ELLA: Yes.

SHORTY: You made up wit yer family?

ELLA: No chance.

SHORTY: Livin' alone?

ELLA: In Brooklyn.

SHORTY: Workin'?

ELLA: In a factory.

SHORTY: You're a sucker. There's lots of softer snaps fer
   you, kid—

ELLA: I know what you mean. No.

SHORTY: Don't yuh wanter step out no more—have fun
   —live?

ELLA: I'm through.

SHORTY (*mockingly*): Jump in de river, huh? T'ink it
   over, baby. I kin start yuh right in my stable. No one'll
   bodder yuh den. I got influence.

ELLA (*without emphasis*): You're a dirty dog. Why doesn't someone kill you?

SHORTY: Is dat so! What're you? They say you been travelin' round with Jim Crow.

ELLA: He's been my only friend.

SHORTY: A nigger!

ELLA: The only white man in the world! Kind and white. You're all black—black to the heart.

SHORTY: Nigger-lover! (*He throws the money in her face. It falls to the street*) Listen, you! Mickey says he's off of yuh fer keeps. Dis is de finish! Dat's what he sent me to tell you. (*Glances at her searchingly—a pause*) Yuh won't make no trouble?

ELLA: Why should I? He's free. The kid's dead. I'm free. No hard feelings—only—I'll be there in spirit at his next fight, tell him! I'll take your tip—the other corner —second the punch—nine—ten—out! He's free! That's all. (*She grins horribly at* SHORTY) Go away, Shorty.

SHORTY (*looking at her and shaking his head—maudlinly*): Groggy! Groggy! We're all groggy! Gluttons for punishment! Me for a drink. So long. (*He goes. A Salvation Army band comes toward the corner. They are playing and singing "Till We Meet at Jesus' Feet." They reach the end as they enter and stop before* ELLA. THE CAPTAIN *steps forward.*)

CAPTAIN: Sister—

ELLA (*picks up the money and drops it in his hat—mockingly*): Here. Go save yourself. Leave me alone.

A WOMAN SALVATIONIST: Sister—

ELLA: Never mind that. I'm not in your line—yet. (*As they hesitate, wonderingly*) I want to be alone. (*To the thud of the big drum they march off.* ELLA *sits down on a box, her hands hanging at her sides. Presently* JIM

HARRIS *comes in. He has grown into a quietly-dressed studious-looking Negro with an intelligent yet queerly baffled face.*)

JIM (*with a joyous but bewildered cry*): Ella! I just saw Shorty—

ELLA (*smiling at him with frank affection*): He had a message from Mickey.

JIM (*sadly*): Ah!

ELLA (*pointing to the box behind her*): Sit down. (*He does so. A pause—then she says indifferently*) It's finished. I'm free, Jim.

JIM (*wearily*): We're never free—except to do what we have to do.

ELLA: What are you getting gloomy about all of a sudden?

JIM: I've got the report from the school. I've flunked again.

ELLA: Poor Jim.

JIM: Don't pity me. I'd like to kick myself all over the block. Five years—and I'm still plugging away where I ought to have been at the end of two.

ELLA: Why don't you give it up?

JIM: No!

ELLA: After all, what's being a lawyer?

JIM: A lot—to me—what it means. (*Intensely*) Why, if I was a Member of the Bar right now, Ella, I believe I'd almost have the courage to—

ELLA: What?

JIM: Nothing. (*After a pause—gropingly*) I can't explain—just—but it hurts like fire. It brands me in my pride. I swear I know more'n any member of my class. I ought to, I study harder. I work like the devil. It's all in my head—all fine and correct to a T. Then when

I'm called on—I stand up—all the white faces looking at me—and I can feel their eyes—I hear my own voice sounding funny, trembling—and all of a sudden it's all gone in my head—there's nothing remembered—and I hear myself stuttering—and give up—sit down— They don't laugh, hardly ever. They're kind. They're good people. (*In a frenzy*) They're considerate, damn them! But I feel branded!

ELLA: Poor Jim.

JIM (*going on painfully*): And it's the same thing in the written exams. For weeks before I study all night. I can't sleep anyway. I learn it all, I see it, I understand it. Then they give me the paper in the exam room. I look it over, I know each answer—perfectly. I take up my pen. On all sides are white men starting to write. They're so sure—even the ones that I know know nothing. But I know it all—but I can't remember any more— it fades—it goes—it's gone. There's a blank in my head— stupidity—I sit like a fool fighting to remember a little bit here, a little bit there—not enough to pass—not enough for anything—when I know it all!

ELLA (*compassionately*): Jim. It isn't worth it. You don't need to—

JIM: I need it more than anyone ever needed anything. I need it to live.

ELLA: What'll it prove?

JIM: Nothing at all much—but everything to me.

ELLA: You're so much better than they are in every other way.

JIM (*looking up at her*): Then—you understand?

ELLA: Of course. (*Affectionately*) Don't I know how fine you've been to me! You've been the only one in the world who's stood by me—the only understanding person—and all after the rotten way I used to treat you.

JIM: But before that—way back so high—you treated me good. (*He smiles.*)

ELLA: You've been white to me, Jim. (*She takes his hand.*)

JIM: White—to you!

ELLA: Yes.

JIM: All love is white. I've always loved you. (*This with the deepest humility.*)

ELLA: Even now—after all that's happened!

JIM: Always.

ELLA: I like you, Jim—better than anyone else in the world.

JIM: That's more than enough, more than I ever hoped for. (*The organ grinder comes to the corner. He plays the chorus of "Annie Laurie." They sit listening, hand in hand*) Would you ever want to marry me, Ella?

ELLA: Yes, Jim.

JIM (*as if this quick consent alarmed him*): No, no, don't answer now. Wait! Turn it over in your mind! Think what it means to you! Consider it—over and over again! I'm in no hurry, Ella. I can wait months—years—

ELLA: I'm alone. I've got to be helped. I've got to help someone—or it's the end—one end or another.

JIM (*eagerly*): Oh, I'll help—I know I can help—I'll give my life to help you—that's what I've been living for—

ELLA: But can I help you? Can I help you?

JIM: Yes! Yes! We'll go abroad where a man is a man—where it don't make that difference—where people are kind and wise to see the souls under skins. I don't ask you to love me—I don't dare to hope nothing like that! I don't want nothing—only to wait—to know you like me—to be near you—to keep harm away—to make up for the past—to never let you suffer any more—to serve you—to lie at your feet like a dog that loves you —to kneel by your bed like a nurse that watches over you sleeping—to preserve and protect and shield you from evil and sorrow—to give my life and my blood and all the strength that's in me to give you peace and joy—to become your slave!—yes, be your slave—your black slave that adores you as sacred! (*He has sunk to his knees. In a frenzy of self-abnegation, as he says the last words he beats his head on the flagstones.*)

ELLA (*overcome and alarmed*): Jim! Jim! You're crazy! I want to help you, Jim—I want to help—

Curtain

ACT ONE
Scene IV

SOME *weeks or so later. A street in the same ward in front of an old brick church. The church sets back from the sidewalk in a yard enclosed by a rusty iron railing with a gate at center. On each side of this yard are tenements. The buildings have a stern, forbidding look. All the shades on the windows are drawn down, giving an effect of staring, brutal eyes that pry callously at human beings without acknowledging them. Even the two tall, narrow church windows on either side of the arched door are blanked with dull green shades. It is a bright sunny*

morning. The district is unusually still, as if it were wait-
ing, holding its breath.

From the street of the blacks to the right a Negro tenor
sings in a voice of shadowy richness—the first stanza
with a contented, child-like melancholy—

> *Sometimes I feel like a mourning dove,*
> *Sometimes I feel like a mourning dove,*
> *Sometimes I feel like a mourning dove,*
> *I feel like a mourning dove.*
> *Feel like a mourning dove.*

The second with a dreamy, boyish exultance—

> *Sometimes I feel like an eagle in the air,*
> *Sometimes I feel like an eagle in the air,*
> *Sometimes I feel like an eagle in the air,*
> *I feel like an eagle in the air.*
> *Feel like an eagle in the air.*

The third with a brooding, earthbound sorrow—

> *Sometimes I wish that I'd never been born,*
> *Sometimes I wish that I'd never been born,*
> *Sometimes I wish that I'd never been born,*
> *I wish that I'd never been born.*
> *Wish that I'd never been born.*

As the music dies down there is a pause of waiting
stillness. This is broken by one startling, metallic clang
of the church-bell. As if it were a signal, people—
men, women, children—pour from the two tene-
ments, whites from the tenement to the left, blacks
from the one to the right. They hurry to form into
two racial lines on each side of the gate, rigid and
unyielding, staring across at each other with bitter

*hostile eyes. The halves of the big church door swing
open and* JIM *and* ELLA *step out from the darkness
within into the sunlight. The doors slam behind
them like wooden lips of an idol that has spat them
out.* JIM *is dressed in black.* ELLA *in white, both with
extreme plainness. They stand in the sunlight,
shrinking and confused. All the hostile eyes are now
concentrated on them. They become aware of the
two lines through which they must pass; they hesitate and tremble; then stand there staring back at the
people, as fixed and immovable as they are. The organ grinder comes in from the right. He plays the
chorus of "Old Black Joe." As he finishes the bell of
the church clangs one more single stroke, insistently
dismissing.*

JIM (*as if the sound had awakened him from a trance,
reaches out and takes her hand*): Come. Time we got
to the steamer. Time we sailed away over the sea.
Come, Honey! (*She tries to answer but her lips tremble; she cannot take her eyes off the eyes of people; she
is unable to move. He sees this and, keeping the same
tone of profound, affectionate kindness, he points upward in the sky, and gradually persuades her eyes to
look up*) Look up, Honey! See the sun! Feel his warm
eye lookin' down! Feel how kind he looks! Feel his
blessing deep in your heart, your bones! Look up,
Honey! (*Her eyes are fixed on the sky now. Her face is
calm. She tries to smile bravely back at the sun. Now
he pulls her by the hand, urging her gently to walk
with him down through the yard and gate, through the
lines of people. He is maintaining an attitude to support them through the ordeal only by a terrible effort,*

which manifests itself in the hysteric quality of ecstasy which breaks into his voice) And look at the sky! Ain't it kind and blue! Blue for hope. Don't they say blue's for hope? Hope! That's for us, Honey. All those blessings in the sky! What's it the Bible says? Falls on just and unjust alike? No, that's the sweet rain. Pshaw, what am I saying? All mixed up. There's no unjust about it. We're all the same—equally just—under the sky—under the sun—under God—sailing over the sea— to the other side of the world—the side where Christ was born—the kind side that takes count of the soul— over the sea—the sea's blue, too—. Let's not be late— let's get that steamer! (*They have reached the curb now, passed the lines of people. She is looking up to the sky with an expression of trance-like calm and peace. He is on the verge of collapse, his face twitching, his eyes staring. He calls hoarsely*): Taxi! Where is he? Taxi!

Curtain

ACT TWO
Scene I

TWO *years later. A flat of the better sort in the Negro district near the corner of Act One. This is the parlor. Its furniture is a queer clash. The old pieces are cheaply ornate, naïvely, childishly gaudy—the new pieces give evidence of a taste that is diametrically opposed, severe to the point of somberness. On one wall, in a heavy gold frame, is a colored photograph—the portrait of an elderly Negro with an able, shrewd face but dressed in an outlandish lodge regalia, a get-up adorned with medals, sashes, a cocked hat with frills—the whole effect as absurd to contemplate as one of Napoleon's Marshals in full uniform. In the left corner, where a window lights it effectively, is a Negro primitive mask from the Congo— a grotesque face, inspiring obscure, dim connotations in one's mind, but beautifully done, conceived in a true religious spirit. In this room, however, the mask acquires an arbitrary accentuation. It dominates by a diabolical quality that contrast imposes upon it.*

There are two windows on the left looking out in the street. In the rear, a door to the hall of the building. In the right, a doorway with red and gold portières leading into the bedroom and the rest of the flat. Everything is cleaned and polished. The dark brown wallpaper is new, the brilliantly figured carpet also. There is a round mahogany table at center. In a rocking chair by the table MRS. HARRIS *is sitting. She is a mild-looking, gray-haired Negress of sixty-five, dressed in an old-fashioned Sunday-*

best dress. Walking about the room nervously is HATTIE, *her daughter,* JIM's *sister, a woman of about thirty with a high-strung, defiant face—an intelligent head showing both power and courage. She is dressed severely, mannishly.*

It is a fine morning in Spring. Sunshine comes through the windows at the left.

MRS. HARRIS: Time dey was here, ain't it?

HATTIE (*impatiently*): Yes.

MRS. H. (*worriedly*): You ain't gwine ter kick up a fuss, is you—like you done wid Jim befo' de weddin'?

HATTIE: No. What's done is done.

MRS. H.: We mustn't let her see we hold it agin' her—de bad dat happened to her wid dat no-count fighter.

HATTIE: I certainly never give that a thought. It's what she's done to Jim—making him run away and give up his fight—!

MRS. H.: Jim loves her a powerful lot, must be.

HATTIE (*after a pause—bitterly*): I wonder if she loves Jim!

MRS. H.: She must, too. Yes, she must, too. Don't you forget dat it was hard for her—mighty, mighty hard— harder for de white dan for de black!

HATTIE (*indignantly*): Why should it be?

MRS. H. (*shaking her head*): I ain't talkin' of shoulds. It's too late for shoulds. Dey's o'ny one should. (*Solemnly*) De white and de black shouldn't mix dat close. Dere's one road where de white goes on alone; dere's anudder road where de black goes on alone—

HATTIE: Yes, if they'd only leave us alone!

MRS. H.: Dey leaves your Pa alone. He comes to de top till he's got his own business, lots o' money in de bank, he owns a building even befo' he die. (*She looks up proudly at the picture.* HATTIE *sighs impatiently—then her mother goes on*)Dey leaves me alone. I bears four children into dis worl', two dies, two lives, I helps you two grow up fine an' healthy and eddicated wid schoolin' and money fo' yo' comfort—

HATTIE (*impatiently*): Ma!

MRS. H.: I does de duty God set for me in dis worl'. Dey leaves me alone. (HATTIE *goes to the window to hide her exasperation. The mother broods for a minute—then goes on*) The worl' done change. Dey ain't no satisfaction wid nuffin' no more.

HATTIE: Oh! (*Then after a pause*) They'll be here any minute now.

MRS. H.: Why didn't you go meet 'em at de dock like I axed you?

HATTIE: I couldn't. My face and Jim's among those hundreds of white faces— (*With a harsh laugh*) It would give her too much advantage!

MRS. H. (*impatiently*): Don't talk dat way! What makes you so proud? (*Then after a pause—sadly*) Hattie.

HATTIE (*turning*): Yes, Ma.

MRS. H.: I want to see Jim again—my only boy—but—all de same I'd ruther he stayed away. He say in his letter he's happy, she's happy, dey likes it dere, de folks don't think nuffin' but what's natural at seeing 'em married. Why don't dey stay?

HATTIE. (*vehemently*): No! They were cowards to run away. If they believe in what they've done, then let them face it out, live it out here, be strong enough to conquer all prejudice!

MRS. H.: Strong? Dey ain't many strong. Dey ain't many happy neider. Dey was happy ovah yondah.

HATTIE: We don't deserve happiness till we've fought the fight of our race and won it! (*In the pause that follows there is a ring from back in the flat*) It's the door bell! You go, Ma. I—I—I'd rather not. (*Her mother looks at her rebukingly and goes out agitatedly through the portières.* HATTIE *waits, nervously walking about, trying to compose herself. There is a long pause. Finally the portières are parted and* JIM *enters. He looks much older, graver, worried.*)

JIM: Hattie!

HATTIE: Jim! (*They embrace with great affection.*)

JIM: It's great to see you again! You're looking fine.

HATTIE (*looking at him searchingly*): You look well, too—thinner maybe—and tired. (*Then as she sees him frowning*) But where's Ella?

JIM: With Ma. (*Apologetically*) She sort of—broke down—when we came in. The trip wore her out.

HATTIE (*coldly*): I see.

JIM: Oh, it's nothing serious. Nerves. She needs a rest.

HATTIE: Wasn't living in France restful?

JIM: Yes, but—too lonely—especially for her.

HATTIE (*resentfully*): Why! Didn't the people there want to associate—?

JIM (*quickly*): Oh, no indeedy, they didn't think anything of that. (*After a pause*) But—she did. For the first year it was all right. Ella liked everything a lot. She went out with French folks and got so she could talk a little—and I learned it—a little. We were having a right nice time. I never thought then we'd ever want to come back here.

HATTIE (*frowning*): But—what happened to change you?

JIM (*after a pause—haltingly*): Well—you see—the first

year—she and I were living around—like friends—like a brother and sister—like you and I might.

HATTIE (*her face becoming more and more drawn and tense*): You mean—then—? (*She shudders—then after a pause*) She loves you, Jim?

JIM: If I didn't know that I'd have to jump in the river.

HATTIE: Are you sure she loves you?

JIM: Isn't that why she's suffering?

HATTIE (*letting her breath escape through her clenched teeth*): Ah!

JIM (*suddenly springs up and shouts almost hysterically*): Why d'you ask me all those damn questions? Are you trying to make trouble between us?

HATTIE (*controlling herself—quietly*): No, Jim.

JIM (*after a pause—contritely*): I'm sorry, Hattie. I'm kind of on edge today. (*He sinks down on his chair— then goes on as if something forced him to speak*) After that we got to living housed in. Ella didn't want to see nobody, she said just the two of us was enough. I was happy then—and I really guess she was happy, too—in a way—for a while. (*Again a pause*) But she never did get to wanting to go out any place again. She got to saying she felt she'd be sure to run into someone she knew—from over here. So I moved us out to the country where no tourist ever comes—but it didn't make any difference to her. She got to avoiding the French folks the same as if they were Americans and I couldn't get it out of her mind. She lived in the house and got paler and paler, and more and more nervous and scary, always imagining things—until I got to imagining things, too. I got to feeling blue. Got to sneering at myself that I wasn't any better than a quitter because I sneaked away right after getting married, didn't face nothing, gave up trying to become a Member of the Bar—and I got to suspecting Ella must feel that way about me, too—that I wasn't a *real man!*

HATTIE (*indignantly*): She couldn't!

JIM (*with hostility*): You don't need to tell me! All this was only in my own mind. We never quarreled a single bit. We never said a harsh word. We were as close to each other as could be. We were all there was in the world to each other. We were alone together! (*A pause*) Well, one day I got so I couldn't stand it. I could see she couldn't stand it. So I just up and said: Ella, we've got to have a plain talk, look everything straight in the face, hide nothing, come out with the exact truth of the way we feel.

HATTIE: And you decided to come back!

JIM: Yes. We decided the reason we felt sort of ashamed was we'd acted like cowards. We'd run away from the thing—and taken it with us. We decided to come back and face it and live it down in ourselves, and prove to ourselves we were strong in our love—and then, and that way only, by being brave we'd free ourselves, and gain confidence, and be really free inside and able then to go anywhere and live in peace and equality with ourselves and the world without any guilty, uncomfortable feeling coming up to rile us. (*He has talked himself now into a state of happy confidence.*)

HATTIE (*bending over and kissing him*): Good for you! I admire you so much, Jim! I admire both of you! And are you going to begin studying right away and get admitted to the Bar?

JIM: You bet I am!

HATTIE: You must, Jim! Our race needs men like you to come to the front and help— (*As voices are heard*

*approaching she stops, stiffens, and her face grows
cold.*)

JIM (*noticing this—warningly*): Remember Ella's been
sick! (*Losing control—threateningly*) You be nice to
her, you hear! (MRS. HARRIS *enters, showing* ELLA *the
way. The colored woman is plainly worried and per-
plexed.* ELLA *is pale, with a strange, haunted expression in her eyes. She runs to* JIM *as to a refuge, clutch-
ing his hands in both of hers, looking from* MRS. HARRIS
to HATTIE *with a frightened defiance.*)

MRS. H.: Dere he is, child, big's life! She was afraid
we'd done kidnapped you away, Jim.

JIM (*patting her hand*): This place ought to be familiar,
Ella. Don't you remember playing here with us sometimes as a kid?

ELLA (*queerly—with a frown of effort*): I remember
playing marbles one night—but that was on the street.

JIM: Don't you remember Hattie?

HATTIE (*coming forward with a forced smile*): It was a
long time ago—but I remember Ella. (*She holds out
her hand.*)

ELLA (*taking it—looking at* HATTIE *with the same queer
defiance*): I remember. But you've changed so much.

HATTIE (*stirred to hostility by* ELLA's *manner—conde-
scendingly*): Yes, I've grown older, naturally. (*Then
in a tone which, as if in spite of herself, becomes
bragging*) I've worked so hard. First I went away
to college, you know—then I took up post-graduate
study—when suddenly I decided I'd accomplish more
good if I gave up learning and took up teaching. (*She
suddenly checks herself, ashamed, and stung by* ELLA's
indifference) But this sounds like stupid boasting. I
don't mean that. I was only explaining—

ELLA (*indifferently*): I didn't know you'd been to school so long. (*A pause*) Where are you teaching? In a colored school, I suppose. (*There is an indifferent superiority in her words that is maddening to* HATTIE.)

HATTIE (*controlling herself*): Yes. A private school endowed by some wealthy members of our race.

ELLA (*suddenly—even eagerly*): Then you must have taken lots of examinations and managed to pass them, didn't you?

HATTIE (*biting her lips*): I always passed with honors!

ELLA: Yes, we both graduated from the same High School, didn't we? That was dead easy for me. Why I hardly even looked at a book. But Jim says it was awfully hard for him. He failed one year, remember? (*She turns and smiles at* JIM—*a tolerant, superior smile but one full of genuine love.* HATTIE *is outraged, but* JIM *smiles.*)

JIM: Yes, it was hard for me, Honey.

ELLA: And the law school examinations Jim hardly ever could pass at all. Could you? (*She laughs lovingly.*)

HATTIE (*harshly*): Yes, he could! He can! He'll pass them now—if you'll give him a chance!

JIM (*angrily*): Hattie!

MRS. HARRIS: Hold yo' fool tongue!

HATTIE (*sullenly*): I'm sorry. (ELLA *has shrunk back against* JIM. *She regards* HATTIE *with a sort of wondering hatred. Then she looks away about the room. Suddenly her eyes fasten on the primitive mask and she gives a stifled scream.*)

JIM: What's the matter, Honey?

ELLA (*pointing*): That! For God's sake, what is it?

HATTIE (*scornfully*): It's a Congo mask. (*She goes and*

picks it up) I'll take it away if you wish. I thought you'd like it. It was my wedding present to Jim.

ELLA: What is it?

HATTIE: It's a mask which used to be worn in religious ceremonies by my people in Africa. But, aside from that, it's beautifully made, a work of Art by a real artist —as real in his way as your Michelangelo. (*Forces* ELLA *to take it*) Here. Just notice the workmanship.

ELLA (*defiantly*): I'm not scared of it if you're not. (*Looking at it with disgust*) Beautiful? Well, some people certainly have queer notions! It looks ugly to me and stupid—like a kid's game—making faces. (*She slaps it contemptuously*) Pooh! You needn't look hard at me. I'll give you the laugh. (*She goes to put it back on the stand.*)

JIM: Maybe, if it disturbs you, we better put it in some other room.

ELLA (*defiantly aggressive*): No. I want it here where I can give it the laugh! (*She sets it there again—then turns suddenly on* HATTIE *with aggressive determination*) Jim's not going to take any more examinations! I won't let him!

HATTIE (*bursting forth*): Jim! Do you hear that? There's white justice!—their fear for their superiority!—

ELLA (*with a terrified pleading*): Make her go away, Jim!

JIM (*losing control—furiously to his sister*): Either you leave here—or we will!

MRS. H. (*weeping—throws her arms around* HATTIE): Let's go, child! Let's go!

HATTIE (*calmly now*): Yes, Ma. All right. (*They go through the portières. As soon as they are gone,* JIM *suddenly collapses into a chair and hides his head in his hands.* ELLA *stands beside him for a moment. She stares distractedly about her, at the portrait, at the mask, at the furniture, at* JIM. *She seems fighting to escape from some weight on her mind. She throws this off and, completely her old self for the moment, kneels by* JIM *and pats his shoulder.*)

ELLA (*with kindness and love*): Don't, Jim! Don't cry, please! You don't suppose I really meant that about the examinations, do you? Why, of course, I didn't mean a word! I couldn't mean it! I want you to take the examinations! I want you to pass! I want you to be a lawyer! I want you to be the best lawyer in the country! I want you to show 'em—all the dirty sneaking, gossiping liars that talk behind our backs—what a man I married. I want the whole world to know you're the whitest of the white! I want you to climb and climb—and step on 'em, stamp right on their mean faces! I love you, Jim! You know that!

JIM (*calm again—happily*): I hope so, Honey—and I'll make myself worthy.

HATTIE (*appears in the doorway—quietly*): We're going now, Jim.

ELLA: No. Don't go.

HATTIE: We were going to, anyway. This is your house—Mother's gift to you, Jim.

JIM (*astonished*): But I can't accept— Where are you going?

HATTIE: We've got a nice flat in the Bronx—(*with bitter pride*) in the heart of the Black Belt—the Congo—among our own people!

JIM (*angrily*): You're crazy—I'll see Ma— (*He goes out.* HATTIE *and* ELLA *stare at each other with scorn and hatred for a moment, then* HATTIE *goes.* ELLA *remains kneeling for a moment by the chair, her eyes dazed and strange as she looks about her. Then she gets to her feet and stands before the portrait of* JIM's *father—with a sneer.*)

ELLA: It's his Old Man—all dolled up like a circus horse! Well, they can't help it. It's in the blood, I suppose. They're ignorant, that's all there is to it. (*She moves to the mask—forcing a mocking tone*) Hello, sport! Who d'you think you're scaring? Not me! I'll give you the laugh. He won't pass, you wait and see. Not in a thousand years! (*She goes to the window and looks down at the street and mutters*) All black! Every one of them! (*Then with sudden excitement*) No, there's one. Why, it's Shorty! (*She throws the window open and calls*) Shorty! Shorty! Hello, Shorty! (*She leans out and waves—then stops, remains there for a moment looking down, then shrinks back on the floor suddenly as if she wanted to hide—her whole face in an anguish*) Say! Say! I wonder—No, he didn't hear you. Yes, he did, too! He must have! I yelled so loud you could hear me in Jersey! No, what are you talking about? How would he hear with all the kids yelling down there? He never heard a word, I tell you! He did, too! He didn't want to hear you! He didn't want to let anyone know he knew you! Why don't you acknowledge it? What are you lying about? I'm not! Why shouldn't he? Where does he come in to—for God's sake, who is Shorty, anyway? A pimp! Yes, and a dope-peddler, too! D'you mean to say he'd have the nerve to hear me call him and then deliberately—? Yes, I mean to say it! I do say it! And it's true, and you know it, and you might as well be honest for a change and admit it! He heard you but he didn't want to hear you! He doesn't want to know you any more. No, not even him! He's afraid it'd get him in wrong with the old gang. Why? You know well enough! Because you married a—a—a—well, I won't say it, but you know without my mentioning names! (ELLA *springs to her feet in horror and shakes off her obsession with a frantic effort*) Stop! (*Then whimpering like a frightened child*) Jim! Jim! Jim! Where are you? I want you, Jim! (*She runs out of the room as the curtain falls.*)

ACT TWO
Scene II

THE *same. Six months later. It is evening. The walls of the room appear shrunken in, the ceiling lowered, so that the furniture, the portrait, the mask look unnaturally large and domineering.* JIM *is seated at the table studying, law books piled by his elbows. He is keeping his attention concentrated only by a driving physical effort which gives his face the expression of a runner's near the tape. His forehead shines with perspiration. He mutters one sentence from Blackstone over and over again, tapping his forehead with his fist in time to the rhythm he gives the stale words. But, in spite of himself, his attention wanders, his eyes have an uneasy, hunted look, he starts at every sound in the house or from the street. Finally, he remains rigid, Blackstone forgotten, his eyes fixed on the portières with tense grief. Then he groans, slams the book shut, goes to the window and throws it open and sinks down beside it, his arms on the sill, his head resting wearily on his arms, staring out into the night, the pale glare from the arc-lamp on the corner throwing his face into relief. The portières on the right are parted and* HATTIE *comes in.*

HATTIE (*not seeing him at the table*): Jim! (*Discovering him*) Oh, there you are. What're you doing?

JIM (*turning to her*): Resting. Cooling my head. (*Forcing a smile*) These law books certainly are a sweating proposition! (*Then anxiously*) How is she?

HATTIE: She's asleep now. I felt it was safe to leave her for a minute. (*After a pause*) What did the doctor tell you, Jim?

JIM: The same old thing. She must have rest, he says, her mind needs rest— (*Bitterly*) But he can't tell me any prescription for that rest—leastways not any that'd work.

HATTIE(*after a pause*): I think you ought to leave her, Jim—or let her leave you—for a while, anyway.

JIM (*angrily*): You're like the doctor. Everything's so simple and easy. Do this and that happens. Only it don't. Life isn't simple like that—not in this case, anyway—no, it isn't simple a bit. (*After a pause*) I can't leave her. She can't leave me. And there's a million little reasons combining to make one big reason why we can't. (*A pause*) For her sake—if it'd do her good —I'd go—I'd leave—I'd do anything—because I love her. I'd kill myself even—jump out of this window this second—I've thought it over, too—but that'd only make matters worse for her. I'm all she's got in the world!

Yes, that isn't bragging or fooling myself. I know that for a fact! Don't you know that's true? (*There is a pleading for the certainty he claims.*)

HATTIE: Yes, I know she loves you, Jim. I know that now.

JIM (*simply*): Then we've got to stick together to the end, haven't we, whatever comes—and hope and pray for the best? (*A pause—then hopefully*) I think maybe this is the crisis in her mind. Once she settles this in herself, she's won to the other side. And me—once I become a Member of the Bar—then I win, too! We're both free—by our own fighting down our own weakness! We're both really, truly free! Then we can be happy with ourselves here or anywhere. She'll be proud then! Yes, she's told me again and again, she says she'll be actually proud!

HATTIE (*turning away to conceal her emotion*): Yes, I'm sure—but you mustn't study too hard, Jim. You mustn't study too awfully hard!

JIM (*gets up and goes to the table and sits down wearily*): Yes, I know. Oh, I'll pass easily. I haven't got that scary feeling about that any more. And I'm doing two years' work in one here alone. That's better than schools, eh?

HATTIE (*doubtfully*): It's wonderful, Jim.

JIM (*his spirit evaporating*): If I can only hold out! It's hard! I'm worn out. I don't sleep. I get to thinking and thinking. My head aches and burns like fire with thinking. Round and round my thoughts go chasing like crazy chickens hopping and flapping before the wind. It gets me crazy mad—'cause I can't stop!

HATTIE (*watching him for a while and seeming to force herself to speak*): The doctor didn't tell you all, Jim.

JIM (*dully*): What's that?

HATTIE: He told me you're liable to break down too, if you don't take care of yourself.

JIM (*abjectly weary*): Let 'er come! I don't care what happens to me. Maybe if I get sick she'll get well. There's only so much bad luck allowed to one family, maybe. (*He forces a wan smile.*)

HATTIE (*hastily*): Don't give in to that idea, for the Lord's sake!

JIM: I'm tired—and blue—that's all.

HATTIE (*after another long pause*): I've got to tell you something else, Jim.

JIM (*dully*): What?

HATTIE: The doctor said Ella's liable to be sick like this a very long time.

JIM: He told me that too—that it'd be a long time before she got back her normal strength. Well, I suppose that's got to be expected.

HATTIE (*slowly*): He didn't mean convalescing—what he told me. (*A long pause.*)

JIM (*evasively*): I'm going to get other doctors in to see Ella—specialists. This one's a damn fool.

HATTIE: Be sensible, Jim. You'll have to face the truth—sooner or later.

JIM (*irritably*): I know the truth about Ella better'n any doctor.

HATTIE (*persuasively*): She'd get better so much sooner if you'd send her away to some nice sanitarium—

JIM: No! She'd die of shame there!

HATTIE: At least until after you've taken your examinations—

JIM: To hell with me!

HATTIE: Six months. That wouldn't be long to be parted.

JIM: What are you trying to do—separate us? (*He gets to his feet—furiously*) Go on out! Go on out!

HATTIE (*calmly*): No, I won't. (*Sharply*) There's something that's got to be said to you and I'm the only one with the courage— (*Intensely*) Tell me, Jim, have you heard her raving when she's out of her mind?

JIM (*with a shudder*): No!

HATTIE: You're lying, Jim. You must have—if you don't stop your ears—and the doctor says she may develop a violent mania, dangerous for you—get worse and worse until—Jim, you'll go crazy too—living this way. Today she raved on about "Black! Black!" and cried because she said her skin was turning black—that you had poisoned her—

JIM (*in anguish*): That's only when she's out of her mind.

HATTIE: And then she suddenly called me a dirty nigger.

JIM: No! She never said that ever! She never would!

HATTIE: She did—and kept on and on! (*A tense pause*) She'll be saying that to you soon.

JIM (*torturedly*): She don't mean it! She isn't responsible for what she's saying!

HATTIE: I know she isn't—yet she is just the same. It's deep down in her or it wouldn't come out.

JIM: Deep down in her people—not deep in her.

HATTIE: I can't make such distinctions. The race in me, deep in me, can't stand it. I can't play nurse to her any more, Jim,—not even for your sake. I'm afraid—afraid of myself—afraid sometime I'll kill her dead to set you free! (*She loses control and begins to cry.*)

JIM (*after a long pause—somberly*): Yes, I guess you'd better stay away from here. Good-by.

HATTIE: Who'll you get to nurse her, Jim,—a white woman?

JIM: Ella'd die of shame. No, I'll nurse her myself.

HATTIE: And give up your studies?

JIM: I can do both.

HATTIE: You can't! You'll get sick yourself! Why, you look terrible even as it is—and it's only beginning!

JIM: I can do anything for her! I'm all she's got in the world! I've got to prove I can be all to her! I've got to prove worthy! I've got to prove she can be proud of me! I've got to prove I'm the whitest of the white!

HATTIE (*stung by this last—with rebellious bitterness*): Is that the ambition she's given you? Oh, you soft, weak-minded fool, you traitor to your race! And the thanks you'll get—to be called a dirty nigger—to hear her cursing you because she can never have a child because it'll be born black—!

JIM (*in a frenzy*): Stop!

HATTIE: I'll say what must be said even though you'll kill me, Jim. Send her to an asylum before you both have to be sent to one together.

JIM (*with a sudden wild laugh*): Do you think you're threatening me with something dreadful now? Why, I'd like that. Sure, I'd like that! Maybe she'd like it better, too. Maybe we'd both find it all simple then— like you think it is now. Yes. (*He laughs again.*)

HATTIE (*frightenedly*): Jim!

JIM: Together! You can't scare me even with hell fire if you say she and I go together. It's heaven then for me! (*With sudden savagery*) You go out of here! All you've ever been aiming to do is to separate us so we can't be together!

HATTIE: I've done what I did for your own good.

JIM: I have no own good. I only got a good together with her. I'm all she's got in the world! Let her call me nigger! Let her call me the whitest of the white! I'm all she's got in the world, ain't I? She's all I've got! You with your fool talk of the black race and the white race! Where does the human race get a chance to come in? I suppose that's simple for you. You lock it up in asylums and throw away the key! (*With fresh violence*) Go along! There isn't going to be no more people coming in here to separate—excepting the doctor. I'm going to lock the door and it's going to stay locked, you hear? Go along, now!

HATTIE (*confusedly*): Jim!

JIM (*pushes her out gently and slams the door after her —vaguely*): Go along! I got to study. I got to nurse Ella, too. Oh, I can do it! I can do anything for her! (*He sits down at the table and, opening the book, begins to recite the line from Blackstone in a meaningless rhythm, tapping his forehead with his fist. ELLA enters noiselessly through the portières. She wears a red dressing-gown over her nightdress but is in her bare feet. She has a carving-knife in her right hand. Her eyes fasten on JIM with a murderous mania. She creeps up behind him. Suddenly he senses something and turns. As he sees her he gives a cry, jumping up and catching her wrist. She stands fixed, her eyes growing bewildered and frightened.*)

JIM (*aghast*): Ella! For God's sake! Do you want to murder me? (*She does not answer. He shakes her.*)

ELLA (*whimperingly*): They kept calling me names as I was walking along—I can't tell you what, Jim—and then I grabbed a knife—

JIM: Yes! See! This! (*She looks at it frightenedly.*)

ELLA: Where did I—? I was having a nightmare— Where did they go—I mean, how did I get here? (*With sudden terrified pleading—like a little girl*) Oh, Jim—don't ever leave me alone! I have such terrible dreams, Jim —promise you'll never go away!

JIM: I promise, Honey.

ELLA (*her manner becoming more and more childishly silly*): I'll be a little girl—and you'll be old Uncle Jim who's been with us for years and years— Will you play that?

JIM: Yes, Honey. Now you better go back to bed.

ELLA (*like a child*): Yes, Uncle Jim. (*She turns to go. He pretends to be occupied by his book. She looks at him for a second—then suddenly asks in her natural woman's voice*) Are you studying hard, Jim?

JIM: Yes, Honey. Go to bed now. You need to rest, you know.

ELLA (*stands looking at him, fighting with herself. A startling transformation comes over her face. It grows mean, vicious, full of jealous hatred. She cannot contain herself but breaks out harshly with a cruel, venomous grin*): You dirty nigger!

JIM (*starting as if he'd been shot*): Ella! For the good Lord's sake!

ELLA (*coming out of her insane mood for a moment, aware of something terrible, frightened*): Jim! Jim! Why are you looking at me like that?

JIM: What did you say to me just then?

ELLA (*gropingly*): Why, I—I said—I remember saying, are you studying hard, Jim? Why? You're not mad at that, are you?

JIM: No, Honey. What made you think I was mad? Go to bed now.

ELLA (*obediently*): Yes, Jim. (*She passes behind the portières.* JIM *stares before him. Suddenly her head is thrust out at the side of the portières. Her face is again that of a vindictive maniac*) Nigger! (*The face disappears —she can be heard running away, laughing with cruel satisfaction.* JIM *bows his head on his outstretched arms but he is too stricken for tears.*)

Curtain

ACT TWO
Scene III

THE *same, six months later. The sun has just gone down. The Spring twilight sheds a vague, gray light about the room, picking out the Congo mask on the stand by the window. The walls appear shrunken in still more, the ceiling now seems barely to clear the people's heads, the furniture and the characters appear enormously magnified. Law books are stacked in two great piles on each side of the table.* ELLA *comes in from the right, the carving-knife in her hand. She is pitifully thin, her face is wasted, but her eyes glow with a mad energy, her movements are abrupt and spring-like. She looks stealthily about the room, then advances and stands before the mask, her arms akimbo, her attitude one of crazy mockery, fear and bravado. She is dressed in the red dressing-gown, grown dirty and ragged now, and is in her bare feet.*

ELLA: I'll give you the laugh, wait and see! (*Then in a confidential tone*) He thought I was asleep! He called, Ella, Ella—but I kept my eyes shut, I pretended to snore. I fooled him good. (*She gives a little hoarse laugh*) This is the first time he's dared to leave me alone for months and months. I've been wanting to talk to you every day but this is the only chance— (*With sudden violence—flourishing her knife*) What're you grinning about, you dirty nigger, you? How dare you grin at me? I guess you forget what you are! That's always the way. Be kind to you, treat you decent, and in a second you've got a swelled head, you think you're somebody, you're all over the place putting on airs; why, it's got so I can't even walk down the street without seeing niggers, niggers everywhere. Hanging around, grinning, grinning—going to school—pretending they're white—taking examinations— (*She stops, arrested by the word, then suddenly*) That's where he's gone—down to the mail-box—to see if there's a letter from the Board—telling him— But why is he so long? (*She calls pitifully*) Jim! (*Then in a terrified whimper*) Maybe he's passed! Maybe he's passed! (*In a frenzy*) No! No! He can't! I'd kill him! I'd kill myself! (*Threatening the Congo mask*) It's you who're to blame for this! Yes, you! Oh, I'm on to you! (*Then appealingly*) But why d'you want to do this to us? What have I ever done wrong to you? What have you got against me? I married you, didn't I? Why don't you let Jim alone? Why don't you let him be happy as he is— with me? Why don't you let me be happy? He's white, isn't he—the whitest man that ever lived? Where do you come in to interfere? Black! Black! Black as dirt! You've poisoned me! I can't wash myself clean! Oh, I hate you! I hate you! Why don't you let Jim and me be happy? (*She sinks down in his chair, her arms outstretched on the table. The door from the hall is slowly opened and* JIM *appears. His bloodshot, sleepless eyes stare from deep hollows. His expression is one of crushed numbness. He holds an open letter in his hand.*)

JIM (*seeing* ELLA—*in an absolutely dead voice*): Honey —I thought you were asleep.

ELLA (*starts and wheels about in her chair*): What's that? You got—you got a letter—?

JIM (*turning to close the door after him*): From the Board of Examiners for admission to the Bar, State of New York—God's country! (*He finishes up with a chuckle of ironic self-pity so spent as to be barely audible.*)

ELLA (*writhing out of her chair like some fierce animal, the knife held behind her—with fear and hatred*): You didn't—you didn't—you didn't pass, did you?

JIM (*looking at her wildly*): Pass? Pass? (*He begins to chuckle and laugh between sentences and phrases, rich, Negro laughter, but heart-breaking in its mocking grief*) Good Lord, child, how come you can ever imagine such a crazy idea? Pass? Me? Jim Crow Harris? Nigger Jim Harris—become a full-fledged Member of the Bar! Why the mere notion of it is enough to kill you with laughing! It'd be against all natural laws, all human right and justice. It'd be miraculous, there'd be earthquakes and catastrophes, the seven Plagues'd come again and locusts'd devour all the money in the banks, the second Flood'd come roaring and Noah'd fall overboard, the sun'd drop out of the sky like a ripe fig, and the Devil'd perform miracles, and God'd be tipped head first right out of the Judgment seat! (*He laughs, maudlinly uproarious.*)

ELLA (*her face beginning to relax, to light up*): Then you—you didn't pass?

JIM (*spent—giggling and gasping idiotically*): Well, I should say not! I should certainly say not!

ELLA (*with a cry of joy, pushes all the law books crashing to the floor—then with childish happiness she grabs* JIM *by both hands and dances up and down*): Oh, Jim, I knew it! I knew you couldn't! Oh, I'm so glad, Jim! I'm so happy! You're still my old Jim—and I'm so glad! (*He looks at her dazedly, a fierce rage slowly gathering on his face. She dances away from him. His eyes follow her. His hands clench. She stands in front of the mask—triumphantly*) There! What did I tell you? I told you I'd give you the laugh! (*She begins to laugh with wild unrestraint, grabs the mask from its place, sets it in the middle of the table and plunging the knife down through it pins it to the table*) There! Who's got the laugh now?

JIM (*his eyes bulging—hoarsely*): You devil! You white devil woman! (*In a terrible roar, raising his fists above her head*) You devil!

ELLA (*looking up at him with a bewildered cry of terror*): Jim! (*Her appeal recalls him to himself. He lets his arms slowly drop to his sides, bowing his head.* ELLA *points tremblingly to the mask*) It's all right, Jim! It's dead. The devil's dead. See! It couldn't live—unless you passed. If you'd passed it would have lived in you. Then I'd have had to kill you, Jim, don't you see?—or it would have killed me. But now I've killed it. (*She pats his hand*) So you needn't ever be afraid any more, Jim.

JIM (*dully*): I've got to sit down, Honey. I'm tired. I haven't had much chance for sleep in so long— (*He slumps down in the chair by the table.*)

ELLA (*sits down on the floor beside him and holds his hand. Her face is gradually regaining an expression that is happy, childlike and pretty*): I know, Jim! That was my fault. I wouldn't let you sleep. I couldn't let you. I kept thinking if he sleeps good then he'll be sure to study good and then he'll pass—and the devil'll win!

JIM (*with a groan*): Don't, Honey!

ELLA (*with a childish grin*): That was why I carried that knife around—(*she frowns—puzzled*)—one reason—to keep you from studying and sleeping by scaring you.

JIM: I wasn't scared of being killed. I was scared of what they'd do to you after.

ELLA (*after a pause—like a child*): Will God forgive me, Jim?

JIM: Maybe He can forgive what you've done to me; and maybe He can forgive what I've done to you; but I don't see how He's going to forgive—Himself.

ELLA: I prayed and prayed. When you were away taking the examinations and I was alone with the nurse, I closed my eyes and pretended to be asleep but I was praying with all my might: O God, don't let Jim pass!

JIM (*with a sob*): Don't, Honey, don't! For the good Lord's sake! You're hurting me!

ELLA (*frightenedly*): How, Jim? Where? (*Then after a pause—suddenly*) I'm sick, Jim. I don't think I'll live long.

JIM (*simply*): Then I won't either. Somewhere yonder maybe—together—our luck'll change. But I wanted—

here and now—before you—we—I wanted to prove to you—to myself—to become a full-fledged Member—so you could be proud— (*He stops. Words fail and he is beyond tears.*)

ELLA (*brightly*): Well, it's all over, Jim. Everything'll be all right now. (*Chattering along*) I'll be just your little girl, Jim—and you'll be my little boy—just as we used to be, remember, when we were beaux; and I'll put shoe-blacking on my face and pretend I'm black and you can put chalk on your face and pretend you're white just as we used to do—and we can play marbles —only you mustn't all the time be a boy. Sometimes you must be my old kind Uncle Jim who's been with us for years and years. Will you, Jim?

JIM (*with utter resignation*): Yes, Honey.

ELLA: And you'll never, never, never, never leave me, Jim?

JIM: Never, Honey.

ELLA: 'Cause you're all I've got in the world—and I love you, Jim. (*She kisses his hand as a child might, tenderly and gratefully.*)

JIM (*suddenly throws himself on his knees and raises his shining eyes, his transfigured face*): Forgive me, God —and make me worthy! Now I see Your Light again! Now I Hear Your Voice! (*He begins to weep in an ecstasy of religious humility*) Forgive me, God, for blaspheming You! Let this fire of burning suffering purify me of selfishness and make me worthy of the child You send me for the woman You take away!

ELLA (*jumping to her feet—excitedly*): Don't cry, Jim! You mustn't cry! I've got only a little time left and I want to play. Don't be old Uncle Jim now. Be my little boy, Jim. Pretend you're Painty Face and I'm Jim Crow. Come and play!

JIM (*still deeply exalted*): Honey, Honey, I'll play right up to the gates of Heaven with you! (*She tugs at one of his hands, laughingly trying to pull him up from his knees as the curtain falls.*)

Beyond the Horizon

❀

A PLAY IN THREE ACTS

CHARACTERS

JAMES MAYO, *a farmer*

KATE MAYO, *his wife*

CAPTAIN DICK SCOTT, *of the bark "Sunda," her brother*

ANDREW MAYO ⎫
⎬ *sons of* JAMES MAYO
ROBERT MAYO ⎭

RUTH ATKINS

MRS. ATKINS, *her widowed mother*

MARY

BEN, *a farm hand*

DOCTOR FAWCETT

SCENES

ACT ONE
Scene I

A SECTION of *country highway. The road runs diagonally from the left, forward, to the right, rear, and can be seen in the distance winding toward the horizon like a pale ribbon between the low, rolling hills with their freshly plowed fields clearly divided from each other, checkerboard fashion, by the lines of stone walls and rough snake-fences.*

The forward triangle cut off by the road is a section of a field from the dark earth of which myriad bright-green blades of fall-sown rye are sprouting. A straggling line of piled rocks, too low to be called a wall, separates this field from the road.

To the rear of the road is a ditch with a sloping, grassy bank on the far side. From the center of this an old, gnarled apple tree, just budding into leaf, strains its twisted branches heavenwards, black against the pallor of distance. A snake-fence sidles from left to right along the top of the bank, passing beneath the apple tree.

The hushed twilight of a day in May is just beginning. The horizon hills are still rimmed by a faint line of flame, and the sky above them glows with the crimson flush of the sunset. This fades gradually as the action of the scene progresses.

At the rise of the curtain, ROBERT MAYO *is discovered sitting on the fence. He is a tall, slender young man of twenty-three. There is a touch of the poet about him expressed in his high forehead and wide, dark eyes. His fea-*

tures are delicate and refined, leaning to weakness in the mouth and chin. He is dressed in gray corduroy trousers pushed into high laced boots, and a blue flannel shirt with a bright colored tie. He is reading a book by the fading sunset light. He shuts this, keeping a finger in to mark the place, and turns his head toward the horizon, gazing out over the fields and hills. His lips move as if he were reciting something to himself.

His brother ANDREW *comes along the road from the right, returning from his work in the fields. He is twenty-seven years old, an opposite type to* ROBERT—*husky, sun-bronzed, handsome in a large-featured, manly fashion—a son of the soil, intelligent in a shrewd way, but with nothing of the intellectual about him. He wears overalls, leather boots, a gray flannel shirt open at the neck, and a soft, mud-stained hat pushed back on his head. He stops to talk to* ROBERT, *leaning on the hoe he carries.*

ANDREW (*seeing* ROBERT *has not noticed his presence—in a loud shout*): Hey there! (ROBERT *turns with a start. Seeing who it is, he smiles*) Gosh, you do take the prize for day-dreaming! And I see you've toted one of the old books along with you. (*He crosses the ditch and sits on the fence near his brother*) What is it this time—poetry, I'll bet. (*He reaches for the book*) Let me see.

ROBERT (*handing it to him rather reluctantly*): Look out you don't get it full of dirt.

ANDREW (*glancing at his hands*): That isn't dirt—it's good clean earth. (*He turns over the pages. His eyes read something and he gives an exclamation of disgust*) Hump! (*With a provoking grin at his brother he reads aloud in a doleful, sing-song voice*) "I have loved wind and light and the bright sea. But Holy and most sacred night, not as I love and have loved thee." (*He hands the book back*) Here! Take it and bury it. I suppose it's that year in college gave you a liking for that kind of stuff. I'm darn glad I stopped at High School, or maybe I'd been crazy too. (*He grins and slaps* ROBERT *on the back affectionately*) Imagine me reading poetry and plowing at the same time. The team'd run away, I'll bet.

ROBERT (*laughing*): Or picture me plowing.

ANDREW: You should have gone back to college last fall, like I know you wanted to. You're fitted for that sort of thing—just as I ain't.

ROBERT: You know why I didn't go back, Andy. Pa didn't like the idea, even if he didn't say so; and I know he wanted the money to use improving the farm. And besides, I'm not keen on being a student, just because you see me reading books all the time. What I want to do now is keep on moving so that I won't take root in any one place.

ANDREW: Well, the trip you're leaving on tomorrow will keep you moving all right. (*At this mention of the trip they both fall silent. There is a pause. Finally* ANDREW *goes on, awkwardly, attempting to speak casually*) Uncle says you'll be gone three years.

ROBERT: About that, he figures.

ANDREW (*moodily*): That's a long time.

ROBERT: Not so long when you come to consider it. You know the "Sunda" sails around the Horn for Yokohama first, and that's a long voyage on a sailing ship; and if we go to any of the other places Uncle Dick mentions—India, or Australia, or South Africa, or South America—they'll be long voyages, too.

ANDREW: You can have all those foreign parts for all of

me. (*After a pause*) Ma's going to miss you a lot, Rob.

ROBERT: Yes—and I'll miss her.

ANDREW: And Pa ain't feeling none too happy to have you go—though he's been trying not to show it.

ROBERT: I can see how he feels.

ANDREW: And you can bet that I'm not giving any cheers about it. (*He puts one hand on the fence near* ROBERT.)

ROBERT (*putting one hand on top of* ANDREW's *with a gesture almost of shyness*): I know that, too, Andy.

ANDREW: I'll miss you as much as anybody, I guess. You see, you and I ain't like most brothers—always fighting and separated a lot of the time, while we've always been together—just the two of us. It's different with us. That's why it hits so hard, I guess.

ROBERT (*with feeling*): It's just as hard for me, Andy— believe that! I hate to leave you and the old folks—but —I feel I've got to. There's something calling me— (*He points to the horizon*) Oh, I can't just explain it to you, Andy.

ANDREW: No need to, Rob. (*Angry at himself*) Hell! You want to go—that's all there is to it; and I wouldn't have you miss this chance for the world.

ROBERT: It's fine of you to feel that way, Andy.

ANDREW: Huh! I'd be a nice son-of-a-gun if I didn't, wouldn't I? When I know how you need this sea trip to make a new man of you—in the body, I mean—and give you your full health back.

ROBERT (*a trifle impatiently*): All of you seem to keep harping on my health. You were so used to seeing me lying around the house in the old days that you never will get over the notion that I'm a chronic invalid. You don't realize how I've bucked up in the past few years. If I had no other excuse for going on Uncle Dick's ship

but just my health, I'd stay right here and start in plowing.

ANDREW: Can't be done. Farming ain't your nature.
There's all the difference shown in just the way us two
feel about the farm. You—well, you like the home part
of it, I expect; but as a place to work and grow things,
you hate it. Ain't that right?

ROBERT: Yes, I suppose it is. For you it's different. You're
a Mayo through and through. You're wedded to the
soil. You're as much a product of it as an ear of corn is,
or a tree. Father is the same. This farm is his life-work,
and he's happy in knowing that another Mayo, inspired
by the same love, will take up the work where he leaves
off. I can understand your attitude, and Pa's; and I
think it's wonderful and sincere. But I—well, I'm not
made that way.

ANDREW: No, you ain't; but when it comes to understanding, I guess I realize that you've got your own
angle of looking at things.

ROBERT (*musingly*): I wonder if you do, really.

ANDREW (*confidently*): Sure I do. You've seen a bit of the
world, enough to make the farm seem small, and
you've got the itch to see it all.

ROBERT: It's more than that, Andy.

ANDREW: Oh, of course. I know you're going to learn
navigation, and all about a ship, so's you can be an officer. That's natural, too. There's fair pay in it, I expect,
when you consider that you've always got a home and
grub thrown in; and if you're set on traveling, you can
go anywhere you're a mind to without paying fare.

ROBERT (*with a smile that is half sad*): It's more than
that, Andy.

ANDREW: Sure it is. There's always a chance of a good

thing coming your way in some of those foreign ports or other. I've heard there are great opportunities for a young fellow with his eyes open in some of those new countries that are just being opened up. (*Jovially*) I'll bet that's what you've been turning over in your mind under all your quietness! (*He slaps his brother on the back with a laugh*) Well, if you get to be a millionaire all of a sudden, call 'round once in a while and I'll pass the plate to you. We could use a lot of money right here on the farm without hurting it any.

ROBERT (*forced to laugh*): I've never considered that practical side of it for a minute, Andy.

ANDREW: Well, you ought to.

ROBERT: No, I oughtn't. (*Pointing to the horizon— dreamily*) Supposing I was to tell you that it's just Beauty that's calling me, the beauty of the far off and unknown, the mystery and spell of the East which lures me in the books I've read, the need of the freedom of great wide spaces, the joy of wandering on and on—in quest of the secret which is hidden over there, beyond the horizon? Suppose I told you that was the one and only reason for my going?

ANDREW: I should say you were nutty.

ROBERT (*frowning*): Don't, Andy. I'm serious.

ANDREW: Then you might as well stay here, because we've got all you're looking for right on this farm. There's wide space enough, Lord knows; and you can have all the sea you want by walking a mile down to the beach; and there's plenty of horizon to look at, and beauty enough for anyone, except in the winter. (*He grins*) As for the mystery and spell, I haven't met 'em yet, but they're probably lying around somewheres. I'll have you understand this is a first class farm with all the fixings. (*He laughs.*)

ROBERT (*joining in the laughter in spite of himself*): It's no use talking to you, you chump!

ANDREW: You'd better not say anything to Uncle Dick about spells and things when you're on the ship. He'll likely chuck you overboard for a Jonah. (*He jumps down from fence*) I'd better run along. I've got to wash up some as long as Ruth's Ma is coming over for supper.

ROBERT (*pointedly—almost bitterly*): And Ruth.

ANDREW (*confused—looking everywhere except at* ROBERT *—trying to appear unconcerned*): Yes, Ruth'll be staying too. Well, I better hustle, I guess, and— (*He steps over the ditch to the road while he is talking.*)

ROBERT (*who appears to be fighting some strong inward emotion—impulsively*): Wait a minute, Andy! (*He jumps down from the fence*) There is something I want to— (*He stops abruptly, biting his lips, his face coloring.*)

ANDREW (*facing him; half-defiantly*): Yes?

ROBERT (*confusedly*): No—never mind—it doesn't matter, it was nothing.

ANDREW (*after a pause, during which he stares fixedly at* ROBERT'S *averted face*): Maybe I can guess what—you were going to say—but I guess you're right not to talk about it. (*He pulls* ROBERT'S *hand from his side and grips it tensely; the two brothers stand looking into each other's eyes for a minute*) We can't help those things, Rob. (*He turns away, suddenly releasing* ROBERT'S *hand*) You'll be coming along shortly, won't you?

ROBERT (*dully*): Yes.

ANDREW: See you later, then. (*He walks off down the road to the left.* ROBERT *stares after him for a moment; then climbs to the fence rail again, and looks out over the hills, an expression of deep grief on his face. After a moment or so,* RUTH *enters hurriedly from the left. She is a healthy, blonde, out-of-door girl of twenty, with a graceful, slender figure. Her face, though inclined to roundness, is undeniably pretty, its large eyes of a deep blue set off strikingly by the sun-bronzed complexion. Her small, regular features are marked by a certain strength—an underlying, stubborn fixity of purpose hidden in the frankly-appealing charm of her fresh youthfulness. She wears a simple white dress but no hat.*)

RUTH (*seeing him*): Hello, Rob!

ROBERT (*startled*): Hello, Ruth!

RUTH (*jumps the ditch and perches on the fence beside him*): I was looking for you.

ROBERT (*pointedly*): Andy just left here.

RUTH: I know. I met him on the road a second ago. He told me you were here. (*Tenderly playful*) I wasn't looking for Andy, Smarty, if that's what you mean. I was looking for *you.*

ROBERT: Because I'm going away tomorrow?

RUTH: Because your mother was anxious to have you come home and asked me to look for you. I just wheeled Ma over to your house.

ROBERT (*perfunctorily*): How is your mother?

RUTH (*a shadow coming over her face*): She's about the same. She never seems to get any better or any worse. Oh, Rob, I do wish she'd try to make the best of things that can't be helped.

ROBERT: Has she been nagging at you again?

RUTH (*nods her head, and then breaks forth rebelliously*): She never stops nagging. No matter what I do for her she finds fault. If only Pa was still living— (*She stops as if ashamed of her outburst*) I suppose I shouldn't complain this way. (*She sighs*) Poor Ma, Lord knows it's hard enough for her. I suppose it's natural to be cross when you're not able ever to walk a step. Oh, I'd like to be going away some place—like you!

ROBERT: It's hard to stay—and equally hard to go, sometimes.

RUTH: There! If I'm not the stupid body! I swore I wasn't going to speak about your trip—until after you'd gone; and there I go, first thing!

ROBERT: Why didn't you want to speak of it?

RUTH: Because I didn't want to spoil this last night you're here. Oh, Rob, I'm going to—we're all going to miss you so awfully. Your mother is going around looking as if she'd burst out crying any minute. You ought to know how I feel. Andy and you and I—why it seems as if we'd always been together.

ROBERT (*with a wry attempt at a smile*): You and Andy will still have each other. It'll be harder for me without anyone.

RUTH: But you'll have new sights and new people to take your mind off; while we'll be here with the old, familiar place to remind us every minute of the day. It's a shame you're going—just at this time, in spring, when everything is getting so nice. (*With a sigh*) I oughtn't to talk that way when I know going's the best thing for you. You're bound to find all sorts of opportunities to get on, your father says.

ROBERT (*heatedly*): I don't give a damn about that! I

wouldn't take a voyage across the road for the best opportunity in the world of the kind Pa thinks of. (*He
smiles at his own irritation*) Excuse me, Ruth, for getting worked up over it; but Andy gave me an overdose
of the practical considerations.

RUTH (*slowly, puzzled*): Well, then, if it isn't— (*With
sudden intensity*) Oh, Rob, why *do* you want to go?

ROBERT (*turning to her quickly, in surprise—slowly*):
Why do you ask that, Ruth?

RUTH (*dropping her eyes before his searching glance*):
Because— (*Lamely*) It seems such a shame.

ROBERT (*insistently*): Why?

RUTH: Oh, because—everything.

ROBERT: I could hardly back out now, even if I wanted
to. And I'll be forgotten before you know it.

RUTH (*indignantly*): You won't! I'll never forget— (*She
stops and turns away to hide her confusion.*)

ROBERT (*softly*): Will you promise me that?

RUTH (*evasively*): Of course. It's mean of you to think
that any of us would forget so easily.

ROBERT (*disappointedly*): Oh!

RUTH (*with an attempt at lightness*): But you haven't
told me your reason for leaving yet.

ROBERT (*moodily*): I doubt if you'll understand. It's difficult to explain, even to myself. Either you feel it, or you
don't. I can remember being conscious of it first when
I was only a kid—you haven't forgotten what a sickly
specimen I was then, in those days, have you?

RUTH (*with a shudder*): Let's not think about them.

ROBERT: You'll have to, to understand. Well, in those
days, when Ma was fixing meals, she used to get me out
of the way by pushing my chair to the west window

and telling me to look out and be quiet. That wasn't
hard. I guess I was always quiet.

RUTH (*compassionately*): Yes, you always were—and
you suffering so much, too!

ROBERT (*musingly*): So I used to stare out over the fields
to the hills, out there— (*He points to the horizon*) and
somehow after a time I'd forget any pain I was in, and
start dreaming. I knew the sea was over beyond those
hills—the folks had told me—and I used to wonder
what the sea was like, and try to form a picture of it in
my mind. (*With a smile*) There was all the mystery in
the world to me then about that—far-off sea—and there
still is! It called to me then just as it does now. (*After
a slight pause*) And other times my eyes would follow
this road, winding off into the distance, toward the hills,
as if it, too, was searching for the sea. And I'd promise myself that when I grew up and was strong, I'd follow that road, and it and I would find the sea together.
(*With a smile*) You see, my making this trip is only
keeping that promise of long ago.

RUTH (*charmed by his low, musical voice telling the
dreams of his childhood*): Yes, I see.

ROBERT: Those were the only happy moments of my life
then, dreaming there at the window. I liked to be all
alone—those times. I got to know all the different kinds
of sunsets by heart. And all those sunsets took place
over there— (*He points*) beyond the horizon. So gradually I came to believe that all the wonders of the
world happened on the other side of those hills. There
was the home of the good fairies who performed beautiful miracles. I believed in fairies then. (*With a smile*)
Perhaps I still do believe in them. Anyway, in those

days they were real enough, and sometimes I could actually hear them calling to me to come out and play with them, dance with them down the road in the dusk in a game of hide-and-seek to find out where the sun was hiding himself. They sang their little songs to me, songs that told of all the wonderful things they had in their home on the other side of the hills; and they promised to show me all of them, if I'd only come, come! But I couldn't come then, and I used to cry sometimes and Ma would think I was in pain. (*He breaks off suddenly with a laugh*) That's why I'm going now, I suppose. For I can still hear them calling. But the horizon is as far away and as luring as ever. (*He turns to her—softly*) Do you understand now, Ruth?

RUTH (*spellbound, in a whisper*): Yes.

ROBERT: You feel it then?

RUTH: Yes, yes, I do! (*Unconsciously she snuggles close against his side. His arm steals about her as if he were not aware of the action*) Oh, Rob, how could I help feeling it? You tell things so beautifully!

ROBERT (*suddenly realizing that his arm is around her, and that her head is resting on his shoulder, gently takes his arm away.* RUTH, *brought back to herself, is overcome with confusion*): So now you know why I'm going. It's for that reason—that and one other.

RUTH: You've another? Then you must tell me that, too.

ROBERT (*looking at her searchingly. She drops her eyes before his gaze*): I wonder if I ought to! You'll promise not to be angry—whatever it is?

RUTH (*softly, her face still averted*): Yes, I promise.

ROBERT (*simply*): I love you. That's the other reason.

RUTH (*hiding her face in her hands*): Oh, Rob!

ROBERT: I wasn't going to tell you, but I feel I have to. It can't matter now that I'm going so far away, and for so long—perhaps forever. I've loved you all these years, but the realization never came 'til I agreed to go away with Uncle Dick. Then I thought of leaving you, and the pain of that thought revealed to me in a flash—that I loved you, had loved you as long as I could remember. (*He gently pulls one of* RUTH's *hands away from her face*) You mustn't mind my telling you this, Ruth. I realize how impossible it all is—and I understand; for the revelation of my own love seemed to open my eyes to the love of others. I saw Andy's love for you— and I knew that you must love him.

RUTH (*breaking out stormily*): I don't! I don't love Andy! I don't! (ROBERT *stares at her in stupid astonishment.* RUTH *weeps hysterically*) Whatever—put such a fool notion into—into your head? (*She suddenly throws her arms about his neck and hides her head on his shoulder*) Oh, Rob! Don't go away! Please! You mustn't, now! You can't! I won't let you! It'd break my —my heart!

ROBERT (*the expression of stupid bewilderment giving way to one of overwhelming joy. He presses her close to him—slowly and tenderly*): Do you mean that— that you love me?

RUTH (*sobbing*): Yes, yes—of course I do—what d'you s'pose? (*She lifts up her head and looks into his eyes with a tremulous smile*) You stupid thing! (*He kisses her*) I've loved you right along.

ROBERT (*mystified*): But you and Andy were always together!

RUTH: Because you never seemed to want to go any place with me. You were always reading an old book, and

not paying any attention to me. I was too proud to let
you see I cared because I thought the year you had away
to college had made you stuck-up, and you thought
yourself too educated to waste any time on me.

ROBERT (*kissing her*): And I was thinking— (*With a
laugh*) What fools we've both been!

RUTH (*overcome by a sudden fear*): You won't go away
on the trip, will you, Rob? You'll tell them you can't go
on account of me, won't you? You can't go now! You
can't!

ROBERT (*bewildered*): Perhaps—you can come too.

RUTH: Oh, Rob, don't be so foolish. You know I can't.
Who'd take care of Ma? Don't you see I couldn't go—
on her account? (*She clings to him imploringly*) Please
don't go—not now. Tell them you've decided not to.
They won't mind. I know your mother and father'll be
glad. They'll all be. They don't want you to go so far
away from them. Please, Rob! We'll be so happy here
together where it's natural and we know things. Please
tell me you won't go!

ROBERT (*face to face with a definite, final decision, betrays
the conflict going on within him*): But—Ruth—I—
Uncle Dick—

RUTH: He won't mind when he knows it's for your happiness to stay. How could he? (*As* ROBERT *remains silent
she bursts into sobs again*) Oh, Rob! And you said—
you loved me!

ROBERT (*conquered by this appeal—an irrevocable decision
in his voice*): I won't go, Ruth. I promise you. There!
Don't cry! (*He presses her to him, stroking her hair
tenderly. After a pause he speaks with happy hopeful-
ness*) Perhaps after all Andy was right—righter than
he knew—when he said I could find all the things I

was seeking for here, at home on the farm. I think love must have been the secret—the secret that called to me from over the world's rim—the secret beyond every horizon; and when I did not come, it came to me. (*He clasps* RUTH *to him fiercely*) Oh, Ruth, our love is sweeter than any distant dream! (*He kisses her passionately and steps to the ground, lifting* RUTH *in his arms and carrying her to the road where he puts her down.*)

RUTH (*with a happy laugh*): My, but you're strong!

ROBERT: Come! We'll go and tell them at once.

RUTH (*dismayed*): Oh, no, don't, Rob, not 'til after I've gone. There'd be bound to be such a scene with them all together.

ROBERT (*kissing her—gayly*): As you like—little Miss Common Sense!

RUTH: Let's go, then. (*She takes his hand, and they start to go off left.* ROBERT *suddenly stops and turns as though for a last look at the hills and the dying sunset flush.*)

ROBERT (*looking upward and pointing*): See! The first star. (*He bends down and kisses her tenderly*) Our star!

RUTH (*in a soft murmur*): Yes. Our very own star. (*They stand for a moment looking up at it, their arms around each other. Then* RUTH *takes his hand again and starts to lead him away*) Come, Rob, let's go. (*His eyes are fixed again on the horizon as he half turns to follow her.* RUTH *urges*) We'll be late for supper, Rob.

ROBERT (*shakes his head impatiently, as though he were throwing off some disturbing thought—with a laugh*): All right. We'll run then. Come on! (*They run off laughing as the curtain falls.*)

ACT ONE
Scene II

THE *small sitting room of the Mayo farmhouse about nine o'clock same night. On the left, two windows looking out on the fields. Against the wall between the windows, an old-fashioned walnut desk. In the left corner, rear, a sideboard with a mirror. In the rear wall to the right of the sideboard, a window looking out on the road. Next to the window a door leading out into the yard. Farther right, a black horsehair sofa, and another door opening on a bedroom. In the corner, a straight-backed chair. In the right wall, near the middle, an open doorway leading to the kitchen. Farther forward a double-heater stove with coal scuttle, etc. In the center of the newly-carpeted floor, an oak dining-room table with a red cover. In the center of the table, a large oil reading lamp. Four chairs, three rockers with crocheted tidies on their backs, and one straight-backed, are placed about the table. The walls are papered a dark red with a scrolly-figured pattern.*

Everything in the room is clean, well-kept, and in its exact place, yet there is no suggestion of primness about the whole. Rather the atmosphere is one of the orderly comfort of a simple, hard-earned prosperity, enjoyed and maintained by the family as a unit.

JAMES MAYO, *his wife, her brother,* CAPTAIN DICK SCOTT, *and* ANDREW *are discovered.* MAYO *is his son* ANDREW *over again in body and face—an* ANDREW *sixty-five years old with a short, square, white beard.* MRS. MAYO *is a slight,*

*round-faced, rather prim-looking woman of fifty-five who
had once been a school teacher. The labors of a farmer's
wife have bent but not broken her, and she retains a certain refinement of movement and expression foreign to
the* MAYO *part of the family. Whatever of resemblance*
ROBERT *has to his parents may be traced to her. Her
brother, the* CAPTAIN, *is short and stocky, with a weather-
beaten, jovial face and a white mustache—a typical old
salt, loud of voice and given to gesture. He is fifty-eight
years old.*

JAMES MAYO *sits in front of the table. He wears spectacles, and a farm journal which he has been reading lies
in his lap. The* CAPTAIN *leans forward from a chair in the
rear, his hands on the table in front of him.* ANDREW *is
tilted back on the straight-backed chair to the left, his
chin sunk forward on his chest, staring at the carpet, preoccupied and frowning.*

As the Curtain rises the CAPTAIN *is just finishing the re-
lation of some sea episode. The others are pretending an
interest which is belied by the absent-minded expressions
on their faces.*

THE CAPTAIN (*chuckling*): And that mission woman, she
hails me on the dock as I was acomin' ashore, and she
says—with her silly face all screwed up serious as judgment—"Captain," she says, "would you be so kind as to
tell me where the sea-gulls sleeps at nights?" Blow me
if them warn't her exact words! (*He slaps the table
with the palms of his hands and laughs loudly. The
others force smiles*) Ain't that just like a fool woman's
question? And I looks at her serious as I could. "Ma'm," says I, "I couldn't rightly answer that question. I ain't never seed a sea-gull in his bunk yet. The

next time I hears one snorin'," I says, "I'll make a note of where he's turned in, and write you a letter 'bout it." And then she calls me a fool real spiteful and tacks away from me quick. (*He laughs again uproariously*) So I got rid of her that way. (*The others smile but immediately relapse into expressions of gloom again.*)

MRS. MAYO (*absent-mindedly—feeling that she has to say something*): But when it comes to that, where *do* seagulls sleep, Dick?

SCOTT (*slapping the table*): Ho! Ho! Listen to her, James. 'Nother one! Well, if that don't beat all hell—'scuse me for cussin', Kate.

MAYO (*with a twinkle in his eyes*): They unhitch their wings, Katey, and spreads 'em out on a wave for a bed.

SCOTT: And then they tells the fish to whistle to 'em when it's time to turn out. Ho! Ho!

MRS. MAYO (*with a forced smile*): You men folks are too smart to live, aren't you? (*She resumes her knitting. MAYO pretends to read his paper; ANDREW stares at the floor.*)

SCOTT (*looks from one to the other of them with a puzzled air. Finally he is unable to bear the thick silence a minute longer, and blurts out*): You folks look as if you was settin' up with a corpse. (*With exaggerated concern*) God A'mighty, there ain't anyone dead, be there?

MAYO (*sharply*): Don't play the dunce, Dick! You know as well as we do there ain't no great cause to be feelin' chipper.

SCOTT (*argumentatively*): And there ain't no cause to be wearin' mourning, either, I can make out.

MRS. MAYO (*indignantly*): How can you talk that way,

Dick Scott, when you're taking our Robbie away from us, in the middle of the night, you might say, just to get on that old boat of yours on time! I think you might wait until morning when he's had his breakfast.

SCOTT (*appealing to the others hopelessly*): Ain't that a woman's way o' seein' things for you? God A'mighty, Kate, I can't give orders to the tide that it's got to be high just when it suits me to have it. I ain't gettin' no fun out o' missing sleep and leavin' here at six bells myself. (*Protestingly*) And the "Sunda" ain't an old ship —leastways, not very old—and she's good's she ever was.

MRS. MAYO (*her lips trembling*): I wish Robbie weren't going.

MAYO (*looking at her over his glasses—consolingly*): There, Katey!

MRS. MAYO (*rebelliously*): Well, I *do* wish he wasn't!

SCOTT: You shouldn't be taking it so hard, 's far as I kin see. This vige'll make a man of him. I'll see to it he learns how to navigate, 'n' study for a mate's c'tificate right off—and it'll give him a trade for the rest of his life, if he wants to travel.

MRS. MAYO: But I don't want him to travel all his life. You've got to see he comes home when this trip is over. Then he'll be all well, and he'll want to—to marry— (ANDREW *sits forward in his chair with an abrupt movement*)—and settle down right here. (*She stares down at the knitting in her lap—after a pause*) I never realized how hard it was going to be for me to have Robbie go—or I wouldn't have considered it a minute.

SCOTT: It ain't no good goin' on that way, Kate, now it's all settled.

MRS. MAYO (*on the verge of tears*): It's all right for *you*

to talk. You've never had any children. You don't
know what it means to be parted from them—and Robbie my youngest, too. (ANDREW *frowns and fidgets in
his chair.*)

ANDREW (*suddenly turning to them*): There's one thing
none of you seem to take into consideration—that Rob
wants to go. He's dead set on it. He's been dreaming
over this trip ever since it was first talked about. It
wouldn't be fair to him not to have him go. (*A sudden uneasiness seems to strike him*) At least, not if he
still feels the same way about it he did when he was
talking to me this evening.

MAYO (*with an air of decision*): Andy's right, Katey.
That ends all argyment, you can see that. (*Looking at
his big silver watch*) Wonder what's happened to Robert? He's been gone long enough to wheel the widder
to home, certain. He can't be out dreamin' at the stars
his last night.

MRS. MAYO (*a bit reproachfully*): Why didn't you wheel
Mrs. Atkins back tonight, Andy? You usually do when
she and Ruth come over.

ANDREW (*avoiding her eyes*): I thought maybe Robert
wanted to tonight. He offered to go right away when
they were leaving.

MRS. MAYO: He only wanted to be polite.

ANDREW (*gets to his feet*): Well, he'll be right back, I
guess. (*He turns to his father*) Guess I'll go take a look
at the black cow, Pa—see if she's ailing any.

MAYO: Yes—better had, son. (ANDREW *goes into the
kitchen on the right.*)

SCOTT (*as he goes out—in a low tone*): There's the boy
that would make a good, strong sea-farin' man—if he'd
a mind to.

MAYO (*sharply*): Don't you put no such fool notions in Andy's head, Dick—or you'n' me's goin' to fall out. (*Then he smiles*) You couldn't tempt him, no ways. Andy's a Mayo bred in the bone, and he's a born farmer, and a damn good one, too. He'll live and die right here on this farm, like I expect to. (*With proud confidence*) And he'll make this one of the slickest, best-payin' farms in the state, too, afore he gits through!

SCOTT: Seems to me it's a pretty slick place right now.

MAYO (*shaking his head*): It's too small. We need more land to make it amount to much, and we ain't got the capital to buy it. (ANDREW *enters from the kitchen. His hat is on, and he carries a lighted lantern in his hand. He goes to the door in the rear leading out.*)

ANDREW (*opens the door and pauses*): Anything else you can think of to be done, Pa?

MAYO: No, nothin' I know of. (ANDREW *goes out, shutting the door.*)

MRS. MAYO (*after a pause*): What's come over Andy tonight, I wonder? He acts so strange.

MAYO: He does seem sort o' glum and out of sorts. It's 'count o' Robert leavin,' I s'pose. (*To* SCOTT) Dick, you wouldn't believe how them boys o' mine sticks together. They ain't like most brothers. They've been thick as thieves all their lives, with nary a quarrel I kin remember.

SCOTT: No need to tell me that. I can see how they take to each other.

MRS. MAYO (*pursuing her train of thought*): Did you notice, James, how queer everyone was at supper? Robert seemed stirred up about something; and Ruth was so flustered and giggly; and Andy sat there dumb, look-

ing as if he'd lost his best friend; and all of them only
nibbled at their food.

MAYO: Guess they was all thinkin' about tomorrow,
same as us.

MRS. MAYO (*shaking her head*): No. I'm afraid somethin's happened—somethin' else.

MAYO: You mean—'bout Ruth?

MRS. MAYO: Yes.

MAYO (*after a pause—frowning*): I hope her and Andy
ain't had a serious fallin'-out. I always sorter hoped
they'd hitch up together sooner or later. What d'you
say, Dick? Don't you think them two'd pair up well?

SCOTT (*nodding his head approvingly*): A sweet, whole-
some couple they'd make.

MAYO: It'd be a good thing for Andy in more ways than
one. I ain't what you'd call calculatin' generally, and I
b'lieve in lettin' young folks run their affairs to suit
themselves; but there's advantages for both o' them in
this match you can't overlook in reason. The Atkins
farm is right next to ourn. Jined together they'd make a
jim-dandy of a place, with plenty o' room to work in.
And bein' a widder with only a daughter, and laid up
all the time to boot, Mrs. Atkins can't do nothin' with
the place as it ought to be done. She needs a man, a
first-class farmer, to take hold o' things; and Andy's
just the one.

MRS. MAYO (*abruptly*): I don't think Ruth loves Andy.

MAYO: You don't? Well, maybe a woman's eyes is sharper
in such things, but—they're always together. And if she
don't love him now, she'll likely come around to it in
time. (*As* MRS. MAYO *shakes her head*) You seem
mighty fixed in your opinion, Katey. How d'you know?

MRS. MAYO: It's just—what I feel.

MAYO (*a light breaking over him*): You don't mean to say— (MRS. MAYO *nods.* MAYO *chuckles scornfully*) Shucks! I'm losin' my respect for your eyesight, Katey. Why, Robert ain't got no time for Ruth, 'cept as a friend!

MRS. MAYO (*warningly*): Sss-h-h! (*The door from the yard opens, and* ROBERT *enters. He is smiling happily, and humming a song to himself, but as he comes into the room an undercurrent of nervous uneasiness manifests itself in his bearing.*)

MAYO: So here you be at last! (ROBERT *comes forward and sits on* ANDY'S *chair.* MAYO *smiles slyly at his wife*) What have you been doin' all this time—countin' the stars to see if they all come out right and proper?

ROBERT: There's only one I'll ever look for any more, Pa.

MAYO (*reproachfully*): You might've even not wasted time lookin' for that one—your last night.

MRS. MAYO (*as if she were speaking to a child*): You ought to have worn your coat a sharp night like this, Robbie.

SCOTT (*disgustedly*): God A'mighty, Kate, you treat Robert as if he was one year old!

MRS. MAYO (*notices* ROBERT'S *nervous uneasiness*): You look all worked up over something, Robbie. What is it?

ROBERT (*swallowing hard, looks quickly from one to the other of them—then begins determinedly*): Yes, there *is* something—something I must tell you—all of you. (*As he begins to talk* ANDREW *enters quietly from the rear, closing the door behind him, and setting the lighted lantern on the floor. He remains standing by the door, his arms folded, listening to* ROBERT *with a repressed expression of pain on his face.* ROBERT *is so much taken up with what he is going to say that he*

does not notice ANDREW's *presence*) Something I discovered only this evening—very beautiful and wonderful—something I did not take into consideration previ-
ously because I hadn't dared to hope that such happiness
could ever come to me. (*Appealingly*) You must all remember that fact, won't you?

MAYO (*frowning*): Let's get to the point, son.

ROBERT (*with a trace of defiance*): Well, the point is this,
Pa: I'm not going—I mean—I can't go tomorrow with
Uncle Dick—or at any future time, either.

MRS. MAYO (*with a sharp sigh of joyful relief*): Oh,
Robbie, I'm so glad!

MAYO (*astounded*): You ain't serious, be you, Robert?
(*Severely*) Seems to me it's a pretty late hour in the day
for you to be upsettin' all your plans so sudden!

ROBERT: I asked you to remember that until this evening
I didn't know myself. I had never dared to dream—

MAYO (*irritably*): What is this foolishness you're talkin'
of?

ROBERT (*flushing*): Ruth told me this evening that—she
loved me. It was after I'd confessed I loved her. I told
her I hadn't been conscious of my love until after the
trip had been arranged, and I realized it would mean—
leaving her. That was the truth. I *didn't* know until
then. (*As if justifying himself to the others*) I hadn't
intended telling her anything but—suddenly—I felt I
must. I didn't think it would matter, because I was going away. And I thought she loved—someone else.
(*Slowly—his eyes shining*) And then she cried and
said it was I she'd loved all the time, but I hadn't seen
it.

MRS. MAYO (*rushes over and throws her arms about
him*): I knew it! I was just telling your father when

you came in—and, oh, Robbie, I'm so happy you're not going!

ROBERT (*kissing her*): I knew you'd be glad, Ma.

MAYO (*bewilderedly*): Well, I'll be damned! You do beat all for gettin' folks' minds all tangled up, Robert. And Ruth too! Whatever got into her of a sudden? Why, I was thinkin'—

MRS. MAYO (*hurriedly—in a tone of warning*): Never mind what you were thinking, James. It wouldn't be any use telling us that now. (*Meaningly*) And what you were hoping for turns out just the same almost, doesn't it?

MAYO (*thoughtfully—beginning to see this side of the argument*): Yes; I suppose you're right, Katey. (*Scratching his head in puzzlement*) But how it ever come about! It do beat anything ever I heard. (*Finally he gets up with a sheepish grin and walks over to* ROBERT) We're glad you ain't goin,' your Ma and I, for we'd have missed you terrible, that's certain and sure; and we're glad you've found happiness. Ruth's a fine girl and'll make a good wife to you.

ROBERT (*much moved*): Thank you, Pa. (*He grips his father's hand in his.*)

ANDREW (*his face tense and drawn comes forward and holds out his hand, forcing a smile*): I guess it's my turn to offer congratulations, isn't it?

ROBERT (*with a startled cry when his brother appears before him so suddenly*): Andy! (*Confused*) Why—I—I didn't see you. Were you here when—

ANDREW: I heard everything you said; and here's wishing you every happiness, you and Ruth. You both deserve the best there is.

ROBERT (*taking his hand*): Thanks, Andy, it's fine of you

to— (*His voice dies away as he sees the pain in* ANDREW'S *eyes.*)

ANDREW (*giving his brother's hand a final grip*): Good luck to you both! (*He turns away and goes back to the rear where he bends over the lantern, fumbling with it to hide his emotion from the others.*)

MRS. MAYO (*to the* CAPTAIN, *who has been too flabbergasted by* ROBERT'S *decision to say a word*): What's the matter, Dick? Aren't you going to congratulate Robbie?

SCOTT (*embarrassed*): Of course I be! (*He gets to his feet and shakes* ROBERT'S *hand, muttering a vague*) Luck to you, boy. (*He stands beside* ROBERT *as if he wanted to say something more but doesn't know how to go about it.*)

ROBERT: Thanks, Uncle Dick.

SCOTT: So you're not acomin' on the "Sunda" with me? (*His voice indicates disbelief.*)

ROBERT: I can't, Uncle—not now. I wouldn't miss it for anything in the world under any other circumstances. (*He sighs unconsciously*) But you see I've found—a bigger dream. (*Then with joyous high spirits*) I want you all to understand one thing—I'm not going to be a loafer on your hands any longer. This means the beginning of a new life for me in every way. I'm going to settle right down and take a real interest in the farm, and do my share. I'll prove to you, Pa, that I'm as good a Mayo as you are—or Andy, when I want to be.

MAYO (*kindly but skeptically*): That's the right spirit, Robert. Ain't none of us doubts your willin'ness, but you ain't never learned—

ROBERT: Then I'm going to start learning right away, and you'll teach me, won't you?

MAYO (*mollifyingly*): Of course I will, boy, and be glad to, only you'd best go easy at first.

SCOTT (*who has listened to this conversation in mingled consternation and amazement*): You don't mean to tell me you're going to let him stay, do you, James?

MAYO: Why, things bein' as they be, Robert's free to do as he's a mind to.

MRS. MAYO: *Let him!* The very idea!

SCOTT (*more and more ruffled*): Then all I got to say is, you're a soft, weak-willed critter to be permittin' a boy—and women, too—to be layin' your course for you wherever they damn pleases.

MAYO (*slyly amused*): It's just the same with me as 'twas with you, Dick. You can't order the tides on the seas to suit you, and I ain't pretendin' I can reg'late love for young folks.

SCOTT (*scornfully*): Love! They ain't old enough to know love when they sight it! Love! I'm ashamed of you, Robert, to go lettin' a little huggin' and kissin' in the dark spile your chances to make a man out o' yourself. It ain't common sense—no siree, it ain't—not by a hell of a sight! (*He pounds the table with his fists in exasperation.*)

MRS. MAYO (*laughing provokingly at her brother*): A fine one you are to be talking about love, Dick—an old cranky bachelor like you. Goodness sakes!

SCOTT (*exasperated by their joking*): I've never been a damn fool like most, if that's what you're steerin' at.

MRS. MAYO (*tauntingly*): Sour grapes, aren't they, Dick? (*She laughs.* ROBERT *and his father chuckle.* SCOTT *sputters with annoyance*) Good gracious, Dick, you do act silly, flying into a temper over nothing.

SCOTT (*indignantly*): Nothin'! You talk as if I wasn't concerned nohow in this here business. Seems to me I've got a right to have my say. Ain't I made all arrangements with the owners and stocked up with some special grub all on Robert's account?

ROBERT: You've been fine, Uncle Dick; and I appreciate it. Truly.

MAYO: 'Course; we all does, Dick.

SCOTT (*unplacated*): I've been countin' sure on havin' Robert for company on this vige—to sorta talk to and show things to, and teach, kinda, and I got my mind so set on havin' him I'm goin' to be double lonesome this vige. (*He pounds on the table, attempting to cover up this confession of weakness*) Darn all this silly lovin' business, anyway. (*Irritably*) But all this talk ain't tellin' me what I'm to do with that sta'b'd cabin I fixed up. It's all painted white, an' a bran new mattress on the bunk, 'n' new sheets 'n' blankets 'n' things. And Chips built in a book-case so's Robert could take his books along—with a slidin' bar fixed across't it, mind, so's they couldn't fall out no matter how she rolled. (*With excited consternation*) What d'you suppose my officers is goin' to think when there's no one comes aboard to occupy that sta'b'd cabin? And the men what did the work on it—what'll *they* think? (*He shakes his finger indignantly*) They're liable as not to suspicion it was a *woman* I'd planned to ship along, and that she gave me the go-by at the last moment! (*He wipes his perspiring brow in anguish at this thought*) Gawd A'mighty! They're only lookin' to have the laugh on me for something like that. They're liable to b'lieve anything, those fellers is!

MAYO (*with a wink*): Then there's nothing to it but for

you to get right out and hunt up a wife somewheres
for that spick 'n' span cabin. She'll have to be a pretty
one, too, to match it. (*He looks at his watch with exaggerated concern*) You ain't got much time to find her,
Dick.

SCOTT (*as the others smile—sulkily*): You kin go to
thunder, Jim Mayo!

ANDREW (*comes forward from where he has been standing by the door, rear, brooding. His face is set in a
look of grim determination*): You needn't worry
about that spare cabin, Uncle Dick, if you've a mind
to take me in Robert's place.

ROBERT (*turning to him quickly*): Andy! (*He sees at
once the fixed resolve in his brother's eyes, and realizes
immediately the reason for it—in consternation*) Andy,
you mustn't!

ANDREW: You've made your decision, Rob, and now I've
made mine. You're out of this, remember.

ROBERT (*hurt by his brother's tone*): But Andy—

ANDREW: Don't interfere, Rob—that's all I ask. (*Turning
to his uncle*) You haven't answered my question,
Uncle Dick.

SCOTT (*clearing his throat, with an uneasy side glance at
JAMES MAYO who is staring at his elder son as if he
thought he had suddenly gone mad*): O' course, I'd
be glad to have you, Andy.

ANDREW: It's settled then. I can pack the little I want to
take in a few minutes.

MRS. MAYO: Don't be a fool, Dick. Andy's only joking
you.

SCOTT (*disgruntedly*): It's hard to tell who's jokin' and
who's not in this house.

ANDREW (*firmly*): I'm not joking, Uncle Dick. (*As* SCOTT

looks at him uncertainly) You needn't be afraid I'll go back on my word.

ROBERT (*hurt by the insinuation he feels in* ANDREW's *tone*): Andy! That isn't fair!

MAYO (*frowning*): Seems to me this ain't no subject to joke over—not for Andy.

ANDREW (*facing his father*): I agree with you, Pa, and I tell you again, once and for all, that I've made up my mind to go.

MAYO (*dumbfounded—unable to doubt the determination in* ANDREW's *voice—helplessly*): But why, son? Why?

ANDREW (*evasively*): I've always wanted to go.

ROBERT: Andy!

ANDREW (*half angrily*): You shut up, Rob! (*Turning to his father again*) I didn't ever mention it because as long as Rob was going I knew it was no use; but now Rob's staying on here, there isn't any reason for me not to go.

MAYO (*breathing hard*): No reason? Can you stand there and say that to me, Andrew?

MRS. MAYO (*hastily—seeing the gathering storm*): He doesn't mean a word of it, James.

MAYO (*making a gesture to her to keep silence*): Let me talk, Katey. (*In a more kindly tone*) What's come over you so sudden, Andy? You know's well as I do that it wouldn't be fair o' you to run off at a moment's notice right now when we're up to our necks in hard work.

ANDREW (*avoiding his eyes*): Rob'll hold his end up as soon as he learns.

MAYO: Robert was never cut out for a farmer, and you was.

ANDREW: You can easily get a man to do my work.

MAYO (*restraining his anger with an effort*): It sounds strange to hear you, Andy, that I always thought had good sense, talkin' crazy like that. (*Scornfully*) Get a man to take your place! You ain't been workin' here for no hire, Andy, that you kin give me your notice to quit like you've done. The farm is your'n as well as mine. You've always worked on it with that understanding; and what you're sayin' you intend doin' is just skulkin' out o' your rightful responsibility.

ANDREW (*looking at the floor—simply*): I'm sorry, Pa. (*After a slight pause*) It's no use talking any more about it.

MRS. MAYO (*in relief*): There! I knew Andy'd come to his senses!

ANDREW: Don't get the wrong idea, Ma. I'm not backing out.

MAYO: You mean you're goin' in spite of—everythin'?

ANDREW: Yes. I'm going. I've got to. (*He looks at his father defiantly*) I feel I oughtn't to miss this chance to go out into the world and see things, and—I want to go.

MAYO (*with bitter scorn*): So—you want to go out into the world and see thin's? (*His voice raised and quivering with anger*) I never thought I'd live to see the day when a son o' mine'd look me in the face and tell a bare-faced lie! (*Bursting out*) You're a liar, Andy Mayo, and a mean one to boot!

MRS. MAYO: James!

ROBERT: Pa!

SCOTT: Steady there, Jim!

MAYO (*waving their protests aside*): He is and he knows it.

ANDREW (*his face flushed*): I won't argue with you, Pa.
    You can think as badly of me as you like.

MAYO (*shaking his finger at* ANDY, *in a colde rage*): You
    know I'm speakin' truth—that's why you're afraid to
    argy! You lie when you say you want to go 'way—and
    see thin's! You ain't got no likin' in the world to go. I've
    watched you grow up, and I know your ways, and
    they're my ways. You're runnin' against your own na-
    ture, and you're goin' to be a'mighty sorry for it if you
    do. 'S if I didn't know your real reason for runnin'
    away! And runnin' away's the only words to fit it.
    You're runnin' away 'cause you're put out and riled
    'cause your own brother's got Ruth 'stead o' you, and—

ANDREW (*his face crimson—tensely*): Stop, Pa! I won't
    stand hearing that—not even from you!

MRS. MAYO (*rushing to* ANDY *and putting her arms about
    him protectingly*): Don't mind him, Andy dear. He
    don't mean a word he's saying! (ROBERT *stands rigidly,
    his hands clenched, his face contracted by pain.* SCOTT
    sits dumbfounded and open-mouthed. ANDREW *soothes
    his mother who is on the verge of tears.*)

MAYO (*in angry triumph*): It's the truth, Andy Mayo!
    And you ought to be bowed in shame to think of it!

ROBERT (*protestingly*): Pa!

MRS. MAYO (*coming from* ANDREW *to his father; puts her
    hands on his shoulders as though to try to push him
    back in the chair from which he has risen*): Won't
    you be still, James? Please won't you?

MAYO (*looking at* ANDREW *over his wife's shoulder—stub-
    bornly*): The truth—God's truth!

MRS. MAYO: Sh-h-h! (*She tries to put a finger across his
    lips, but he twists his head away.*)

ANDREW (*who has regained control over himself*): You're wrong, Pa, it isn't truth. (*With defiant assertiveness*) I don't love Ruth. I never loved her, and the thought of such a thing never entered my head.

MAYO (*with an angry snort of disbelief*): Hump! You're pilin' lie on lie.

ANDREW (*losing his temper—bitterly*): I suppose it'd be hard for you to explain anyone's wanting to leave this blessed farm except for some outside reason like that. But I'm sick and tired of it—whether you want to believe me or not—and that's why I'm glad to get a chance to move on.

ROBERT: Andy! Don't! You're only making it worse.

ANDREW (*sulkily*): I don't care. I've done my share of work here. I've earned my right to quit when I want to. (*Suddenly overcome with anger and grief; with rising intensity*) I'm sick and tired of the whole damn business. I hate the farm and every inch of ground in it. I'm sick of digging in the dirt and sweating in the sun like a slave without getting a word of thanks for it. (*Tears of rage starting to his eyes—hoarsely*) I'm through, through for good and all; and if Uncle Dick won't take me on his ship, I'll find another. I'll get away somewhere, somehow.

MRS. MAYO (*in a frightened voice*): Don't you answer him, James. He doesn't know what he's saying. Don't say a word to him 'til he's in his right senses again. Please James, don't—

MAYO (*pushes her away from him; his face is drawn and pale with the violence of his passion. He glares at ANDREW as if he hated him*): You dare to—you dare to speak like that to me? You talk like that 'bout this farm—the Mayo farm—where you was born—you— you— (*He clenches his fist above his head and advances threateningly on* ANDREW) You damned whelp!

MRS. MAYO (*with a shriek*): James! (*She covers her face with her hands and sinks weakly into* MAYO's *chair.* ANDREW *remains standing motionless, his face pale and set.*)

SCOTT (*starting to his feet and stretching his arms across the table toward* MAYO): Easy there, Jim!

ROBERT (*throwing himself between father and brother*): Stop! Are you mad?

MAYO (*grabs* ROBERT'S *arm and pushes him aside—then stands for a moment gasping for breath before* ANDREW. *He points to the door with a shaking finger*): Yes—go —go!— You're no son o' mine—no son o' mine! You can go to hell if you want to! Don't let me find you here—in the mornin'—or—or—I'll *throw* you out!

ROBERT: Pa! For God's sake! (MRS. MAYO *bursts into noisy sobbing.*)

MAYO (*he gulps convulsively and glares at* ANDREW): You go—tomorrow mornin'—and by God—don't come back —don't dare come back—by God, not while I'm livin' —or I'll—I'll (*He shakes over his muttered threat and strides toward the door rear, right.*)

MRS. MAYO (*rising and throwing her arms around him— hysterically*): James! James! Where are you going?

MAYO (*incoherently*): I'm goin'—to bed, Katey. It's late, Katey—it's late. (*He goes out.*)

MRS. MAYO (*following him, pleading hysterically*): James! Take back what you've said to Andy. James! (*She follows him out.* ROBERT *and the* CAPTAIN *stare after them with horrified eyes.* ANDREW *stands rigidly looking straight in front of him, his fists clenched at his sides.*)

SCOTT (*the first to find his voice—with an explosive sigh*):
Well, if he ain't the devil himself when he's roused!
You oughtn't to have talked to him that way, Andy,
'bout the damn farm, knowin' how touchy he is about
it. (*With another sigh*) Well, you won't mind what he's
said in anger. He'll be sorry for it when he's calmed
down a bit.

ANDREW (*in a dead voice*): You don't know him. (*Defiantly*) What's said is said and can't be unsaid; and
I've chosen.

ROBERT (*with violent protest*): Andy! You can't go! This
is all so stupid—and terrible!

ANDREW (*coldly*): I'll talk to you in a minute, Rob.
(*Crushed by his brother's attitude* ROBERT *sinks down
into a chair, holding his head in his hands.*)

SCOTT (*comes and slaps* ANDREW *on the back*): I'm
damned glad you're shippin' on, Andy. I like your spirit,
and the way you spoke up to him. (*Lowering his
voice to a cautious whisper*) The sea's the place for a
young feller like you that isn't half dead 'n' alive. (*He
gives* ANDY *a final approving slap*) You 'n' me'll get
along like twins, see if we don't. I'm goin' aloft to turn
in. Don't forget to pack your dunnage. And git some
sleep, if you kin. We'll want to sneak out extra early
b'fore they're up. It'll do away with more argyments.
Robert can drive us down to the town, and bring back
the team. (*He goes to the door in the rear, left*) Well,
good night.

ANDREW: Good night. (SCOTT *goes out. The two brothers
remain silent for a moment. Then* ANDREW *comes over
to his brother and puts a hand on his back. He speaks
in a low voice, full of feeling*) Buck up, Rob. It ain't

any use crying over spilt milk; and it'll all turn out for the best—let's hope. It couldn't be helped—what's happened.

ROBERT (*wildly*): But it's a lie, Andy, a lie!

ANDREW: Of course it's a lie. You know it and I know it, —but that's all ought to know it.

ROBERT: Pa'll never forgive you. Oh, the whole affair is so senseless—and tragic. Why did you think you must go away?

ANDREW: You know better than to ask that. You know why. (*Fiercely*) I can wish you and Ruth all the good luck in the world, and I do, and I mean it; but you can't expect me to stay around here and watch you two together, day after day—and me alone. I couldn't stand it—not after all the plans I'd made to happen on this place thinking— (*His voice breaks*) thinking she cared for me.

ROBERT (*putting a hand on his brother's arm*): God! It's horrible! I feel so guilty—to think that I should be the cause of your suffering, after we've been such pals all our lives. If I could have foreseen what'd happen, I swear to you I'd have never said a word to Ruth. I swear I wouldn't have, Andy!

ANDREW: I know you wouldn't; and that would've been worse, for Ruth would've suffered then. (*He pats his brother's shoulder*) It's best as it is. It had to be, and I've got to stand the gaff, that's all. Pa'll see how I felt —after a time. (*As* ROBERT *shakes his head*)—and if he don't—well, it can't be helped.

ROBERT: But think of Ma! God, Andy, you can't go! You can't!

ANDREW (*fiercely*): I've got to go—to get away! I've got to, I tell you. I'd go crazy here, bein' reminded every second of the day what a fool I'd made of myself. I've got to get away and try and forget, if I can. And I'd hate the farm if I stayed, hate it for bringin' things back. I couldn't take interest in the work any more, work with no purpose in sight. Can't you see what a hell it'd be? You love her too, Rob. Put yourself in my place, and remember I haven't stopped loving her, and couldn't if I was to stay. Would that be fair to you or to her? Put yourself in my place. (*He shakes his brother fiercely by the shoulder*) What'd you do then? Tell me the truth! You love her. What'd you do?

ROBERT (*chokingly*): I'd—I'd go, Andy! (*He buries his face in his hands with a shuddering sob*) God!

ANDREW (*seeming to relax suddenly all over his body—in a low, steady voice*): Then you know why I got to go; and there's nothing more to be said.

ROBERT (*in a frenzy of rebellion*): Why did this have to happen to us? It's damnable! (*He looks about him wildly, as if his vengeance were seeking the responsible fate.*)

ANDREW (*soothingly—again putting his hands on his brother's shoulder*): It's no use fussing any more, Rob. It's done. (*Forcing a smile*) I guess Ruth's got a right to have who she likes. She made a good choice— and God bless her for it!

ROBERT: Andy! Oh, I wish I could tell you half I feel of how fine you are!

ANDREW (*interrupting him quickly*): Shut up! Let's go to bed. I've got to be up long before sun-up. You, too, if you're going to drive us down.

ROBERT: Yes. Yes.

ANDREW (*turning down the lamp*): And I've got to pack yet. (*He yawns with utter weariness*) I'm as tired as if I'd been plowing twenty-four hours at a stretch. (*Dully*) I feel—dead. (ROBERT *covers his face again with his hands.* ANDREW *shakes his head as if to get rid of his thoughts, and continues with a poor attempt at cheery briskness*) I'm going to douse the light. Come on. (*He slaps his brother on the back.* ROBERT *does not move.* ANDREW *bends over and blows out the lamp. His voice comes from the darkness*) Don't sit there mourning, Rob. It'll all come out in the wash. Come and get some sleep. Everything'll turn out all right in the end. (ROBERT *can be heard stumbling to his feet, and the dark figures of the two brothers can be seen groping their way toward the doorway in the rear as the curtain falls.*)

ACT TWO
Scene I

SAME *as Act One, Scene 2. Sitting room of the farmhouse about half past twelve in the afternoon of a hot, sun-baked day in mid-summer, three years later. All the windows are open, but no breeze stirs the soiled white curtains. A patched screen door is in the rear. Through it the yard can be seen, its small stretch of lawn divided by the dirt path leading to the door from the gate in the white picket fence which borders the road.*

The room has changed, not so much in its outward appearance as in its general atmosphere. Little significant details give evidence of carelessness, of inefficiency, of an industry gone to seed. The chairs appear shabby from lack of paint; the table cover is spotted and askew; holes show in the curtains; a child's doll, with one arm gone, lies under the table; a hoe stands in a corner; a man's coat is flung on the couch in the rear; the desk is cluttered with odds and ends; a number of books are piled carelessly on the sideboard. The noon enervation of the sultry, scorching day seems to have penetrated indoors, causing even inanimate objects to wear an aspect of despondent exhaustion.

A place is set at the end of the table, left, for someone's dinner. Through the open door to the kitchen comes the clatter of dishes being washed, interrupted at intervals by a woman's irritated voice and the peevish whining of a child.

At the rise of the curtain MRS. MAYO *and* MRS. ATKINS *are discovered sitting facing each other,* MRS. MAYO *to the rear,* MRS. ATKINS *to the right of the table.* MRS. MAYO's *face has lost all character, disintegrated, become a weak mask wearing a helpless, doleful expression of being constantly on the verge of comfortless tears. She speaks in an uncertain voice, without assertiveness, as if all power of willing had deserted her.* MRS. ATKINS *is in her wheel chair. She is a thin, pale-faced, unintelligent-looking woman of about forty-eight, with hard, bright eyes. A victim of partial paralysis for many years, condemned to be pushed from day to day of her life in a wheel chair, she has developed the selfish, irritable nature of the chronic invalid. Both women are dressed in black.* MRS. ATKINS *knits nervously as she talks. A ball of unused yarn, with needles stuck through it, lies on the table before* MRS. MAYO.

MRS. ATKINS (*with a disapproving glance at the place set on the table*): Robert's late for his dinner again, as usual. I don't see why Ruth puts up with it, and I've told her so. Many's the time I've said to her, "It's about time you put a stop to his nonsense. Does he suppose you're runnin' a hotel—with no one to help with things?" But she don't pay no attention. She's as bad as he is, a'most—thinks she knows better than an old, sick body like me.

MRS. MAYO (*dully*): Robbie's always late for things. He can't help it, Sarah.

MRS. ATKINS (*with a snort*): Can't help it! How you do go on, Kate, findin' excuses for him! Anybody can help anything they've a mind to—as long as they've got health, and ain't rendered helpless like me—(*She adds as a pious afterthought*)—through the will of God.

MRS. MAYO: Robbie can't.

mrs. atkins: Can't! It do make me mad, Kate Mayo, to see folks that God gave all the use of their limbs to potterin' round and wastin' time doin' everything the wrong way—and me powerless to help and at their mercy, you might say. And it ain't that I haven't pointed the right way to 'em. I've talked to Robert thousands of times and told him how things ought to be done. You know that, Kate Mayo. But d'you s'pose he takes any notice of what I say? Or Ruth, either—my own daughter? No, they think I'm a crazy, cranky old woman, half dead a'ready, and the sooner I'm in the grave and out o' their way the better it'd suit them.

mrs. mayo: You mustn't talk that way, Sarah. They're not as wicked as that. And you've got years and years before you.

mrs. atkins: You're like the rest, Kate. You don't know how near the end I am. Well, at least I can go to my eternal rest with a clear conscience. I've done all a body could do to avert ruin from this house. On their heads be it!

mrs. mayo (*with hopeless indifference*): Things might be worse. Robert never had any experience in farming. You can't expect him to learn in a day.

mrs. atkins (*snappily*): He's had three years to learn, and he's gettin' worse 'stead of better. Not on'y your place but mine too is driftin' to rack and ruin, and I can't do nothin' to prevent.

mrs. mayo (*with a spark of assertiveness*) You can't say but Robbie works hard, Sarah.

mrs. atkins: What good's workin' hard if it don't accomplish anythin', I'd like to know?

mrs. mayo: Robbie's had bad luck against him.

mrs. atkins: Say what you've a mind to, Kate, the proof

of the puddin's in the eatin'; and you can't deny that things have been goin' from bad to worse ever since your husband died two years back.

MRS. MAYO (*wiping tears from her eyes with her handkerchief*): It was God's will that he should be taken.

MRS. ATKINS (*triumphantly*): It was God's punishment on James Mayo for the blasphemin' and denyin' of God he done all his sinful life! (MRS. MAYO *begins to weep softly*) There, Kate, I shouldn't be remindin' you, I know. He's at peace, poor man, and forgiven, let's pray.

MRS. MAYO (*wiping her eyes—simply*): James was a good man.

MRS. ATKINS (*ignoring this remark*): What I was sayin' was that since Robert's been in charge things've been goin' down hill steady. You don't know *how* bad they are. Robert don't let on to you what's happenin'; and you'd never see it yourself if 'twas under your nose. But, thank the Lord, Ruth still comes to me once in a while for advice when she's worried near out of her senses by his goin's-on. Do you know what she told me last night? But I forgot, she said not to tell you—still I think you've got a right to know, and it's my duty not to let such things go on behind your back.

MRS. MAYO (*wearily*): You can tell me if you want to.

MRS. ATKINS (*bending over toward her—in a low voice*): Ruth was almost crazy about it. Robert told her he'd have to mortgage the farm—said he didn't know how he'd pull through 'til harvest without it, and he can't get money any other way. (*She straightens up—indignantly*) Now what do you think of your Robert?

MRS. MAYO (*resignedly*) If it has to be—

MRS. ATKINS: You don't mean to say you're goin' to sign

away your farm, Kate Mayo—after me warnin' you?

MRS. MAYO: I'll do what Robbie says is needful.

MRS. ATKINS (*holding up her hands*): Well, of all the foolishness!—well, it's your farm, not mine, and I've nothin' more to say.

MRS. MAYO: Maybe Robbie'll manage till Andy gets back and sees to things. It can't be long now.

MRS. ATKINS (*with keen interest*): Ruth says Andy ought to turn up any day. When does Robert figger he'll get here?

MRS. MAYO: He says he can't calculate exactly on account o' the "Sunda" being a sail boat. Last letter he got was from England, the day they were sailing for home. That was over a month ago, and Robbie thinks they're overdue now.

MRS. ATKINS: We can praise to God then that he'll be back in the nick o' time. He ought to be tired of travelin' and anxious to get home and settle down to work again.

MRS. MAYO: Andy *has* been working. He's head officer on Dick's boat, he wrote Robbie. You know that.

MRS. ATKINS: That foolin' on ships is all right for a spell, but he must be right sick of it by this.

MRS. MAYO (*musingly*): I wonder if he's changed much. He used to be so fine-looking and strong. (*With a sigh*) Three years! It seems more like three hundred. (*Her eyes filling—piteously*) Oh, if James could only have lived 'til he came back—and forgiven him!

MRS. ATKINS: He never would have—not James Mayo! Didn't he keep his heart hardened against him till the last in spite of all you and Robert did to soften him?

MRS. MAYO (*with a feeble flash of anger*): Don't you dare say that! (*Brokenly*) Oh, I know deep down in his heart he forgave Andy, though he was too stubborn ever to own up to it. It was that brought on his death—breaking his heart just on account of his stubborn pride. (*She wipes her eyes with her handkerchief and sobs.*)

MRS. ATKINS (*piously*): It was the will of God. (*The whining crying of the child sounds from the kitchen.* MRS. ATKINS *frowns irritably*) Drat that young one! Seems as if she cries all the time on purpose to set a body's nerves on edge.

MRS. MAYO (*wiping her eyes*): It's the heat upsets her. Mary doesn't feel any too well these days, poor little child!

MRS. ATKINS: She gets it right from her Pa—being sickly all the time. You can't deny Robert was always ailin' as a child. (*She sighs heavily*) It was a crazy mistake for them two to get married. I argyed against it at the time, but Ruth was so spelled with Robert's wild poetry notions she wouldn't listen to sense. Andy was the one would have been the match for her.

MRS. MAYO: I've often thought since it might have been better the other way. But Ruth and Robbie seem happy enough together.

MRS. ATKINS: At any rate it was God's work—and His will be done. (*The two women sit in silence for a moment.* RUTH *enters from the kitchen, carrying in her arms her two-year-old daughter,* MARY, *a pretty but sickly and anemic-looking child with a tear-stained face.* RUTH *has aged appreciably. Her face has lost its youth and freshness. There is a trace in her expression of something hard and spiteful. She sits in the rocker in front of the table and sighs wearily. She wears a gingham dress with a soiled apron tied around her waist.*)

RUTH: Land sakes, if this isn't a scorcher! That kitchen's

like a furnace. Phew! (*She pushes the damp hair back from her forehead.*)

MRS. MAYO: Why didn't you call me to help with the dishes?

RUTH (*shortly*): No. The heat in there'd kill you.

MARY (*sees the doll under the table and struggles on her mother's lap*): Dolly, Mama! Dolly!

RUTH (*pulling her back*): It's time for your nap. You can't play with Dolly now.

MARY (*commencing to cry whiningly*): Dolly!

MRS. ATKINS (*irritably*): Can't you keep that child still? Her racket's enough to split a body's ears. Put her down and let her play with the doll if it'll quiet her.

RUTH (*lifting MARY to the floor*): There! I hope you'll be satisfied and keep still. (MARY *sits down on the floor before the table and plays with the doll in silence.* RUTH *glances at the place set on the table*) It's a wonder Rob wouldn't try to get to meals on time once in a while.

MRS. MAYO (*dully*): Something must have gone wrong again.

RUTH (*wearily*): I s'pose so. Something always going wrong these days, it looks like.

MRS. ATKINS (*snappily*): It wouldn't if you possessed a bit of spunk. The idea of you permittin' him to come in to meals at all hours—and you doin' the work! I never heard of such a thin'. You're too easy goin', that's the trouble.

RUTH: Do stop your nagging at me, Ma! I'm sick of hearing you. I'll do as I please about it; and thank you for not interfering. (*She wipes her moist forehead—wearily*) Phew! It's too hot to argue. Let's talk of something pleasant. (*Curiously*) Didn't I hear you speaking about Andy a while ago?

MRS. MAYO: We were wondering when he'd get home.

RUTH (*brightening*): Rob says any day now he's liable to drop in and surprise us—him and the Captain. It'll certainly look natural to see him around the farm again.

MRS. ATKINS: Let's hope the farm'll look more natural, too, when he's had a hand at it. The way thin's are now!

RUTH (*irritably*): Will you stop harping on that, Ma? We all know things aren't as they might be. What's the good of your complaining all the time?

MRS. ATKINS: There, Kate Mayo! Ain't that just what I told you? I can't say a word of advice to my own daughter even, she's that stubborn and self-willed.

RUTH (*putting her hands over her ears—in exasperation*): For goodness sakes, Ma!

MRS. MAYO (*dully*): Never mind. Andy'll fix everything when he comes.

RUTH (*hopefully*): Oh, yes, I know he will. He always did know just the right thing ought to be done. (*With weary vexation*) It's a shame for him to come home and have to start in with things in such a topsy-turvy.

MRS. MAYO: Andy'll manage.

RUTH (*sighing*): I s'pose it isn't Rob's fault things go wrong with him.

MRS. ATKINS (*scornfully*): Hump! (*She fans herself nervously*) Land o' Goshen, but it's bakin' in here! Let's go out in under the trees where there's a breath of fresh air. Come, Kate. (MRS. MAYO *gets up obediently and starts to wheel the invalid's chair toward the screen door*) You better come too, Ruth. It'll do you good. Learn him a lesson and let him get his own dinner. Don't be such a fool.

RUTH (*going and holding the screen door open for them*

—*listlessly*): He wouldn't mind. He doesn't eat much. But I can't go anyway. I've got to put baby to bed.

MRS. ATKINS: Let's go, Kate. I'm boilin' in here. (MRS. MAYO *wheels her out and off left.* RUTH *comes back and sits down in her chair.*)

RUTH (*mechanically*): Come and let me take off your shoes and stockings, Mary, that's a good girl. You've got to take your nap now. (*The child continues to play as if she hadn't heard, absorbed in her doll. An eager expression comes over* RUTH's *tired face. She glances toward the door furtively—then gets up and goes to the desk. Her movements indicate a guilty fear of discovery. She takes a letter from a pigeon-hole and retreats swiftly to her chair with it. She opens the envelope and reads the letter with great interest, a flush of excitement coming to her cheeks.* ROBERT *walks up the path and opens the screen door quietly and comes into the room. He, too, has aged. His shoulders are stooped as if under too great a burden. His eyes are dull and lifeless, his face burned by the sun and unshaven for days. Streaks of sweat have smudged the layer of dust on his cheeks. His lips drawn down at the corners give him a hopeless, resigned expression. The three years have accentuated the weakness of his mouth and chin. He is dressed in overalls, laced boots, and a flannel shirt open at the neck.*)

ROBERT (*throwing his hat over on the sofa—with a great sigh of exhaustion*): Phew! The sun's hot today! (RUTH *is startled. At first she makes an instinctive motion as if to hide the letter in her bosom. She immediately thinks better of this and sits with the letter in her hands looking at him with defiant eyes. He bends down and kisses her.*)

RUTH (*feeling of her cheek—irritably*): Why don't you shave? You look awful.

ROBERT (*indifferently*): I forgot—and it's too much trouble this weather.

MARY (*throwing aside her doll, runs to him with a happy cry*): Dada! Dada!

ROBERT (*swinging her up above his head—lovingly*): And how's this little girl of mine this hot day, eh?

MARY (*screeching happily*): Dada! Dada!

RUTH (*in annoyance*): Don't do that to her! You know it's time for her nap and you'll get her all waked up; then I'll be the one that'll have to sit beside her till she falls asleep.

ROBERT (*sitting down in the chair on the left of table and cuddling* MARY *on his lap*): You needn't bother. I'll put her to bed.

RUTH (*shortly*): You've got to get back to your work, I s'pose.

ROBERT (*with a sigh*): Yes, I was forgetting. (*He glances at the open letter on* RUTH's *lap*) Reading Andy's letter again? I should think you'd know it by heart by this time.

RUTH (*coloring as if she'd been accused of something—defiantly*): I've got a right to read it, haven't I? He says it's meant for all of us.

ROBERT (*with a trace of irritation*): Right? Don't be so silly. There's no question of right. I was only saying that you must know all that's in it after so many readings.

RUTH: Well, I don't (*She puts the letter on the table and gets wearily to her feet*) I s'pose you'll be wanting your dinner now.

ROBERT (*listlessly*): I don't care. I'm not hungry.

RUTH: And here I been keeping it hot for you!

ROBERT (*irritably*): Oh, all right then. Bring it in and I'll try to eat.

RUTH: I've got to get her to bed first. (*She goes to lift* MARY *off his lap*) Come, dear. It's after time and you can hardly keep your eyes open now.

MARY (*crying*): No, no! (*Appealing to her father*) Dada! No!

RUTH (*accusingly to* ROBERT): There! Now see what you've done! I told you not to—

ROBERT (*shortly*): Let her alone, then. She's all right where she is. She'll fall asleep on my lap in a minute if you'll stop bothering her.

RUTH (*hotly*): She'll not do any such thing! She's got to learn to mind me! (*Shaking her finger at* MARY) You naughty child! Will you come with Mama when she tells you for your own good?

MARY (*clinging to her father*): No, Dada!

RUTH (*losing her temper*): A good spanking's what you need, my young lady—and you'll get one from me if you don't mind better, d'you hear? (MARY *starts to whimper frightenedly.*)

ROBERT (*with sudden anger*): Leave her alone! How often have I told you not to threaten her with whipping? I won't have it. (*Soothing the wailing* MARY) There! There, little girl! Baby mustn't cry. Dada won't like you if you do. Dada'll hold you and you must promise to go to sleep like a good little girl. Will you when Dada asks you?

MARY (*cuddling up to him*): Yes, Dada.

RUTH (*looking at them, her pale face set and drawn*): A fine one you are to be telling folks how to do things! (*She bites her lips. Husband and wife look into each other's eyes with something akin to hatred in their expressions; then* RUTH *turns away with a shrug of affected indifference*) All right, take care of her then, if you think it's so easy. (*She walks away into the kitchen.*)

ROBERT (*smoothing* MARY'S *hair—tenderly*): We'll show Mama you're a good little girl, won't we?

MARY (*crooning drowsily*): Dada, Dada.

ROBERT: Let's see: Does your mother take off your shoes and stockings before your nap?

MARY (*nodding with half-shut eyes*): Yes, Dada.

ROBERT (*taking off her shoes and stockings*): We'll show Mama we know how to do those things, won't we? There's one old shoe off—and there's the other old shoe —and here's one old stocking—and there's the other old stocking. There we are, all nice and cool and comfy. (*He bends down and kisses her*) And now will you promise to go right to sleep if Dada takes you to bed? (MARY *nods sleepily*) That's the good little girl. (*He gathers her up in his arms carefully and carries her into the bedroom. His voice can be heard faintly as he lulls the child to sleep.* RUTH *comes out of the kitchen and gets the plate from the table. She hears the voice from the room and tiptoes to the door to look in. Then she starts for the kitchen but stands for a moment thinking, a look of ill-concealed jealousy on her face. At a noise from inside she hurriedly disappears into the kitchen. A moment later* ROBERT *re-enters. He comes forward and picks up the shoes and stockings which he shoves carelessly under the table. Then, seeing no one about, he goes to the sideboard and selects a book. Coming back to his chair, he sits down and immediately becomes absorbed in reading.* RUTH *returns from the kitchen bringing his plate heaped with food, and a cup of tea. She sets those before him and sits down in her former place.* ROBERT *continues to read, oblivious to the food on the table.*)

RUTH (*after watching him irritably for a moment*): For heaven's sakes, put down that old book! Don't you see your dinner's getting cold?

ROBERT (*closing his book*): Excuse me, Ruth. I didn't notice. (*He picks up his knife and fork and begins to eat gingerly, without appetite.*)

RUTH: I should think you might have some feeling for me, Rob, and not always be late for meals. If you think it's fun sweltering in that oven of a kitchen to keep things warm for you, you're mistaken.

ROBERT: I'm sorry, Ruth, really I am. Something crops up every day to delay me. I mean to be here on time.

RUTH (*with a sigh*): Mean-tos don't count.

ROBERT (*with a conciliating smile*): Then punish me, Ruth. Let the food get cold and don't bother about me.

RUTH: I'd have to wait just the same to wash up after you.

ROBERT: But I can wash up.

RUTH: A nice mess there'd be then!

ROBERT (*with an attempt at lightness*): The food is lucky to be able to get cold this weather. (*As* RUTH *doesn't answer or smile he opens his book and resumes his reading, forcing himself to take a mouthful of food every now and then.* RUTH *stares at him in annoyance.*)

RUTH: And besides, you've got your own work that's got to be done.

ROBERT (*absent-mindedly, without taking his eyes from the book*): Yes, of course.

RUTH (*spitefully*): Work you'll never get done by reading books all the time.

ROBERT (*shutting the book with a snap*): Why do you persist in nagging at me for getting pleasure out of reading? Is it because—(*He checks himself abruptly.*)

RUTH (*coloring*): Because I'm too stupid to understand them, I s'pose you were going to say.

ROBERT (*shame-facedly*): No—no. (*In exasperation*) Why do you goad me into saying things I don't mean? Haven't I got my share of troubles trying to work this cursed farm without your adding to them? You know how hard I've tried to keep things going in spite of bad luck—

RUTH (*scornfully*): Bad luck!

ROBERT: And my own very apparent unfitness for the job, I was going to add; but you can't deny there's been bad luck to it, too. Why don't you take things into consideration? Why can't we pull together? We used to. I know it's hard on you also. Then why can't we help each other instead of hindering?

RUTH (*sullenly*): I do the best I know how.

ROBERT (*gets up and puts his hand on her shoulder*): I know you do. But let's both of us try to do better. We can improve. Say a word of encouragement once in a while when things go wrong, even if it is my fault. You know the odds I've been up against since Pa died. I'm not a farmer. I've never claimed to be one. But there's nothing else I can do under the circumstances, and I've got to pull things through somehow. With your help, I can do it. With you against me— (*He shrugs his shoulders. There is a pause. Then he bends down and kisses her hair—with an attempt at cheerfulness*) So you promise that; and I'll promise to be here when the clock strikes—and anytime else you tell me to. Is it a bargain?

RUTH (*dully*): I s'pose so. (*They are interrupted by the sound of a loud knock at the kitchen door*) There's someone at the kitchen door. (*She hurries out. A moment later she reappears*) It's Ben.

ROBERT (*frowning*): What's the trouble now, I wonder?
(*In a loud voice*) Come on in here, Ben. (BEN *slouches
in from the kitchen. He is a hulking, awkward young
fellow with a heavy, stupid face and shifty, cunning eyes.
He is dressed in overalls, boots, etc., and wears a broad-
brimmed hat of coarse straw pushed back on his head*)
Well, Ben, what's the matter?

BEN (*drawlingly*): The mowin' machine's bust.

ROBERT: Why, that can't be. The man fixed it only last
week.

BEN: It's bust just the same.

ROBERT: And can't you fix it?

BEN: No. Don't know what's the matter with the goll-
darned thing. 'Twon't work, anyhow.

ROBERT (*getting up and going for his hat*): Wait a minute
and I'll go look it over. There can't be much the matter
with it.

BEN (*impudently*): Don't make no diff'rence t' me
whether there be or not. I'm quittin'.

ROBERT (*anxiously*): You don't mean you're throwing up
your job here?

BEN: That's what! My month's up today and I want
what's owin' t' me.

ROBERT: But why are you quitting now, Ben, when you
know I've so much work on hand? I'll have a hard time
getting another man at such short notice.

BEN: That's for you to figger. I'm quittin'.

ROBERT: But what's your reason? You haven't any com-
plaint to make about the way you've been treated, have
you?

BEN: No. 'Tain't that. (*Shaking his finger*) Look-a-here.
I'm sick o' being made fun at, that's what; an' I got
a job up to Timms' place; an' I'm quittin' here.

ROBERT: Being made fun of? I don't understand you. Who's making fun of you?

BEN: They all do. When I drive down with the milk in the mornin' they all laughs and jokes at me—that boy up to Harris' and the new feller up to Slocum's, and Bill Evans down to Meade's, and all the rest on 'em.

ROBERT: That's a queer reason for leaving me flat. Won't they laugh at you just the same when you're working for Timms?

BEN: They wouldn't dare to. Timms is the best farm hereabouts. They was laughin' at me for workin' for *you,* that's what! "How're things up to the Mayo place?" they hollers every mornin'. "What's Robert doin' now —pasturin' the cattle in the cornlot? Is he seasonin' his hay with rain this year, same as last?" they shouts. "Or is he inventin' some 'lectrical milkin' engine to fool them dry cows o' his into givin' hard cider?" (*Very much ruffled*) That's like they talks; and I ain't goin' to put up with it no longer. Everyone's always knowed me as a first-class hand hereabouts, and I ain't wantin' 'em to get no different notion. So I'm quittin' you. And I wants what's comin' to me.

ROBERT (*coldly*): Oh, if that's the case, you can go to the devil. You'll get your money tomorrow when I get back from town—not before!

BEN (*turning to doorway to kitchen*): That suits me. (*As he goes out he speaks back over his shoulder*) And see that I do get it, or there'll be trouble. (*He disappears and the slamming of the kitchen door is heard.*)

ROBERT (*as* RUTH *comes from where she has been standing by the doorway and sits down dejectedly in her old place*): The stupid damn fool! And now what about the haying? That's an example of what I'm up against. No one can say I'm responsible for that.

RUTH: He wouldn't dare act that way with anyone else! (*Spitefully, with a glance at* ANDREW's *letter on the table*) It's lucky Andy's coming back.

ROBERT (*without resentment*): Yes, Andy'll see the right thing to do in a jiffy. (*With an affectionate smile*) I wonder if the old chump's changed much? He doesn't seem to from his letters, does he? (*Shaking his head*) But just the same I doubt if he'll want to settle down to a humdrum farm life, after all he's been through.

RUTH (*resentfully*): Andy's not like you. He likes the farm.

ROBERT (*immersed in his own thoughts—enthusiastically*): Gad, the things he's seen and experienced! Think of the places he's been! All the wonderful far places I used to dream about! God, how I envy him! What a trip! (*He springs to his feet and instinctively goes to the window and stares out at the horizon.*)

RUTH (*bitterly*): I s'pose you're sorry now you didn't go?

ROBERT (*too occupied with his own thoughts to hear her —vindictively*): Oh, those cursed hills out there that I used to think promised me so much! How I've grown to hate the sight of them! They're like the walls of a narrow prison yard shutting me in from all the freedom and wonder of life! (*He turns back to the room with a gesture of loathing*) Sometimes I think if it wasn't for you, Ruth, and— (*His voice softening*)—little Mary, I'd chuck everything up and walk down the road with just one desire in my heart—to put the whole rim of the world between me and those hills, and be able to breathe freely once more! (*He sinks down into his chair and*

smiles with bitter self-scorn) There I go dreaming again
—my old fool dreams.

RUTH (*in a low, repressed voice—her eyes smoldering*):
You're not the only one!

ROBERT (*buried in his own thoughts—bitterly*): And
Andy, who's had the chance—what has he got out of it?
His letters read like the diary of a—of a farmer! "We're
in Singapore now. It's a dirty hole of a place and hotter
than hell. Two of the crew are down with fever and
we're short-handed on the work. I'll be damn glad when
we sail again, although tacking back and forth in these
blistering seas is a rotten job too!" (*Scornfully*) That's
about the way he summed up his impressions of the
East.

RUTH (*her repressed voice trembling*): You needn't make
fun of Andy.

ROBERT: When I think—but what's the use? You know
I wasn't making fun of Andy personally, but his attitude
toward things is—

RUTH (*her eyes flashing—bursting into uncontrollable
rage*): You was too making fun of him! And I ain't
going to stand for it! You ought to be ashamed of yourself! (ROBERT *stares at her in amazement. She continues
furiously*) A fine one to talk about anyone else—after
the way you've ruined everything with your lazy loafing!—and the stupid way you do things!

ROBERT (*angrily*): Stop that kind of talk, do you hear?

RUTH: You findin' fault—with your own brother who's
ten times the man you ever was or ever will be! You're
jealous, that's what! Jealous because he's made a man
of himself, while you're nothing but a—but a— (*She
stutters incoherently, overcome by rage.*)

ROBERT: Ruth! Ruth! You'll be sorry for talking like that.

RUTH: I won't! I won't never be sorry! I'm only saying what I've been thinking for years.

ROBERT (*aghast*): Ruth! You can't mean that!

RUTH: What do you think—living with a man like you —having to suffer all the time because you've never been man enough to work and do things like other people. But no! You never own up to that. You think you're so much better than other folks, with your college education, where you never learned a thing, and always reading your stupid books instead of working. I s'pose you think I ought to be *proud* to be your wife—a poor, ignorant thing like me! (*Fiercely*) But I'm not. I hate it! I hate the sight of you. Oh, if I'd only known! If I hadn't been such a fool to listen to your cheap, silly, poetry talk that you learned out of books! If I could have seen how you were in your true self—like you are now—I'd have killed myself before I'd have married you! I was sorry for it before we'd been together a month. I knew what you were really like—when it was too late.

ROBERT (*his voice raised loudly*): And now—I'm finding out what you're really like—what a—a creature I've been living with. (*With a harsh laugh*) God! It wasn't that I haven't guessed how mean and small you are—but I've kept on telling myself that I must be wrong—like a fool!—like a damned fool!

RUTH: You were saying you'd go out on the road if it wasn't for me. Well, you can go, and the sooner the better! I don't care! I'll be glad to get rid of you! The farm'll be better off too. There's been a curse on it ever since you took hold. So go! Go and be a tramp like you've always wanted. It's all you're good for. I can get along without you, don't you worry. (*Exulting fiercely*) Andy's coming back, don't forget that! He'll attend to things like they should be. He'll show what a man can do! I don't need you. Andy's coming!

ROBERT (*they are both standing.* ROBERT *grabs her by the shoulders and glares into her eyes*): What do you mean? (*He shakes her violently*) What are you thinking of? What's in your evil mind, you—you— (*His voice is a harsh shout.*)

RUTH (*in a defiant scream*): Yes, I do mean it! I'd say it if you was to kill me! I do love Andy. I do! I do! I always loved him. (*Exultantly*) And he loves me! He loves me! I know he does. He always did! And you know he did, too! So go! Go if you want to!

ROBERT (*throwing her away from him. She staggers back against the table—thickly*): You—you slut! (*He stands glaring at her as she leans back, supporting herself by the table, gasping for breath. A loud frightened whimper sounds from the awakened child in the bedroom. It continues. The man and woman stand looking at one another in horror, the extent of their terrible quarrel suddenly brought home to them. A pause. The noise of a horse and carriage comes from the road before the house. The two, suddenly struck by the same premonition, listen to it breathlessly, as to a sound heard in a dream. It stops. They hear* ANDY's *voice from the road shouting a long hail—"Ahoy there!"*)

RUTH (*with a strangled cry of joy*): Andy! Andy! (*She rushes and grabs the knob of the screen door, about to fling it open.*)

ROBERT (*in a voice of command that forces obedience*): Stop! (*He goes to the door and gently pushes the trembling* RUTH *away from it. The child's crying rises to a louder pitch*) I'll meet Andy. You better go in to Mary,

Ruth. (*She looks at him defiantly for a moment, but there is something in his eyes that makes her turn and walk slowly into the bedroom.*)

ANDY'S VOICE (*in a louder shout*): Ahoy there, Rob!

ROBERT (*in an answering shout of forced cheeriness*): Hello, Andy! (*He opens the door and walks out as the curtain falls.*)

ACT TWO
Scene II

THE *top of a hill on the farm. It is about eleven o'clock the next morning. The day is hot and cloudless. In the distance the sea can be seen.*

The top of the hill slopes downward slightly toward the left. A big boulder stands in the center toward the rear. Further right, a large oak tree. The faint trace of a path leading upward to it from the left foreground can be detected through the bleached, sun-scorched grass.

ROBERT *is discovered sitting on the boulder, his chin resting on his hands, staring out toward the horizon seaward. His face is pale and haggard, his expression one of utter despondency.* MARY *is sitting on the grass near him in the shade, playing with her doll, singing happily to herself. Presently she casts a curious glance at her father, and, propping her doll up against the tree, comes over and clambers to his side.*

MARY (*pulling at his hand—solicitously*): Dada sick?

ROBERT (*looking at her with a forced smile*): No, dear. Why?

MARY: Play wif Mary.

ROBERT (*gently*): No, dear, not today. Dada doesn't feel like playing today.

MARY (*protestingly*): Yes, Dada!

ROBERT: No, dear. Dada does feel sick—a little. He's got a bad headache.

MARY: Mary see. (*He bends his head. She pats his hair*) Bad head.

ROBERT (*kissing her—with a smile*): There! It's better now, dear, thank you. (*She cuddles up close against him. There is a pause during which each of them looks out seaward. Finally* ROBERT *turns to her tenderly*) Would you like Dada to go away?—far, far away?

MARY (*tearfully*): No! No! No, Dada, no!

ROBERT: Don't you like Uncle Andy—the man that came yesterday—not the old man with the white mustache— the other?

MARY: Mary loves Dada.

ROBERT (*with fierce determination*): He won't go away, baby. He was only joking. He couldn't leave his little Mary. (*He presses the child in his arms.*)

MARY (*with an exclamation of pain*): Oh! Hurt!

ROBERT: I'm sorry, little girl. (*He lifts her down to the grass*) Go play with Dolly, that's a good girl; and be careful to keep in the shade. (*She reluctantly leaves him and takes up her doll again. A moment later she points down the hill to the left.*)

MARY: Mans, Dada.

ROBERT (*looking that way*): It's your Uncle Andy. (*A moment later* ANDREW *comes up from the left, whistling cheerfully. He has changed but little in appearance, except for the fact that his face has been deeply bronzed by his years in the tropics; but there is a decided change*

in his manner. The old easy-going good nature seems
to have been partly lost in a breezy, business-like brisk-
ness of voice and gesture. There is an authoritative note
in his speech as though he were accustomed to give
orders and have them obeyed as a matter of course. He
is dressed in the simple blue uniform and cap of a
merchant ship's officer.)

ANDREW: Here you are, eh?

ROBERT: Hello, Andy.

ANDREW (*going over to* MARY): And who's this young
lady I find you all alone with, eh? Who's this pretty
young lady? (*He tickles the laughing, squirming* MARY,
then lifts her up arm's length over his head) Upsy—
daisy! (*He sets her down on the ground again*) And
there you are! (*He walks over and sits down on the*
boulder beside ROBERT *who moves to one side to make*
room for him) Ruth told me I'd probably find you up
top-side here; but I'd have guessed it, anyway. (*He*
digs his brother in the ribs affectionately) Still up to
your old tricks, you old beggar! I can remember how
you used to come up here to mope and dream in the old
days.

ROBERT (*with a smile*): I come up here now because it's
the coolest place on the farm. I've given up dreaming.

ANDREW (*grinning*): I don't believe it. You can't have
changed that much. (*After a pause—with boyish en-*
thusiasm) Say, it sure brings back old times to be up
here with you having a chin all by our lonesomes again.
I feel great being back home.

ROBERT: It's great for us to have you back.

ANDREW (*after a pause—meaningly*): I've been looking
over the old place with Ruth. Things don't seem to
be—

ROBERT (*his face flushing—interrupts his brother shortly*): Never mind the damn farm! Let's talk about something interesting. This is the first chance I've had to have a word with you alone. Tell me about your trip.

ANDREW: Why, I thought I told you everything in my letters.

ROBERT (*smiling*): Your letters were—sketchy, to say the least.

ANDREW: Oh, I know I'm no author. You needn't be afraid of hurting my feelings. I'd rather go through a typhoon again than write a letter.

ROBERT (*with eager interest*): Then you were through a typhoon?

ANDREW: Yes—in the China sea. Had to run before it under bare poles for two days. I thought we were bound down for Davy Jones, sure. Never dreamed waves could get so big or the wind blow so hard. If it hadn't been for Uncle Dick being such a good skipper we'd have gone to the sharks, all of us. As it was we came out minus a main topmast and had to beat back to Hong-Kong for repairs. But I must have written you all this.

ROBERT: You never mentioned it.

ANDREW: Well, there was so much dirty work getting things ship-shape again I must have forgotten about it.

ROBERT (*looking at* ANDREW—*marveling*): Forget a typhoon? (*With a trace of scorn*) You're a strange combination, Andy. And is what you've told me all you remember about it?

ANDREW: Oh, I could give you your bellyful of details if I wanted to turn loose on you. It was all-wool-and-a-yard-wide-Hell, I'll tell you. You ought to have been there. I remember thinking about you at the worst of it, and saying to myself: "This'd cure Rob of them ideas of his about the beautiful sea, if he could see it." And it would have too, you bet! (*He nods emphatically.*)

ROBERT (*dryly*): The sea doesn't seem to have impressed you very favorably.

ANDREW: I should say it didn't! I'll never set foot on a ship again if I can help it—except to carry me some place I can't get to by train.

ROBERT: But you studied to become an officer!

ANDREW: Had to do something or I'd gone mad. The days were like years. (*He laughs*) And as for the East you used to rave about—well, you ought to see it, and *smell* it! One walk down one of their filthy narrow streets with the tropic sun beating on it would sicken you for life with the "wonder and mystery" you used to dream of.

ROBERT (*shrinking from his brother with a glance of aversion*): So all you found in the East was a stench?

ANDREW: *A* stench! Ten thousand of them!

ROBERT: But you did like some of the places, judging from your letters—Sydney, Buenos Aires—

ANDREW: Yes, Sydney's a good town. (*Enthusiastically*) But Buenos Aires—there's the place for you. Argentine's a country where a fellow has a chance to make good. You're right I like it. And I'll tell you, Rob, that's right where I'm going just as soon as I've seen you folks a while and can get a ship. I can get a berth as second officer, and I'll jump the ship when I get there. I'll need every cent of the wages Uncle's paid me to get a start at something in B.A.

ROBERT (*staring at his brother—slowly*): So you're not going to stay on the farm?

ANDREW: Why sure not! Did you think I was? There wouldn't be any sense. One of us is enough to run this little place.

ROBERT: I suppose it does seem small to you now.

ANDREW (*not noticing the sarcasm in* ROBERT's *tone*): You've no idea, Rob, what a splendid place Argentine is. I had a letter from a marine insurance chap that I'd made friends with in Hong-Kong to his brother, who's in the grain business in Buenos Aires. He took quite a fancy to me, and what's more important, he offered me a job if I'd come back there. I'd have taken it on the spot, only I couldn't leave Uncle Dick in the lurch, and I'd promised you folks to come home. But I'm going back there, you bet, and then you watch me get on! (*He slaps* ROBERT *on the back*) But don't you think it's a big chance, Rob?

ROBERT: It's fine—for you, Andy.

ANDREW: We call this a farm—but you ought to hear about the farms down there—ten square miles where we've got an acre. It's a new country where big things are opening up—and I want to get in on something big before I die. I'm no fool when it comes to farming, and I know something about grain. I've been reading up a lot on it, too, lately. (*He notices* ROBERT's *absent-minded expression and laughs*) Wake up, you old poetry bookworm, you! I know my talking about business makes you want to choke me, doesn't it?

ROBERT (*with an embarrassed smile*): No, Andy, I—I just happened to think of something else. (*Frowning*) There've been lots of times lately that I wished I had some of your faculty for business.

ANDREW (*soberly*): There's something I want to talk about, Rob—the farm. You don't mind, do you?

ROBERT: No.

ANDREW: I walked over it this morning with Ruth—and she told me about things— (*Evasively*) I could see the place had run down; but you mustn't blame yourself. When luck's against anyone—

ROBERT: Don't, Andy! It *is* my fault. You know it as well as I do. The best I've ever done was to make ends meet.

ANDREW (*after a pause*): I've got over a thousand saved, and you can have that.

ROBERT (*firmly*): No. You need that for your start in Buenos Aires.

ANDREW: I don't. I can—

ROBERT (*determinedly*): No, Andy! Once and for all, no! I won't hear of it!

ANDREW (*protestingly*): You obstinate old son of a gun!

ROBERT: Oh, everything'll be on a sound footing after harvest. Don't worry about it.

ANDREW (*doubtfully*): Maybe. (*After a pause*) It's too bad Pa couldn't have lived to see things through. (*With feeling*) It cut me up a lot—hearing he was dead. He never—softened up, did he—about me, I mean?

ROBERT: He never understood, that's a kinder way of putting it. He does now.

ANDREW (*after a pause*): You've forgotten all about what —caused me to go, haven't you, Rob? (ROBERT *nods but keeps his face averted*) I was a slushier damn fool in those days than you were. But it was an act of Providence I did go. It opened my eyes to how I'd been fooling myself. Why, I'd forgotten all about—that—before I'd been at sea six months.

ROBERT (*turns and looks into* ANDREW's *eyes searchingly*): You're speaking of—Ruth?

ANDREW (*confused*): Yes. I didn't want you to get false notions in your head, or I wouldn't say anything. (*Looking* ROBERT *squarely in the eyes*) I'm telling you the truth when I say I'd forgotten long ago. It don't sound well for me, getting over things so easy, but I guess it never really amounted to more than a kid idea I was letting rule me. I'm certain now I never was in love—I was getting fun out of thinking I was—and being a hero to myself. (*He heaves a great sigh of relief*) There! Gosh, I'm glad that's off my chest. I've been feeling sort of awkward ever since I've been home, thinking of what you two might think. (*A trace of appeal in his voice*) You've got it all straight now, haven't you, Rob?

ROBERT (*in a low voice*): Yes, Andy.

ANDREW: And I'll tell Ruth, too, if I can get up the nerve. She must feel kind of funny having me round—after what used to be—and not knowing how I feel about it.

ROBERT (*slowly*): Perhaps—for her sake—you'd better not tell her.

ANDREW: For her sake? Oh, you mean she wouldn't want to be reminded of my foolishness? Still, I think it'd be worse if—

ROBERT (*breaking out—in an agonized voice*): Do as you please, Andy; but for God's sake, let's not talk about it! (*There is a pause.* ANDREW *stares at* ROBERT *in hurt stupefaction.* ROBERT *continues after a moment in a voice which he vainly attempts to keep calm*) Excuse me, Andy. This rotten headache has my nerves shot to pieces.

ANDREW (*mumbling*): It's all right, Rob—long as you're not sore at me.

ROBERT: Where did Uncle Dick disappear to this morning?

ANDREW: He went down to the port to see to things on the "Sunda." He said he didn't know exactly when he'd be back. I'll have to go down and tend to the ship when he comes. That's why I dressed up in these togs.

MARY (*pointing down to the hill to the left*): See! Mama! Mama! (*She struggles to her feet.* RUTH *appears at left. She is dressed in white, shows she has been fixing up. She looks pretty, flushed and full of life.*)

MARY (*running to her mother*): Mama!

RUTH (*kissing her*): Hello, dear! (*She walks toward the rock and addresses* ROBERT *coldly*) Jake wants to see you about something. He finished working where he was. He's waiting for you at the road.

ROBERT (*getting up—wearily*): I'll go down right away. (*As he looks at* RUTH, *noting her changed appearance, his face darkens with pain.*)

RUTH: And take Mary with you, please. (*To* MARY) Go with Dada, that's a good girl. Grandma has your dinner 'most ready for you.

ROBERT (*shortly*): Come, Mary!

MARY (*taking his hand and dancing happily beside him*): Dada! Dada! (*They go down the hill to the left.* RUTH *looks after them for a moment, frowning—then turns to* ANDY *with a smile*) I'm going to sit down. Come on, Andy. It'll be like old times. (*She jumps lightly to the top of the rock and sits down*) It's so fine and cool up here after the house.

ANDREW (*half-sitting on the side of the boulder*): Yes. It's great.

RUTH: I've taken a holiday in honor of your arrival.

(*Laughing excitedly*) I feel so free I'd like to have wings and fly over the sea. You're a man. You can't know how awful and stupid it is—cooking and washing dishes all the time.

ANDREW (*making a wry face*): I can guess.

RUTH: Besides, your mother just insisted on getting your first dinner to home, she's that happy at having you back. You'd think I was planning to poison you the flurried way she shooed me out of the kitchen.

ANDREW: That's just like Ma, bless her!

RUTH: She's missed you terrible. We all have. And you can't deny the farm has, after what I showed you and told you when we was looking over the place this morning.

ANDREW (*with a frown*): Things are run down, that's a fact! It's too darn hard on poor old Rob.

RUTH (*scornfully*): It's his own fault. He never takes any interest in things.

ANDREW (*reprovingly*): You can't blame him. He wasn't born for it; but I know he's done his best for your sake and the old folks and the little girl.

RUTH (*indifferently*): Yes, I suppose he has. (*Gaily*) But thank the Lord, all those days are over now. The "hard luck" Rob's always blaming won't last long when you take hold, Andy. All the farm's ever needed was someone with the knack of looking ahead and preparing for what's going to happen.

ANDREW: Yes, Rob hasn't got that. He's frank to own up to that himself. I'm going to try and hire a good man for him—an experienced farmer—to work the place on a salary and percentage. That'll take it off of Rob's hands, and he needn't be worrying himself to death any more. He looks all worn out, Ruth. He ought to be careful.

RUTH (*absent-mindedly*): Yes, I s'pose. (*Her mind is filled with premonitions by the first part of his statement*) Why do you want to hire a man to oversee things? Seems as if now that you're back it wouldn't be needful.

ANDREW: Oh, of course I'll attend to everything while I'm here. I mean after I'm gone.

RUTH (*as if she couldn't believe her ears*): Gone!

ANDREW: Yes. When I leave for the Argentine again.

RUTH (*aghast*): You're going away to sea!

ANDREW: Not to sea, no; I'm through with the sea for good as a job. I'm going down to Buenos Aires to get in the grain business.

RUTH: But—that's far off—isn't it?

ANDREW (*easily*): Six thousand miles more or less. It's quite a trip. (*With enthusiasm*) I've got a peach of a chance down there, Ruth. Ask Rob if I haven't. I've just been telling him all about it.

RUTH (*a flush of anger coming over her face*): And didn't he try to stop you from going?

ANDREW (*in surprise*): No, of course not. Why?

RUTH (*slowly and vindictively*): That's just like him—not to.

ANDREW (*resentfully*): Rob's too good a chum to try and stop me when he knows I'm set on a thing. And he could see just as soon's I told him what a good chance it was.

RUTH (*dazedly*): And you're bound on going?

ANDREW: Sure thing. Oh, I don't mean right off. I'll have to wait for a ship sailing there for quite a while, likely.

Anyway, I want to stay to home and visit with you folks a spell before I go.

RUTH (*dumbly*): I s'pose. (*With sudden anguish*) Oh, Andy, you can't go! You can't. Why we've all thought —we've all been hoping and praying you was coming home to stay, to settle down on the farm and see to things. You mustn't go! Think of how your Ma'll take on if you go—and how the farm'll be ruined if you leave it to Rob to look after. You can see that.

ANDREW (*frowning*): Rob hasn't done so bad. When I get a man to direct things the farm'll be safe enough.

RUTH (*insistently*): But your Ma—think of her.

ANDREW: She's used to me being away. She won't object when she knows it's best for her and all of us for me to go. You ask Rob. In a couple of years down there, I'll make my pile, see if I don't; and then I'll come back and settle down and turn this farm into the crackiest place in the whole state. In the meantime, I can help you both from down there. (*Earnestly*) I tell you, Ruth, I'm going to make good right from the minute I land, if working hard and a determination to get on can do it; and I *know* they can! (*Excitedly—in a rather boastful tone*) I tell you, I feel ripe for bigger things than settling down here. The trip did that for me, anyway. It showed me the world is a larger proposition than ever I thought it was in the old days. I couldn't be content any more stuck here like a fly in molasses. It all seems trifling, somehow. You ought to be able to understand what I feel.

RUTH (*dully*): Yes—I s'pose I ought. (*After a pause—a sudden suspicion forming in her mind*) What did Rob tell you—about me?

ANDREW: Tell? About you? Why, nothing.

RUTH (*staring at him intensely*): Are you telling me the truth, Andy Mayo? Didn't he say—I— (*She stops confusedly.*)

ANDREW (*surprised*): No, he didn't mention you, I can remember. Why? What made you think he did?

RUTH (*wringing her hands*): Oh, I wish I could tell if you're lying or not!

ANDREW (*indignantly*): What're you talking about? I didn't used to lie to you, did I? And what in the name of God is there to lie for?

RUTH (*still unconvinced*): Are you sure—will you swear —it isn't the reason— (*She lowers her eyes and half turns away from him*) The same reason that made you go last time that's driving you away again? 'Cause if it is—I was going to say—you mustn't go—on that account. (*Her voice sinks to a tremulous, tender whisper as she finishes.*)

ANDREW (*confused—forces a laugh*): Oh, is *that* what you're driving at? Well, you needn't worry about that no more— (*Soberly*) I don't blame you, Ruth, feeling embarrassed having me round again, after the way I played the dumb fool about going away last time.

RUTH (*her hope crushed—with a gasp of pain*): Oh, Andy!

ANDREW (*misunderstanding*): I know I oughtn't to talk about such foolishness to you. Still I figure it's better to get it out of my system so's we three can be together same's years ago, and not be worried thinking one of us might have the wrong notion.

RUTH: Andy! Please! Don't!

ANDREW: Let me finish now that I've started. It'll help clear things up. I don't want you to think once a fool always a fool, and be upset all the time I'm here on my fool account. I want you to believe I put all that silly nonsense back of me a long time ago—and now—it seems—well—as if you'd always been my sister, that's what, Ruth.

RUTH (*at the end of her endurance—laughing hysterically*): For God's sake, Andy—won't you please stop talking! (*She again hides her face in her hands, her bowed shoulders trembling.*)

ANDREW (*ruefully*): Seems if I put my foot in it whenever I open my mouth today. Rob shut me up with almost the same words when I tried speaking to him about it.

RUTH (*fiercely*): You told him—what you've told me?

ANDREW (*astounded*): Why sure! Why not?

RUTH (*shuddering*): Oh, my God!

ANDREW (*alarmed*): Why? Shouldn't I have?

RUTH (*hysterically*): Oh, I don't care what you do! I don't care! Leave me alone! (ANDREW *gets up and walks down the hill to the left, embarrassed, hurt, and greatly puzzled by her behavior.*)

ANDREW (*after a pause—pointing down the hill*): Hello! Here they come back—and the Captain's with them. How'd he come to get back so soon, I wonder? That means I've got to hustle down to the port and get on board. Rob's got the baby with him. (*He comes back to the boulder.* RUTH *keeps her face averted from him*) Gosh, I never saw a father so tied up in a kid as Rob is! He just watches every move she makes. And I don't blame him. You both got a right to feel proud of her. She's surely a little winner. (*He glances at* RUTH *to see if this very obvious attempt to get back in her good graces is having any effect*) I can see the likeness to Rob standing out all over her, can't you? But there's no denying she's your young one, either. There's something about her eyes—

RUTH (*piteously*): Oh, Andy, I've a headache! I don't want to talk! Leave me alone, won't you please?

ANDREW (*stands staring at her for a moment—then walks away saying in a hurt tone*): Everybody hereabouts seems to be on edge today. I begin to feel as if I'm not wanted around. (*He stands near the path, left, kicking at the grass with the toe of his shoe. A moment later* CAPTAIN DICK SCOTT *enters, followed by* ROBERT *carrying* MARY. *The* CAPTAIN *seems scarcely to have changed at all from the jovial, booming person he was three years before. He wears a uniform similar to* ANDREW'S. *He is puffing and breathless from his climb and mops wildly at his perspiring countenance.* ROBERT *casts a quick glance at* ANDREW, *noticing the latter's discomfited look, and then turns his eyes on* RUTH *who, at their approach, has moved so her back is toward them, her chin resting on her hands as she stares out seaward.*)

MARY: Mama! Mama! (ROBERT *puts her down and she runs to her mother.* RUTH *turns and grabs her up in her arms with a sudden fierce tenderness, quickly turning away again from the others. During the following scene she keeps* MARY *in her arms.*)

SCOTT (*wheezily*): Phew! I got great news for you, Andy. Let me get my wind first. Phew! God A'mighty, mountin' this damned hill is worser'n goin' aloft to the skys'l yard in a blow. I got to lay to a while. (*He sits down on the grass, mopping his face.*)

ANDREW: I didn't look for you this soon, Uncle.

SCOTT: I didn't figger it, neither; but I run across a bit o' news down to the Seamen's Home made me 'bout ship and set all sail back here to find you.

ANDREW (*eagerly*): What is it, Uncle?

SCOTT: Passin' by the Home I thought I'd drop in an' let 'em know I'd be lackin' a mate next trip count o' your leavin'. Their man in charge o' the shippin' asked after you 'special curious. "Do you think he'd consider a berth as Second on a steamer, Captain?" he asks. I was going to say no when I thinks o' you wantin' to get back down south to the Plate agen; so I asks him: "What is she and where's she bound?" "She's the 'El Paso,' a brand new tramp," he says, "and she's bound for Buenos Aires."

ANDREW (*his eyes lighting up—excitedly*): Gosh, that is luck! When does she sail?

SCOTT: Tomorrow mornin'. I didn't know if you'd want to ship away agen so quick an' I told him so. "Tell him I'll hold the berth open for him until late this afternoon," he says. So there you be, an' you can make your own choice.

ANDREW: I'd like to take it. There may not be another ship for Buenos Aires with a vacancy in months. (*His eyes roving from* ROBERT *to* RUTH *and back again—uncertainly*) Still—damn it all—tomorrow morning *is* soon. I wish she wasn't leaving for a week or so. That'd give me a chance—it seems hard to go right away again when I've just got home. And yet it's a chance in a thousand— (*Appealing to* ROBERT) What do you think, Rob? What would you do?

ROBERT (*forcing a smile*): He who hesitates, you know. (*Frowning*) It's a piece of good luck thrown in your way—and—I think you owe it to yourself to jump at it. But don't ask me to decide for you.

RUTH (*turning to look at* ANDREW—*in a tone of fierce re-*

sentment): Yes, go, Andy! (*She turns quickly away again. There is a moment of embarrassed silence.*)

ANDREW (*thoughtfully*): Yes, I guess I will. It'll be the best thing for all of us in the end, don't you think so, Rob? (ROBERT *nods but remains silent.*)

SCOTT (*getting to his feet*): Then, that's settled.

ANDREW (*now that he has definitely made a decision his voice rings with hopeful strength and energy*): Yes, I'll take the berth. The sooner I go the sooner I'll be back, that's a certainty; and I won't come back with empty hands next time. You bet I won't!

SCOTT: You ain't got so much time, Andy. To make sure you'd best leave here soon's you kin. I got to get right back aboard. You'd best come with me.

ANDREW: I'll go to the house and repack my bag right away.

ROBERT (*quietly*): You'll both be here for dinner, won't you?

ANDREW (*worriedly*): I don't know. Will there be time? What time is it now, I wonder?

ROBERT (*reproachfully*): Ma's been getting dinner especially for you, Andy.

ANDREW (*flushing—shamefacedly*): Hell! And I was forgetting! Of course I'll stay for dinner if I missed every damned ship in the world. (*He turns to the* CAPTAIN—*briskly*) Come on, Uncle. Walk down with me to the house and you can tell me more about this berth on the way. I've got to pack before dinner. (*He and the* CAPTAIN *start down to the left.* ANDREW *calls back over his shoulder*) You're coming soon, aren't you, Rob?

ROBERT: Yes. I'll be right down. (ANDREW *and the* CAPTAIN *leave.* RUTH *puts* MARY *on the ground and hides her face in her hands. Her shoulders shake as if she were sobbing.* ROBERT *stares at her with a grim, somber expression.* MARY *walks backward toward* ROBERT, *her wondering eyes fixed on her mother.*)

MARY (*her voice vaguely frightened, taking her father's hand*): Dada, Mama's cryin', Dada.

ROBERT (*bending down and stroking her hair—in a voice he endeavors to keep from being harsh*): No, she isn't, little girl. The sun hurts her eyes, that's all. Aren't you beginning to feel hungry, Mary?

MARY (*decidedly*): Yes, Dada.

ROBERT (*meaningly*): It must be your dinner time now.

RUTH (*in a muffled voice*): I'm coming, Mary. (*She wipes her eyes quickly and, without looking at* ROBERT, *comes and takes* MARY'S *hand—in a dead voice*) Come on and I'll get your dinner for you. (*She walks out left, her eyes fixed on the ground, the skipping* MARY *tugging at her hand.* ROBERT *waits a moment for them to get ahead and then slowly follows as the curtain falls.*)

ACT THREE
Scene I

SMALL *as Act Two, Scene I— The sitting room of the farm-house about six o'clock in the morning of a day toward the end of October five years later. It is not yet dawn, but as the action progresses the darkness outside the windows gradually fades to gray.*

The room, seen by the light of the shadeless oil lamp with a smoky chimney which stands on the table, presents an appearance of decay, of dissolution. The curtains at the windows are torn and dirty and one of them is missing. The closed desk is gray with accumulated dust as if it had not been used in years. Blotches of dampness disfigure the wall paper. Threadbare trails, leading to the kitchen and outer doors, show in the faded carpet. The top of the coverless table is stained with the imprints of hot dishes and spilt food. The rung of one rocker has been clumsily mended with a piece of plain board. A brown coating of rust covers the unblacked stove. A pile of wood is stacked up carelessly against the wall by the stove.

The whole atmosphere of the room, contrasted with that of former years, is one of an habitual poverty too hopelessly resigned to be any longer ashamed or even conscious of itself.

At the rise of the curtain RUTH *is discovered sitting by the stove, with hands outstretched to the warmth as if the air in the room were damp and cold. A heavy shawl is wrapped about her shoulders, half-concealing her dress of deep mourning. She has aged horribly. Her pale, deeply-lined face has the stony lack of expression of one to whom nothing more can ever happen, whose capacity for emotion has been exhausted. When she speaks her voice is without timbre, low and monotonous. The negligent disorder of her dress, the slovenly arrangement of her hair, now streaked with gray, her muddied shoes run down at the heel, give full evidence of the apathy in which she lives.*

Her mother is asleep in her wheel chair beside the stove toward the rear, wrapped up in a blanket.

There is a sound from the open bedroom door in the rear as if someone were getting out of bed. RUTH *turns in that direction with a look of dull annoyance. A moment later* ROBERT *appears in the doorway, leaning weakly against it for support. His hair is long and unkempt, his face and body emaciated. There are bright patches of crimson over his cheek bones and his eyes are burning with fever. He is dressed in corduroy pants, a flannel shirt, and wears worn carpet slippers on his bare feet.*

RUTH (*dully*): S-s-s-h! Ma's asleep.

ROBERT (*speaking with an effort*): I won't wake her. (*He walks weakly to a rocker by the side of the table and sinks down in it exhausted.*)

RUTH (*staring at the stove*): You better come near the fire where it's warm.

ROBERT: No. I'm burning up now.

RUTH: That's the fever. You know the doctor told you not to get up and move round.

ROBERT (*irritably*): That old fossil! He doesn't know anything. Go to bed and stay there—that's his only prescription.

RUTH (*indifferently*): How are you feeling now?

ROBERT (*buoyantly*): Better! Much better than I've felt in ages. Really I'm fine now—only very weak. It's the turning point, I guess. From now on I'll pick up so quick I'll surprise you—and no thanks to that old fool of a country quack, either.

RUTH: He's always tended to us.

ROBERT: Always helped us to die, you mean! He "tended" to Pa and Ma and— (*His voice breaks*) and to—Mary.

RUTH (*dully*): He did the best he knew, I s'pose. (*After a pause*) Well, Andy's bringing a specialist with him when he comes. That ought to suit you.

ROBERT (*bitterly*): Is that why you're waiting up all night?

RUTH: Yes.

ROBERT: For Andy?

RUTH (*without a trace of feeling*): Somebody had got to. It's only right for someone to meet him after he's been gone five years.

ROBERT (*with bitter mockery*): Five years! It's a long time.

RUTH: Yes.

ROBERT (*meaningly*): To *wait!*

RUTH (*indifferently*): It's past now.

ROBERT: Yes, it's past. (*After a pause*) Have you got his two telegrams with you? (RUTH *nods*) Let me see them, will you? My head was so full of fever when they came I couldn't make head or tail to them. (*Hastily*) But I'm feeling fine now. Let me read them again. (RUTH *takes them from the bosom of her dress and hands them to him.*)

RUTH: Here. The first one's on top.

ROBERT (*opening it*): New York. "Just landed from steamer. Have important business to wind up here. Will be home as soon as deal is completed." (*He smiles bit-terly*) Business first was always Andy's motto. (*He reads*) "Hope you are all well. Andy." (*He repeats ironically*) "Hope you are all well!"

RUTH (*dully*): He couldn't know you'd been took sick till I answered that and told him.

ROBERT (*contritely*): Of course he couldn't. I'm a fool. I'm touchy about nothing lately. Just what did you say in your reply?

RUTH (*inconsequentially*): I had to send it collect.

ROBERT (*irritably*): What did you say was the matter with me?

RUTH: I wrote you had lung trouble.

ROBERT (*flying into a petty temper*): You *are* a fool! How often have I explained to you that it's *pleurisy* is the matter with me. You can't seem to get it in your head that the pleura is outside the lungs, not in them!

RUTH (*callously*): I only wrote what Doctor Smith told me.

ROBERT (*angrily*): He's a damned ignoramus!

RUTH (*dully*): Makes no difference. I had to tell Andy something, didn't I?

ROBERT (*after a pause, opening the other telegram*): He sent this last evening. Let's see. (*He reads*) "Leave for home on midnight train. Just received your wire. Am bringing specialist to see Rob. Will motor to farm from Port." (*He calculates*) What time is it now?

RUTH: Round six, must be.

ROBERT: He ought to be here soon. I'm glad he's bringing a doctor who knows something. A specialist will tell you in a second that there's nothing the matter with my lungs.

RUTH (*stolidly*): You've been coughing an awful lot lately.

ROBERT (*irritably*): What nonsense! For God's sake, haven't you ever had a bad cold yourself? (RUTH *stares at the stove in silence.* ROBERT *fidgets in his chair. There is a pause. Finally* ROBERT's *eyes are fixed on the sleeping* MRS. ATKINS) Your mother is lucky to be able to sleep so soundly.

RUTH: Ma's tired. She's been sitting up with me most of the night.

ROBERT (*mockingly*): Is she waiting for Andy, too? (*There is a pause.* ROBERT *sighs*) I couldn't get to sleep to save my soul. I counted ten million sheep if I counted one. No use! I gave up trying finally and just laid there in the dark thinking. (*He pauses, then continues in a tone of tender sympathy*) I was thinking about you, Ruth—of how hard these last years must have been for you. (*Appealingly*) I'm sorry, Ruth.

RUTH (*in a dead voice*): I don't know. They're past now. They were hard on all of us.

ROBERT: Yes; on all of us but Andy. (*With a flash of sick jealousy*) Andy's made a big success of himself—the kind he wanted. (*Mockingly*) And now he's coming home to let us admire his greatness. (*Frowning—irritably*) What am I talking about? My brain must be sick, too. (*After a pause*) Yes, these years have been terrible for both of us. (*His voice is lowered to a trembling whisper*) Especially the last eight months since Mary—died. (*He forces back a sob with a convulsive shudder—then breaks out in a passionate agony*) Our last hope of happiness! I could curse God from the bottom of my soul—if there was a God! (*He is racked by a violent fit of coughing and hurriedly puts his handkerchief to his lips.*)

RUTH (*without looking at him*): Mary's better off—being dead.

ROBERT (*gloomily*): We'd all be better off for that matter. (*With a sudden exasperation*) You tell that mother of yours she's got to stop saying that Mary's death was due to a weak constitution inherited from me. (*On the verge of tears of weakness*) It's got to stop, I tell you!

RUTH (*sharply*): S-h-h! You'll wake her; and then she'll nag at me—not you.

ROBERT (*coughs and lies back in his chair weakly—a pause*): It's all because your mother's down on me for not begging Andy for help.

RUTH (*resentfully*): You might have. He's got plenty.

ROBERT: How can *you* of all people think of taking money from *him?*

RUTH (*dully*): I don't see the harm. He's your own brother.

ROBERT (*shrugging his shoulders*): What's the use of talking to you? Well, I couldn't. (*Proudly*) And I've managed to keep things going, thank God. You can't deny that without help I've succeeded in— (*He breaks off with a bitter laugh*) My God, what am I boasting of? Debts to this one and that, taxes, interest unpaid! I'm a fool! (*He lies back in his chair closing his eyes for a moment, then speaks in a low voice*) I'll be frank, Ruth. I've been an utter failure, and I've dragged you with me. I couldn't blame you in all justice—for hating me.

RUTH (*without feeling*): I don't hate you. It's been my fault too, I s'pose.

ROBERT: No. You couldn't help loving—Andy.

RUTH (*dully*): I don't love anyone.

ROBERT (*waving her remark aside*): You needn't deny it. It doesn't matter. (*After a pause—with a tender smile*) Do you know, Ruth, what I've been dreaming back there in the dark? (*With a short laugh*) I was planning our future when I get well. (*He looks at her with appealing eyes as if afraid she will sneer at him. Her expression does not change. She stares at the stove. His voice takes on a note of eagerness*) After all, why shouldn't we have a future? We're young yet. If we can only shake off the curse of this farm! It's the farm that's ruined our lives, damn it! And now that Andy's coming back—I'm going to sink my foolish pride, Ruth! I'll borrow the money from him to give us a good start in the city. We'll go where people live instead of stagnating, and start all over again. (*Confidently*) I won't be the failure there that I've been here, Ruth. You won't need to be ashamed of me there. I'll prove to you the reading I've done can be put to some use. (*Vaguely*) I'll write, or something of that sort. I've always wanted to write. (*Pleadingly*) You'll want to do that, won't you, Ruth?

RUTH (*dully*): There's Ma.

ROBERT: She can come with us.

RUTH: She wouldn't.

ROBERT (*angrily*): So that's your answer! (*He trembles with violent passion. His voice is so strange that* RUTH *turns to look at him in alarm*) You're lying, Ruth! Your mother's just an excuse. You want to stay here. You think that because Andy's coming back that— (*He chokes and has an attack of coughing.*)

RUTH (*getting up—in a frightened voice*): What's the matter? (*She goes to him*) I'll go with you, Rob. Stop that coughing for goodness' sake! It's awful bad for you. (*She soothes him in dull tones*) I'll go with you to the city—soon's you're well again. Honest I will, Rob, I promise! (ROB *lies back and closes his eyes. She stands looking down at him anxiously*) Do you feel better now?

ROBERT: Yes. (RUTH *goes back to her chair. After a pause he opens his eyes and sits up in his chair. His face is flushed and happy*) Then you *will* go, Ruth?

RUTH: Yes.

ROBERT (*excitedly*): We'll make a new start, Ruth—just you and I. Life owes us some happiness after what we've been through. (*Vehemently*) It must! Otherwise our suffering would be meaningless—and that is unthinkable.

RUTH (*worried by his excitement*): Yes, yes, of course, Rob, but you mustn't—

ROBERT: Oh, don't be afraid. I feel completely well, really I do—now that I can hope again. Oh if you knew how glorious it feels to have something to look forward to! Can't you feel the thrill of it, too—the vision of a new life opening up after all the horrible years?

RUTH: Yes, yes, but do be—

ROBERT: Nonsense! I won't be careful. I'm getting back all my strength. (*He gets lightly to his feet*) See! I feel light as a feather. (*He walks to her chair and bends down to kiss her smilingly*) One kiss—the first in years, isn't it?—to greet the dawn of a new life together.

RUTH (*submitting to his kiss—worriedly*): Sit down, Rob, for goodness' sake!

ROBERT (*with tender obstinacy—stroking her hair*): I won't sit down. You're silly to worry. (*He rests one hand on the back of her chair*) Listen. All our suffering has been a test through which we had to pass to prove ourselves worthy of a finer realization. (*Exult-ingly*) And we did pass through it! It hasn't broken us! And now the dream is to come true! Don't you see?

RUTH (*looking at him with frightened eyes as if she thought he had gone mad*): Yes, Rob, I see; but won't you go back to bed now and rest?

ROBERT: No. I'm going to see the sun rise. It's an augury of good fortune. (*He goes quickly to the window in the rear left, and pushing the curtains aside, stands looking out.* RUTH *springs to her feet and comes quickly to the table, left, where she remains watching* ROBERT *in a tense, expectant attitude. As he peers out his body seems gradually to sag, to grow limp and tired. His voice is mournful as he speaks*) No sun yet. It isn't time. All I can see is the black rim of the damned hills outlined against a creeping grayness. (*He turns around; letting the curtains fall back, stretching a hand out to the wall to support himself. His false strength of a moment has evaporated leaving his face drawn and hollow-eyed. He makes a pitiful attempt to smile*) That's not a very happy augury, is it? But the sun'll come—soon. (*He sways weakly.*)

RUTH (*hurrying to his side and supporting him*): Please go to bed, won't you, Rob? You don't want to be all wore out when the specialist comes, do you?

ROBERT (*quickly*): No. That's right. He mustn't think I'm sicker than I am. And I feel as if I could sleep now — (*Cheerfully*) a good, sound, restful sleep.

RUTH (*helping him to the bedroom door*): That's what you need most. (*They go inside. A moment later she reappears calling back*) I'll shut this door so's you'll be quiet. (*She closes the door and goes quickly to her mother and shakes her by the shoulder*) Ma! Ma! Wake up!

MRS. ATKINS (*coming out of her sleep with a start*): Glory be! What's the matter with you?

RUTH: It was Rob. He's just been talking to me out here. I put him back to bed. (*Now that she is sure her mother is awake her fear passes and she relapses into dull indifference. She sits down in her chair and stares at the stove—dully*) He acted—funny; and his eyes looked so—so wild like.

MRS. ATKINS (*with asperity*): And is that all you woke me out of a sound sleep for, and scared me near out of my wits?

RUTH: I was afraid. He talked so crazy. I couldn't quiet him. I didn't want to be alone with him that way. Lord knows what he might do.

MRS. ATKINS (*scornfully*): Humph! A help I'd be to you and me not able to move a step! Why didn't you run and get Jake?

RUTH (*dully*): Jake isn't here. He quit last night. He hasn't been paid in three months.

MRS. ATKINS (*indignantly*): I can't blame him. What decent person'd want to work on a place like this? (*With sudden exasperation*) Oh, I wish you'd never married that man!

RUTH (*wearily*): You oughtn't to talk about him now when he's sick in his bed.

MRS. ATKINS (*working herself into a fit of rage*): You know very well, Ruth Mayo, if it wasn't for me helpin' you on the sly out of my savin's, you'd both been in the poor house—and all 'count of his pigheaded pride in not lettin' Andy know the state thin's were in. A nice thin' for me to have to support him out of what I'd saved for my last days—and me an invalid with no one to look to!

RUTH: Andy'll pay you back, Ma. I can tell him so's Rob'll never know.

MRS. ATKINS (*with a snort*): What'd Rob think you and him was livin' on, I'd like to know?

RUTH (*dully*): He didn't think about it, I s'pose. (*After a slight pause*) He said he'd made up his mind to ask Andy for help when he comes. (*As a clock in the kitchen strikes six*) Six o'clock. Andy ought to get here directly.

MRS. ATKINS: D'you think this special doctor'll do Rob any good?

RUTH (*hopelessly*): I don't know. (*The two women remain silent for a time staring dejectedly at the stove.*)

MRS. ATKINS (*shivering irritably*): For goodness' sake put some wood on that fire. I'm most freezin'!

RUTH (*pointing to the door in the rear*): Don't talk so loud. Let him sleep if he can. (*She gets wearily from the chair and puts a few pieces of wood in the stove*) This is the last of the wood. I don't know who'll cut more now that Jake's left. (*She sighs and walks to the window in the rear, left, pulls the curtains aside, and looks out*) It's getting gray out. (*She comes back to the stove*) Looks like it'd be a nice day. (*She stretches out her hands to warm them*) Must've been a heavy frost last night. We're paying for the spell of warm weather we've been having. (*The throbbing whine of a motor sounds from the distance outside.*)

MRS. ATKINS (*sharply*): S-h-h! Listen! Ain't that an auto I hear?

RUTH (*without interest*): Yes. It's Andy, I s'pose.

MRS. ATKINS (*with nervous irritation*): Don't sit there like a silly goose. Look at the state of this room! What'll this strange doctor think of us? Look at that lamp chimney all smoke! Gracious sakes, Ruth—

RUTH (*indifferently*): I've got a lamp all cleaned up in the kitchen.

MRS. ATKINS (*peremptorily*): Wheel me in there this minute. I don't want him to see me looking a sight. I'll lay down in the room the other side. You don't need me now and I'm dead for sleep. (RUTH *wheels her mother off right. The noise of the motor grows louder and finally ceases as the car stops on the road before the farmhouse.* RUTH *returns from the kitchen with a lighted lamp in her hand which she sets on the table beside the other. The sound of footsteps on the path is heard—then a sharp rap on the door.* RUTH *goes and opens it.* ANDREW *enters, folowed by* DOCTOR FAWCETT *carrying a small black bag.* ANDREW *has changed greatly. His face seems to have grown highstrung, hardened by the look of decisiveness which comes from being constantly under a strain where judgments on the spur of the moment are compelled to be accurate. His eyes are keener and more alert. There is even a suggestion of ruthless cunning about them. At present, however, his expression is one of tense anxiety.* DOCTOR FAWCETT *is a short, dark, middle-aged man with a Vandyke beard. He wears glasses.*)

RUTH: Hello, Andy! I've been waiting—

ANDREW (*kissing her hastily*): I got here as soon as I could. (*He throws off his cap and heavy overcoat on the table, introducing* RUTH *and the* DOCTOR *as he does so. He is dressed in an expensive business suit and appears stouter*) My sister-in-law, Mrs. Mayo—Doctor Fawcett. (*They bow to each other silently.* ANDREW *casts a quick glance about the room*) Where's Rob?

RUTH (*pointing*): In there.

ANDREW: I'll take your coat and hat, Doctor. (*As he helps the* DOCTOR *with his things*) Is he very bad, Ruth?

RUTH (*dully*): He's been getting weaker.

ANDREW: Damn! This way, Doctor. Bring the lamp, Ruth. (*He goes into the bedroom, followed by the* DOCTOR *and* RUTH *carrying the clean lamp.* RUTH *reappears almost immediately closing the door behind her, and goes slowly to the outside door, which she opens, and stands in the doorway looking out. The sound of* ANDREW'S *and* ROBERT'S *voices comes from the bedroom. A moment later* ANDREW *re-enters, closing the door softly. He comes forward and sinks down in the rocker on the right of table, leaning his head on his hand. His face is drawn in a shocked expression of great grief. He sighs heavily, staring mournfully in front of him.* RUTH *turns and stands watching him. Then she shuts the door and returns to her chair by the stove, turning it so she can face him.*)

ANDREW (*glancing up quickly—in a harsh voice*): How long has this been going on?

RUTH: You mean—how long has he been sick?

ANDREW (*shortly*): Of course! What else?

RUTH: It was last summer he had a bad spell first, but he's been ailin' ever since Mary died—eight months ago.

ANDREW (*harshly*): Why didn't you let me know—cable me? Do you want him to die, all of you? I'm damned if it doesn't look that way! (*His voice breaking*) Poor old chap! To be sick in this out-of-the-way hole without anyone to attend to him but a country quack! It's a damned shame!

RUTH (*dully*): I wanted to send you word once, but he

only got mad when I told him. He was too proud to ask anything, he said.

ANDREW: Proud? To ask *me?* (*He jumps to his feet and paces nervously back and forth*) I can't understand the way you've acted. Didn't you see how sick he was getting? Couldn't you realize—why, I nearly dropped in my tracks when I saw him! He looks— (*He shudders*) terrible! (*With fierce scorn*) I suppose you're so used to the idea of his being delicate that you took his sickness as a matter of course. God, if I'd only known!

RUTH (*without emotion*): A letter takes some time to get where you were—and we couldn't afford to telegraph. We owed everyone already, and I couldn't ask Ma. She'd been giving me money out of her savings till she hadn't much left. Don't say anything to Rob about it. I never told him. He'd only be mad at me if he knew. But I had to, because—God knows how we'd have got on if I hadn't.

ANDREW: You mean to say— (*His eyes seemed to take in the poverty-stricken appearance of the room for the first time*) You sent that telegram to me collect. Was it because— (RUTH *nods silently.* ANDREW *pounds on the table with his fist*) Good God! And all this time I've been—why I've had everything! (*He sits down in his chair and pulls it close to* RUTH's *impulsively*) But—I can't get it through my head. Why? Why? What has happened? How did it ever come about? Tell me!

RUTH (*dully*): There's nothing much to tell. Things kept getting worse, that's all—and Rob didn't seem to care. He never took any interest since way back when your Ma died. After that he got men to take charge, and they nearly all cheated him—he couldn't tell—and left one after another. Then after Mary died he didn't pay no heed to anything any more—just stayed indoors and took to reading books again. So I had to ask Ma if she wouldn't help us some.

ANDREW (*surprised and horrified*): Why, damn it, this is frightful! Rob must be mad not to have let me know. Too proud to ask help of *me!* What's the matter with him in God's name? (*A sudden, horrible suspicion entering his mind*) Ruth! Tell me the truth. His mind hasn't gone back on him, has it?

RUTH (*dully*): I don't know. Mary's dying broke him up terrible—but he's used to her being gone by this time, I s'pose.

ANDREW (*looking at her queerly*): Do you mean to say *you're* used to it?

RUTH (*in a dead tone*): There's a time comes—when you don't mind any more—anything.

ANDREW (*looks at her fixedly for a moment—with great pity*): I'm sorry, Ruth—if I seemed to blame you. I didn't realize— The sight of Rob lying in bed there, so gone to pieces—it made me furious at everyone. Forgive me, Ruth.

RUTH: There's nothing to forgive. It doesn't matter.

ANDREW (*springing to his feet again and pacing up and down*): Thank God I came back before it was too late. This doctor will know exactly what to do. That's the first thing to think of. When Rob's on his feet again we can get the farm working on a sound basis once more. I'll see to that—before I leave.

RUTH: You're going away again?

ANDREW: I've got to.

RUTH: You wrote Rob you was coming back to stay this time.

ANDREW: I expected to—until I got to New York. Then

I learned certain facts that make it necessary. (*With a short laugh*) To be candid, Ruth, I'm not the rich man you've probably been led to believe by my letters—not now. I was when I wrote them. I made money hand over fist as long as I stuck to legitimate trading; but I wasn't content with that. I wanted it to come easier, so like all the rest of the idiots, I tried speculation. Oh, I won all right! Several times I've been almost a millionaire—on paper—and then come down to earth again with a bump. Finally the strain was too much. I got disgusted with myself and made up my mind to get out and come home and forget it and really live again. (*He gives a harsh laugh*) And now comes the funny part. The day before the steamer sailed I saw what I thought was a chance to become a millionaire again. (*He snaps his fingers*) That easy! I plunged. Then, before things broke, I left—I was so confident I couldn't be wrong. But when I landed in New York —I wired you I had business to wind up, didn't I? Well, it was the business that wound me up! (*He smiles grimly, pacing up and down, his hands in his pockets.*)

RUTH (*dully*): You found—you'd lost everything?

ANDREW (*sitting down again*): Practically. (*He takes a cigar from his pocket, bites the end off, and lights it*) Oh, I don't mean I'm dead broke. I've saved ten thousand from the wreckage, maybe twenty. But that's a poor showing for five years' hard work. That's why I'll have to go back. (*Confidently*) I can make it up in a year or so down there—and I don't need but a shoestring to start with. (*A weary expression comes over his face and he sighs heavily*) I wish I didn't have to. I'm sick of it all.

RUTH: It's too bad—things seem to go wrong so.

ANDREW (*shaking off his depression—briskly*): They might be much worse. There's enough left to fix the farm O.K. before I go. I won't leave 'til Rob's on his feet again. In the meantime I'll make things fly around here. (*With satisfaction*) I need a rest, and the kind of rest I need is hard work in the open—just like I used to do in the old days. (*Stopping abruptly and lowering his voice cautiously*) Not a word to Rob about my losing money! Remember that, Ruth! You can see why. If he's grown so touchy he'd never accept a cent if he thought I was hard up; see?

RUTH: Yes, Andy. (*After a pause, during which* ANDREW *puffs at his cigar abstractedly, his mind evidently busy with plans for the future, the bedroom door is opened and* DR. FAWCETT *enters, carrying a bag. He closes the door quietly behind him and comes forward, a grave expression on his face.* ANDREW *springs out of his chair.*)

ANDREW: Ah, Doctor! (*He pushes a chair between his own and* RUTH's) Won't you have a chair?

FAWCETT (*glancing at his watch*): I must catch the nine o'clock back to the city. It's imperative. I have only a moment. (*Sitting down and clearing his throat—in a perfunctory, impersonal voice*) The case of your brother, Mr. Mayo, is— (*He stops and glances at* RUTH *and says meaningly to* ANDREW) Perhaps it would be better if you and I—

RUTH (*with dogged resentment*): I know what you mean, Doctor. (*Dully*) Don't be afraid I can't stand it. I'm used to bearing trouble by this time; and I can guess what you've found out. (*She hesitates for a moment—then continues in a monotonous voice*) Rob's going to die.

ANDREW (*angrily*): Ruth!

FAWCETT (*raising his hand as if to command silence*): I am afraid my diagnosis of your brother's condition forces me to the same conclusion as Mrs. Mayo's.

ANDREW (*groaning*): But, Doctor, surely—

FAWCETT (*calmly*): Your brother hasn't long to live—perhaps a few days, perhaps only a few hours. It's a marvel that he's alive at this moment. My examination revealed that both of his lungs are terribly affected.

ANDREW (*brokenly*): Good God! (RUTH *keeps her eyes fixed on her lap in a trance-like stare.*)

FAWCETT: I am sorry I have to tell you this. If there was anything that could be done—

ANDREW: There isn't anything?

FAWCETT (*shaking his head*): It's too late. Six months ago there might have—

ANDREW (*in anguish*): But if we were to take him to the mountains—or to Arizona—or—

FAWCETT: That might have prolonged his life six months ago. (ANDREW *groans*) But now— (*He shrugs his shoulders significantly.*)

ANDREW (*appalled by a sudden thought*): Good heavens, you haven't told him this, have you, Doctor?

FAWCETT: No. I lied to him. I said a change of climate — (*He looks at his watch again nervously*) I must leave you. (*He gets up.*)

ANDREW (*getting to his feet—insistently*): But there must still be some chance—

FAWCETT (*as if he were reassuring a child*): There is always that last chance—the miracle. (*He puts on his hat and coat—bowing to* RUTH) Good-by, Mrs. Mayo.

RUTH (*without raising her eyes—dully*): Good-by.

ANDREW (*mechanically*): I'll walk to the car with you,

Doctor. (*They go out of the door.* RUTH *sits motion-lessly. The motor is heard starting and the noise grad-ually recedes into the distance.* ANDREW *re-enters and sits down in his chair, holding his head in his hands*) Ruth! (*She lifts her eyes to his*) Hadn't we better go in and see him? God! I'm afraid to! I know he'll read it in my face. (*The bedroom door is noiselessly opened and* ROBERT *appears in the doorway. His cheeks are flushed with fever, and his eyes appear unusually large and brilliant.* ANDREW *continues with a groan*) It can't be, Ruth. It can't be as hopeless as he said. There's al-ways a fighting chance. We'll take Rob to Arizona. He's got to get well. There *must* be a chance!

ROBERT (*in a gentle tone*): Why must there, Andy? (RUTH *turns and stares at him with terrified eyes.*)

ANDREW (*whirling around*): Rob! (*Scoldingly*) What are you doing out of bed? (*He gets up and goes to him*) Get right back now and obey the Doc, or you're going to get a licking from me!

ROBERT (*ignoring these remarks*): Help me over to the chair, please, Andy.

ANDREW: Like hell I will! You're going right back to bed, that's where you're going, and stay there! (*He takes hold of* ROBERT's *arm.*)

ROBERT (*mockingly*): Stay there 'til I die, eh, Andy? (*Coldly*) Don't behave like a child. I'm sick of lying down. I'll be more rested sitting up. (*As* ANDREW *hesi-tates—violently*) I swear I'll get out of bed every time you put me there. You'll have to sit on my chest, and that wouldn't help my health any. Come on, Andy. Don't play the fool. I want to talk to you, and I'm go-ing to. (*With a grim smile*) A dying man has some rights, hasn't he?

ANDREW (*with a shudder*): Don't talk that way, for God's sake! I'll only let you sit down if you'll promise that. Remember. (*He helps* ROBERT *to the chair between his own and* RUTH's) Easy now! There you are! Wait, and I'll get a pillow for you. (*He goes into the bedroom.* ROBERT *looks at* RUTH *who shrinks away from him in terror.* ROBERT *smiles bitterly.* ANDREW *comes back with the pillow which he places behind* ROBERT's *back*) How's that?

ROBERT (*with an affectionate smile*): Fine! Thank you! (*As* ANDREW *sits down*) Listen, Andy. You've asked me not to talk—and I won't after I've made my position clear. (*Slowly*) In the first place I know I'm dying. (RUTH *bows her head and covers her face with her hands. She remains like this all during the scene between the two brothers.*)

ANDREW: Rob! That isn't so!

ROBERT (*wearily*): It *is* so! Don't lie to me. After Ruth put me to bed before you came, I saw it clearly for the first time. (*Bitterly*) I'd been making plans for our future—Ruth's and mine—so it came hard at first—the realization. Then when the doctor examined me, I knew—although he tried to lie about it. And then to make sure I listened at the door to what he told you. So don't mock me with fairy tales about Arizona, or any such rot as that. Because I'm dying is no reason you should treat me as an imbecile or a coward. Now that I'm sure what's happening I can say Kismet to it with all my heart. It was only the silly uncertainty that hurt. (*There is a pause.* ANDREW *looks around in impotent anguish, not knowing what to say.* ROBERT *regards him with an affectionate smile.*)

ANDREW (*finally blurts out*): It isn't foolish. You *have*

got a chance. If you heard all the Doctor said that ought to prove it to you.

ROBERT: Oh, you mean when he spoke of the miracle? (*Dryly*) I don't believe in miracles—in my case. Besides, I know more than any doctor on earth *could* know—because I *feel* what's coming. (*Dismissing the subject*) But we've agreed not to talk of it. Tell me about yourself, Andy. That's what I'm interested in. Your letters were too brief and far apart to be illuminating.

ANDREW: I meant to write oftener.

ROBERT (*with a faint trance of irony*): I judge from them you've accomplished all you set out to do five years ago?

ANDREW: That isn't much to boast of.

ROBERT (*surprised*): Have you really, honestly reached that conclusion?

ANDREW: Well, it doesn't seem to amount to much now.

ROBERT: But you're rich, aren't you?

ANDREW (*with a quick glance at* RUTH): Yes, I s'pose so.

ROBERT: I'm glad. You can do to the farm all I've undone. But what did you do down there? Tell me. You went in the grain business with that friend of yours?

ANDREW: Yes. After two years I had a share in it. I sold out last year. (*He is answering* ROBERT's *questions with great reluctance.*)

ROBERT: And then?

ANDREW: I went in on my own.

ROBERT: Still in grain?

ANDREW: Yes.

ROBERT: What's the matter? You look as if I were accusing you of something.

ANDREW: I'm proud enough of the first four years. It's after that I'm not boasting of. I took to speculating.

ROBERT: In wheat?

ANDREW: Yes.

ROBERT: And you made money—gambling?

ANDREW: Yes.

ROBERT (*thoughtfully*): I've been wondering what the great change was in you. (*After a pause*) You—a farmer—to gamble in a wheat pit with scraps of paper. There's a spiritual significance in that picture, Andy. (*He smiles bitterly*) I'm a failure, and Ruth's another— but we can both justly lay some of the blame for our stumbling on God. But you're the deepest-dyed failure of the three, Andy. You've spent eight years running away from yourself. Do you see what I mean? You used to be a creator when you loved the farm. You and life were in harmonious partnership. And now— (*He stops as if seeking vainly for words*) My brain is mud- dled. But part of what I mean is that your gambling with the thing you used to love to create proves how far astray— So you'll be punished. You'll have to suffer to win back— (*His voice grows weaker and he sighs wearily*) It's no use. I can't say it. (*He lies back and closes his eyes, breathing pantingly.*)

ANDREW (*slowly*): I think I know what you're driving at, Rob—and it's true, I guess. (ROBERT *smiles gratefully and stretches out his hand, which* ANDREW *takes in his.*)

ROBERT: I want you to promise me to do one thing, Andy, after—

ANDREW: I'll promise anything, as God is my Judge!

ROBERT: Remember, Andy, Ruth has suffered double her share. (*His voice faltering with weakness*) Only through contact with suffering, Andy, will you—awaken. Listen. You must marry Ruth—afterwards.

RUTH (*with a cry*): Rob! (ROBERT *lies back, his eyes closed, gasping heavily for breath.*)

ANDREW (*making signs to her to humor him—gently*): You're tired out, Rob. You better lie down and rest a while, don't you think? We can talk later on.

ROBERT (*with a mocking smile*): Later on! You always were an optimist, Andy! (*He sighs with exhaustion*) Yes, I'll go and rest a while. (*As* ANDREW *comes to help him*) It must be near sunrise, isn't it?

ANDREW: It's after six.

ROBERT (*As* ANDREW *helps him into the bedroom*): Shut the door, Andy. I want to be alone. (ANDREW *reappears and shuts the door softly. He comes and sits down on his chair again, supporting his head on his hands. His face drawn with the intensity of his dry-eyed anguish.*)

RUTH (*glancing at him—fearfully*): He's out of his mind now, isn't he?

ANDREW: He may be a little delirious. The fever would do that. (*With impotent rage*) God, what a shame! And there's nothing we can do but sit and—wait! (*He springs from his chair and walks to the stove.*)

RUTH (*dully*): He was talking—wild—like he used to— only this time it sounded—unnatural, don't you think?

ANDREW: I don't know. The things he said to me had truth in them—even if he did talk them way up in the air, like he always sees things. Still— (*He glances down at* RUTH *keenly*) Why do you suppose he wanted us to promise we'd— (*Confusedly*) You know what he said.

RUTH (*dully*): His mind was wandering, I s'pose.

ANDREW (*with conviction*): No—there was something back of it.

RUTH: He wanted to make sure I'd be all right—after he'd gone, I expect.

ANDREW: No, it wasn't that. He knows very well I'd naturally look after you without—anything like that.

RUTH: He might be thinking of—something happened five years back, the time you came home from the trip.

ANDREW: What happened? What do you mean?

RUTH (*dully*): We had a fight.

ANDREW: A fight? What has that to do with me?

RUTH: It was about you—in a way.

ANDREW (*amazed*): About *me?*

RUTH: Yes, mostly. You see I'd found out I'd made a mistake about Rob soon after we were married—when it was too late.

ANDREW: Mistake? (*Slowly*) You mean—you found out you didn't love Rob?

RUTH: Yes.

ANDREW: Good God!

RUTH: And then I thought that when Mary came it'd be different, and I'd love him; but it didn't happen that way. And I couldn't bear with his blundering and book-reading—and I grew to hate him, almost.

ANDREW: Ruth!

RUTH: I couldn't help it. No woman could. It had to be because I loved someone else, I'd found out. (*She sighs wearily*) It can't do no harm to tell you now—when it's all past and gone—and dead. *You* were the one I really loved—only I didn't come to the knowledge of it 'til too late.

ANDREW (*stunned*): Ruth! Do you know what you're saying?

RUTH: It was true—then. (*With sudden fierceness*) How could I help it? No woman could.

ANDREW: Then—you loved me—that time I came home?

RUTH (*doggedly*): I'd known your real reason for leaving home the first time—everybody knew it—and for three years I'd been thinking—

ANDREW: That I loved you?

RUTH: Yes. Then that day on the hill you laughed about what a fool you'd been for loving me once—and I knew it was all over.

ANDREW: Good God, but I never thought— (*He stops, shuddering at his remembrance*) And did Rob—

RUTH: That was what I'd started to tell. We'd had a fight just before you came and I got crazy mad—and I told him all I've told you.

ANDREW (*gaping at her speechlessly for a moment*): You told Rob—you loved me?

RUTH: Yes.

ANDREW (*shrinking away from her in horror*): You—you—you mad fool, you! How could you do such a thing?

RUTH: I couldn't help it. I'd got to the end of bearing things—without talking.

ANDREW: Then Rob must have known every moment I stayed here! And yet he never said or showed—God, how he must have suffered! Didn't you know how much he loved you?

RUTH (*dully*): Yes. I knew he liked me.

ANDREW: Liked you! What kind of a woman are you? Couldn't you have kept silent? Did you have to torture him? No wonder he's dying! And you've lived together for five years with this between you?

RUTH: We've lived in the same house.

ANDREW: Does he still think—

RUTH: I don't know. We've never spoke a word about it

since that day. Maybe, from the way he went on, he s'poses I care for you yet.

ANDREW: But you don't. It's outrageous. It's stupid! You don't love me!

RUTH (*slowly*): I wouldn't know how to feel love, even if I tried, any more.

ANDREW (*brutally*): And I don't love you, that's sure! (*He sinks into his chair, his head between his hands*) It's damnable such a thing should be between Rob and me. Why, I love Rob better'n anybody in the world and always did. There isn't a thing on God's green earth I wouldn't have done to keep trouble away from him. And I have to be the very one—it's damnable! How am I going to face him again? What can I say to him now? (*He groans with anguished rage. After a pause*) He asked me to promise—what am I going to do?

RUTH: You can promise—so's it'll ease his mind—and not mean anything.

ANDREW: What? Lie to him now—when he's dying? (*Determinedly*): No! It's *you* who'll have to do the lying, since it must be done. You've got a chance now to undo some of all the suffering you've brought on Rob. Go in to him! Tell him you never loved me—it was all a mistake. Tell him you only said so because you were mad and didn't know what you were saying! Tell him something, anything, that'll bring him peace!

RUTH (*dully*): He wouldn't believe me.

ANDREW (*furiously*): You've got to make him believe you, do you hear? You've got to—now—hurry—you never know when it may be too late. (*As she hesitates —imploringly*) For God's sake, Ruth! Don't you see you owe it to him? You'll never forgive yourself if you don't.

RUTH (*dully*): I'll go. (*She gets wearily to her feet and walks slowly toward the bedroom*) But it won't do any good. (ANDREW's *eyes are fixed on her anxiously. She opens the door and steps inside the room. She remains standing there for a minute. Then she calls in a frightened voice*) Rob! Where are you? (*Then she hurries back, trembling with fright*) Andy! Andy! He's gone!

ANDREW (*misunderstanding her—his face pale with dread*): He's not—

RUTH (*interrupting him—hysterically*): He's gone! The bed's empty. The window's wide open. He must have crawled out into the yard!

ANDREW (*springing to his feet. He rushes into the bedroom and returns immediately with an expression of alarmed amazement on his face*): Come! He can't have gone far! (*Grabbing his hat he takes* RUTH's *arm and shoves her toward the door*) Come on! (*Opening the door*) Let's hope to God— (*The door closes behind them, cutting off his words as the curtain falls.*)

ACT THREE
Scene II

SAME *as Act One, Scene 1—A section of country highway. The sky to the east is already alight with bright color and a thin, quivering line of flame is spreading slowly along the horizon rim of the dark hills. The roadside, however, is still steeped in the grayness of the dawn, shadowy and vague. The field in the foreground has a wild uncultivated appearance as if it had been allowed to remain fallow the preceding summer. Parts of the snakefence in the rear have been broken down. The apple tree is leafless and seems dead.*

ROBERT *staggers weakly in from the left. He stumbles into the ditch and lies there for a moment; then crawls with a great effort to the top of the bank where he can see the sun rise, and collapses weakly.* RUTH *and* ANDREW *come hurriedly along the road from the left.*

ANDREW (*stopping and looking about him*): There he is! I knew it! I knew we'd find him here.

ROBERT (*trying to raise himself to a sitting position as they hasten to his side—with a wan smile*): I thought I'd given you the slip.

ANDREW (*with kindly bullying*): Well you didn't, you old scoundrel, and we're going to take you right back where you belong—in bed. (*He makes a motion to lift* ROBERT.)

ROBERT: Don't, Andy. Don't, I tell you!

ANDREW: You're in pain?

ROBERT (*simply*): No. I'm dying. (*He falls back weakly.* RUTH *sinks down beside him with a sob and pillows his head on her lap.* ANDREW *stands looking down at him helplessly.* ROBERT *moves his head restlessly on* RUTH's *lap*) I couldn't stand it back there in the room. It seemed as if all my life—I'd been cooped in a room. So I thought I'd try to end as I might have—if I'd had the courage—alone—in a ditch by the open road— watching the sun rise.

ANDREW: Rob! Don't talk. You're wasting your strength. Rest a while and then we'll carry you—

ROBERT: Still hoping, Andy? Don't. I know. (*There is a pause during which he breathes heavily, straining his eyes toward the horizon*) The sun comes so slowly. (*With an ironical smile*) The doctor told me to go to the far-off places—and I'd be cured. He was right. That was always the cure for me. It's too late—for this life —but— (*He has a fit of coughing which racks his body.*)

ANDREW (*with a hoarse sob*): Rob! (*He clenches his fists in an impotent rage against Fate*) God! God! (RUTH *sobs brokenly and wipes* ROBERT's *lips with her handkerchief.*)

ROBERT (*in a voice which is suddenly ringing with the happiness of hope*): You mustn't feel sorry for me. Don't you see I'm happy at last—free—free!—freed from the farm—free to wander on and on—eternally! (*He raises himself on his elbow, his face radiant, and points to the horizon*) Look! Isn't it beautiful beyond the hills? I can hear the old voices calling me to come— (*Exultantly*) And this time I'm going! It isn't the end. It's a free beginning—the start of my voyage! I've won to my trip—the right of release—beyond the horizon! Oh, you ought to be glad—glad—for my sake! (*He collapses weakly*) Andy! (ANDREW *bends down to him*) Remember Ruth—

ANDREW: I'll take care of her, I swear to you, Rob!

ROBERT: Ruth has suffered—remember, Andy—only through sacrifice—the secret beyond there— (*He suddenly raises himself with his last remaining strength and points to the horizon where the edge of the sun's disc is rising from the rim of the hills*) The sun! (*He remains with his eyes fixed on it for a moment. A rattling noise throbs from his throat. He mumbles*)

Remember! (*And falls back and is still.* RUTH *gives a cry of horror and springs to her feet, shuddering, her hands over her eyes.* ANDREW *bends on one knee beside the body, placing a hand over* ROBERT'S *heart, then he kisses his brother reverentially on the forehead and stands up.*)

ANDREW (*facing* RUTH, *the body between them—in a dead voice*): He's dead. (*With a sudden burst of fury*) God damn you, you never told him!

RUTH (*piteously*): He was so happy without my lying to him.

ANDREW (*pointing to the body—trembling with the violence of his rage*): This is your doing, you damn woman, you coward, you murderess!

RUTH (*sobbing*): Don't, Andy! I couldn't help it—and he knew how I'd suffered, too. He told you—to remember.

ANDREW (*stares at her for a moment, his rage ebbing away, an expression of deep pity gradually coming over his face. Then he glances down at his brother and speaks brokenly in a compassionate voice*): Forgive me, Ruth—for his sake—and I'll remember— (RUTH *lets her hands fall from her face and looks at him uncomprehendingly. He lifts his eyes to hers and forces out falteringly*) I—you—we've both made a mess of things! We must try to help each other—and—in time —we'll come to know what's right— (*Desperately*) And perhaps we— (*But* RUTH, *if she is aware of his words, gives no sign. She remains silent, gazing at him dully with the sad humility of exhaustion, her mind already sinking back into that spent calm beyond the further troubling of any hope.*)

Curtain

The Best of the World's Best Books
COMPLETE LIST OF TITLES IN
THE MODERN LIBRARY

MISCELLANEOUS